Literary Criticism and Morality

Matthew Arnold, J. Middleton Murry and F.R. Leavis

Literary Criticism and Morality

Matthew Arnold, J. Middleton Murry and F.R. Leavis

Ranjana Tripathi

ATLANTIC
PUBLISHERS & DISTRIBUTORS (P) LTD

Published by
ATLANTIC
PUBLISHERS & DISTRIBUTORS (P) LTD
7/22, Ansari Road, Darya Ganj, New Delhi-110002
Phones : +91-11-40775252, 23273880, 23275880, 23280451
Fax : +91-11-23285873
Web : www.atlanticbooks.com
E-mail : orders@atlanticbooks.com

Branch Office
5, Nallathambi Street, Wallajah Road, Chennai-600002
Phones : +91-44-64611085, 32413319
E-mail : chennai@atlanticbooks.com

ISBN 978-81-269-1710-5

Printed in India at Glorious Printers, A-13, D.S.I.D.C., Jhilmil Industrial Area, Delhi-110095

Foreword

I have great pleasure in writing this foreword for Ranjana Tirpathi's book, *Literary Criticism and Morality: Matthew Arnold, J. Middleton Murry and F.R. Leavis*. This book is no ordinary work. It is the labour of love for a subject that will never grow outdated, unlike some of our contemporary critical interests. Where there is literature there will always be its concomitants—literary criticism as well as morality. This subject is not like the more fleeting fashions of literary taste that arrive and depart; it is something that will live on till literature has social and cultural value. Ranjana Tripathi has therefore chosen an area of research which has a great future.

The three critics under discussion in this book, Matthew Arnold, J. Middleton Murry and F.R. Leavis have much in common. They are not merely formalists, studying just the beauty and aesthetics of literature; they also examine the meaning, the criticism of life and the affirmative value that literary texts contain. They continually relate literature to life. These critics assess the worth of literature in accordance with the truth to life that it provides. They are all humanists and humanism is something that has lived on ever since the ancient Greek masters showed interest in it and the European renaissance revived it. Arnold, Murry and Leavis belong to a tradition in that each is tied by the string of humanism. Ranjana's book has looked upon these three moralists as of a piece because their work never ignores the sacredness of humanism. I am impressed by the hard work Ranjana has put into this work. I consider it a work of brilliance. I see this book as a very valuable source book for future research. It is a highly original piece of scholarship for which its author will never be forgotten.

Lakshmi Raj Sharma
Professor, Department of English,
University of Allahabad, Allahabad

Preface

With an increasing shift of values, from the traditional, calm acceptance of social, cultural and religious ways, to the amoral, questioning and scientific attitude to life, man appears to be drifting away from the life-giving sources of existence. With doubt and scepticism looming large before him, religion has been steadily receding into the background. The vacuum thus created has to be filled with other forces and perhaps literature is the chief surrogate for faith, or at least this is what a number of thinkers after the eighteenth century have thought. But if literature has such responsibilities to fulfil, it has primarily to be moral, affirmative and positive. The three great english critics, Matthew Arnold, J. Middleton Murry and F.R. Leavis worked endlessly to establish this view of literature. The book concerns itself with the modern literary criticism with emphasis on these critics.

In my effort to trace the moralistic tradition, a number of views regarding the nature of morality in literature have been put forward from the very beginning to the recent times. While focusing on individual critics, I have assimilated their views on different aspects of literature which largely lie scattered in their voluminous critiques. Consequently, the inherent similarities in their views on life, art, and literature have been brought to light. A search into the meanings of frequently used yet undefined terms have also strengthened the bond unifying them.

I have been singularly fortunate to have received guidance from Prof. L.R. Sharma for which I am thankful. When confusion gripped and solution to the discussions was far to seek, his enlightening comments dispelled the haze and the clue eventually evolved. At times I have looked to Prof. Rajnath for imparting his invaluable views which would have been difficult to attain otherwise. I remain indebted to him for the kind help I received. I also thank Prof. Vandana Sharma who has given me all the encouragement and advice that I was quite often in need of.

The impetus for writing this book has come mainly from my parents for which I am beholden to them. I owe a lot to my husband whose unconditional support has seen this book through. It has been my pleasure to belong to a family that infused the enthusiam I called for. I am extremely grateful to them.

I acknowledge with gratitude the help given by my friends and cousins who have been considerate enough to send me the much needed material from Hyderabad, Kanpur and the UK.

Last but not least, I am thankful to Atlantic Publishers and Distributors (P) Ltd. for the interest evinced in publishing this book.

Ranjana Tripathi

The Argument

With literary criticism racing ahead towards vague and nebulous destinations, it may seem unnecessary and even anachronistic to think seriously of an old approach like the moralistic one. One of the aims of this study is to bring together the best that is found in English moralistic criticism and to show that this approach is one of the few that can save literary criticism from becoming a meaningless activity. M.H. Abrams, J. Hillis Miller and others have shown how with the help of the most recent approaches such as the one adopted by 'deconstruction', every reading of a literary work becomes a misreading. The net result is what the most such approaches can achieve is to bring the reader close to the text. The reader, however, is denied one of the primary fruits of reading literature, namely the thought content of literary works. If there is no certainity of being able to interpret the intention of the author, there is no use in thinking of the aesthetic dimension alone. Literature does teach, and it is a 'criticism of life'. It is only literature that can provide us with some of the most authentic and truly felt experiences of some of the greatest minds. It, therefore, becomes necessary to assert the importance of the moralistic approach and save literature and literary criticism from becoming a meaningless activity.

This study seeks to assert that the richest and the most valid version of moralistic criticism in English literature is contained in the works of Matthew Arnold, J. Middleton Murry, and F.R. Leavis. T.S. Eliot is excluded from the list because Eliot's criticism contains the germs of the criticism which the moralists ultimately oppose. Vincent Buckley groups Eliot with Arnold and Leavis as one of the greatest exponents of the moralistic approach, but the present study argues against

Eliot and supports Murry's inclusion in the tradition of the moralists. Eliot's exclusion from the study is due to the following reasons:

(a) Eliot is against interpretation, in literature. Murry, on the other hand, takes the writer seriously at his word.

(b) Whereas Arnold, Murry and Leavis stand for life and its experience, Eliot seems to stand away from life. This will emerge in the course of this book.

(c) Eliot focuses on the poem rather than the poet. This divorce between the poem and the poet makes the poem a sealed unit and becomes a plea for the formalistic approach which Arnold, Leavis and Murry supported only partially.

This study deals with critical concepts which have been defined by some of the most intelligent minds. It is for this reason that the book brings together a number of statements in the language used by the critics which could not be improved upon. Hence, the reader will find a number of quotations arranged in a certain order. The basic endeavour of this book is one of synthesis. In order to logically present the claims of the three critics, it was necessary to put before the reader a vast number of their quotations. Only after this was it possible to assess their works.

Ranjana Tripathi

Contents

1

Criticism and Morality

Since the moralistic approach to literature is as old as criticism itself, it is not an easy task to trace its history. But it is possible to put together as many views and attitudes to the problem of "Literature and Morality" as are central to our purpose. In this chapter, the method followed is that of M.H. Abrams's *The Mirror and the Lamp*—that stupendous masterpiece—in which Abrams examines exhaustively, the critical opinion in the eighteenth and nineteenth centuries, particularly in England and Germany. The difference between Abrams's work and my own effort is that he limits himself to a certain period and even if he goes beyond it, it is only to return to it again, whereas I have taken the period almost from the beginning of criticism and brought it up to the present. Abrams takes up all the responses to literature in the period in question, but I have limited myself to the moralistic response alone.

In dealing with such a large span of time, it is only natural that some critics will have to be left out. But the effort is to take up at least the most relevant one's. The net result has been that at times, the chapter seems disjointed and sketchy. In this respect, the present chapter will not be found as organically worked out as the rest of the chapters. But since the purpose of this chapter is to examine a large span of time, and the purpose of the other chapters is to focus only on certain points in this large flow, it is only natural that there will be some difference between the intrinsic quality of this chapter and the others.

Various approaches to literature are prevalent today. There are a few discussions among literary scholars which have drawn the attention of more minds than the one relating to literature and morality. Akin to this debate are the ones between form and content, truth and beauty, reason and sensation. To say that a work is aesthetically good is one thing and to say that it is morally of a high standard and can be useful to humanity, is another. Though outwardly both these views seem to be irreconcilable, yet they do have links and are not entirely unrelated.

Form and content exist in a unity. Taking either separately would be at the cost of the other and this would harm the work under consideration. All that is practically possible is giving importance to one while considering the other subservient to it. Content is the subject matter. It refers to the substance, the thought, the reason, the experience and the emotion of a work of art. Form is the style, the diction, the expression of the content. Words are the elements of both form and content. They convey through their meaning, and through their sound value. Those critics who emphasize the aesthetic value of a work are called formalists. In an attempt to define form, R.A. Scott-James says:

> Form...is the objective order that has been imposed on matter by the mind. And we may understand by it either the shape that our ideas take when the creative effort is complete, or the corresponding shape given to the medium through which the artist works.[1]

The ultimate aim of the formalists is to awaken perception. Art is not determined by the action but by the extent to which it activates our senses. Aestheticians view art for its own sake. It is entirely in the interest of poetry. The aim of art is to "exhibit", while that of morality is to "exhort".

According to H.W. Garrod, "the experience of art is the primary consideration"[2] for aestheticians. Morality influences action. It enters a work of art when an artist presents a discussion of life, or of man. Thus the view that the function of poetry is to influence humanity and make it morally better is the presumption of moralists. To evaluate a work wholly or in parts as unravelling the external truth, as presenting a criticism of life, is having "high seriousness", as a means of improving humanity, as a statement of man's relation to God, the universe or men is to judge a work within the framework of ethical theory. Moral, theories refer a work of art to a scheme of moral values existing outside it. The more concrete and explicit this scheme of moral values is, the more concrete and explicit is the moralistic criticism.

Sociological criticism which has gained importance in the twentieth century examines a work of art with reference to the social milieu of its author. The sociological critic treats literature as a social phenomenon and the creation of literature as a social act. Art for him is not created in vacuum. It is not for a particular person alone but it is a creation which has the emblem of the artist, the age, and the environment. Sociological criticism starts with a conviction that the relationship of art and society are vitally important, and that the investigation of these relationships may organize and deepen one's aesthetic response to a work of art. The values that are expressed in a work of art are, for sociological critics, relevant to a group, a class, a nation or to the humanity itself. Moral theory, it should be noted, is the mother of sociological theory of criticism, but all moral theories are not sociological theories. A few eminent sociological critics of our age are F.W. Bateson, John F. Danby and Humphry House. The roots of sociological criticism can be traced back to Vico's criticism of Homer's work in the eighteenth century, as a work exposing the social temper of that age. With the theory of Taine in the nineteenth century it attained individuality. It would not be wrong to say that Marxist criticism is a special form of sociological criticism, with a still narrower perspective of literature. The Marxist position is given clearly in a letter of Engels to Starkenburg, 25th January 1894:

> Political, legal, philosophical, religious, literary, artistic, etc., development is grounded upon economic development. But all of them react, conjointly and separately, one upon another and upon the economic foundation.[3]

That literature is a historical revelation and that the imaginative construct that is expressed is the reality, is the truth of that age, can be accepted. But that literature is grounded in the economics of the nation and it is only this that affects a work is difficult to accept. Engels, himself, in a letter dated 21st September 1890, to Joseph Bloch, admits that he and Marx had over-emphasized the economic factor and understated the role of reciprocal interaction. Plekhanov and Trotsky believe in a limited, independent development of form. Some of the better known writers of this type of criticism are Christopher Caudwell, Granville Hicks, and R.J. Kaufmann. Marxist criticism, towards the 1930s, was good and influential not in its pure form, but rather as an ingredient for those who went their own way in a personal, humanist or national direction, like Edward Wilson, Kenneth Burke, Trilling, and Matthiessen. Thus Marxist criticism opened the gates for the revolutionary writer who may have hesitated to write his criticism or publish his works because of being entirely different to the established form.

Sociological criticism has some shortcomings. A significant one is that it quite often provides no explanation to lyrical works and subjective writing. Thus a large part of creative writing remains inexplicable and unexplored by it. Despite its drawbacks, it has been fortunate enough to attain great heights and has a secure place today.

Both formal and moral criticism may be useful in themselves. To consider literature as a reflection of society or as a means of edification is to overlook the style—the expression. A complete criticism is possible by the synthesis of both the aspects. A possible means for the moralist to achieve this end is to evaluate a work of art in its totality and also show how the form helps to attain the moral end. Formalists, too, besides presenting their approach, can present a synthesis by showing how morality has been a means of attaining the formal end.

Historically, the theories of morality are as old as those of aestheticism itself. Plato, the first to discuss poetry and morality, often considers art as morally dangerous, and at other times morally inspired. These are two broad aspects of moral theories. In his famous works *The Laws* and *The Republic* he admired poets but in his ideal republic he tends to criticise the poets for hampering the growth of ethical values in the tender, young and impressionable minds. As a measure to protect them from works which weakened the senses and distressed the soul, he banned poets. In *The Republic* Plato's desire was to have a council of rulers of a state untouched by the germ of immorality. It was not possible to restrict their access, in their formative years, to works that violate morality. This being his chief concern, he banned poets. In his other works, *Ion* and *Phaedrus* he upheld the virtues of art and considered poets divine. But if asked to choose between art and morality, he would opt for the latter.[4]

Plato's views of poetry have relevance even today. The discussion of poetry and belief, a contentious debate of recent times, has its origin in his theory of poetry. He said that poetry is twice removed from reality. This explicitly means that whatever the poet says has nothing to do with his personal views, values and beliefs. Wimsatt, stating the importance of Plato in criticism today, says:

> What Plato saw as evil of poetry, the mixture of its emotions and the confusion of its advice has become new, under such names as ironic "tension" and "synaesthesis", the richness of aesthetic value. (Verbal Icon, 91)

Aristotle, reversed Plato by considering art as the imitation of a universal or an ideal rather than the imitation of an imitation. Aristotle's way of interpreting poetic imitation is probably his most valuable contribution to poetic theory. The object of poetic imitation is "men in action". The poet first acquired inspiration from the world by the power of his imagination; the art of poetry then imitates this, imaginative inspiration in language. The exciting thing here is to imagine life as it could be rather than as it is. Such imagination becomes a sensation that can inspire a poet. Men may be represented as better than they are in ordinary life, or as worse. The former representation would lead to serious writing like epic or tragedy, while the latter would lead to comedy. Aristotle thus introduces the moral consideration and distinguishes between tragedy and comedy.[5] To study the character, and how far a work is serious is for him, the primary task of the critic. Art is a thing of beauty and affords pleasure appropriate to its own kind. His concept of beauty is that it should have order, proportion and organic unity. Through a tragedy, a serious writing, there is release of emotions that bring about purgation of soul. Catharsis, as he calls it, is a means to attain a moral end to bring about peace of mind.

Horace emphasized the importance of both the usefulness and beauty of poetry, the *utile* and *dulce*, as he calls it. Art brings before us an image of what is better than us, it even affects us by the release we experience through this articulation. Quintillion concentrates on form and has less to say about matter. For him the choice of words is important so that there may be a proper arrangement. A critic should look for clarity, conciseness and design and also the force of the argument, the excitement around, the humour, and the devices that are used to arouse head and heart.

Before Longinus the function of literature was to instruct and to delight. Longinus introduced into the critical vocabulary the term "sublimity" which he said was required in a work of art besides delight and instruction. The choice of words, the ornament of style and the dignity of composition can bring about sublimity, which is in the domain of art. Longinus is more interested in that aspect of art which springs from the nature of the artist. According to him the thought and language are fused, and he is of the view that even if we discuss them separately, they have a combined effect on the soul. Both thought and passion are demanded from a poet by Longinus. This is an idea which Matthew Arnold developed into his concepts of truth and seriousness.

Dante gave importance to the subject of the poet. The best subjects are moral, philosophical and religious. The style should have the quality of loftiness or devotion. This, to a large extent, depends on the excellence of vocabulary. With Philip

Sidney began a new era in criticism. He defended poetry from the attacks of puritans in his work *The Defence of Poetry* (1585). Poetry is for him a superior moral teacher. Philosophy is too abstract, while history is too concrete. Poetry has its place somewhere between them. It presents ideas with concrete examples. Both the virtues and the vices are presented side by side in poetry. His view is truly a humanistic approach. To him poetry is an art of imitation for a specific purpose—to teach and to delight. It is a superior means of communication.

John Dryden was the first to discard the old tangle of conventional morality and art. Delight for him was the chief concern of art, morality could be accepted but only in the second place. Poetry, he believed, instructs through delight. But instruction could not be given by ignoring art. It is art through which instruction can be delivered.

Samuel Johnson belongs to the older traditional school of criticism. He is the spokesman of the classical school, he asserts effectively its doctrines. He was well steeped in the writings "of antiquity", which had formed his reading since the earliest times. Dr Johnson is concerned with literature as a means to basic truths, but he begins with the personal and emotive.[6] Dr Johnson defined a play as a just and lively image of human nature, representing its passions and honours and the changes of fortune to which it is subjected for delight and instruction of mankind. Delight comes from liveliness with which human nature is associated. Knowledge increases when one studies human nature and thus automatically learns about some aspects of life. Dr Johnson has also influenced some major critics like Murry, Eliot, Leavis, A.C. Bradley and Oliver Elton.

A recent book of criticism analyses the importance of Dr Johnson:

> Dr Johnson's common reader in eighteenth century England probably bears little resemblance to what would have to be defined as a common reader in twentieth century, industrial, urban, mass educated America. But if we make some allowance for changes in taste and the literary curriculum from the eighteenth to the twentieth

century, we can perhaps agree that for the most part we are talking about relatively similar types of readers.[7]

The basic function of literature for Plato, Horace, Dr Johnson and his followers is to teach morality and to probe philosophical issues.[8]

Wordsworth and the other Romantics valued art for the sake of experience and self-expression. William Wordsworth has an exalted view of poetry. His interest in humanity drove him towards nature. In the "Preface" to the *Lyrical Ballads* (1800) he calls poetry "...the spontaneous overflow of powerful feelings, it takes its origin, from emotion recollected in tranquility...."[9] He says that the principal objective of writing poems was to choose incidents and situations from common life and to relate or describe them throughout, as far as possible, in a language used by men. He also emphasizes the need of an interesting situation that would give pleasure. His concept of pleasure is moral.

S.T. Coleridge is regarded by many critics as one of the most original English critics. He was a poet and a philosopher too. Literature, he says in *Biographia Literatria* (1817), should give a vision of life revealed by reason. Poetry should be an ideal representation. He stresses the necessity of feeling, emotion or passion in poetry as it should arouse the emotion of the reader. Hence, poetry is not only a means to satisfy the creative impulse of the art or to communicate his state of mind to others. As truth is the object of science, pleasure is of poetry. Pleasure in art is to serve its own end. It may happen to be useful, moral, instructive and health giving.

Charles Augustine Sainte Beuve belonged to the group which brought "Protestantism" in literature and believed in the freedom of art. He had no method and in this way asserted the necessity of some new method.[10] Broadly speaking his method was to judge the author, and understand him. His approach was biographical for he believed that a critic can create only when he enters the imagination of the creator. In this way critic is also a creative artist whose theme is literature. His literary criticism was admired by Matthew Arnold[11] and Irving Babbit;[12] J.M. Murry also adopted the view that the critic must penetrate into the artists' line of thought.

H.A. Taine believed that literature was created by social forces. He presented a doctrine of race, milieu, and moment. His was a scientific way of judgement. According to Taine, "Three different sources contribute to produce this elementary moral state—race, surroundings and epoch."[13]

Nietzsche believed that the essential requirement of art is, "...the beautiful appearance of the dream worlds, in creating which every man is a perfect artist".[14] The other requirement is 'drunkenness', under its influence it causes the "self to vanish into complete self-forgetfulness".[15]

Matthew Arnold worked to promote culture through poetry and criticism. The function of criticism was to evaluate a work and to propagate the best ideas and transfer them to the next generation. In poetry, too, he had immense faith as it had the power "to animate", "to console", "to rejoice" and "to strengthen".[16] He insisted that poetry would one day take the place of religion. Though his chief concern lay in content, he did not ignore form. Some moral qualities, he said, seem to be connected in a man with his power of style. Milton's grand style had "great character elevation". He demanded that the poetic subject should have magnitude and character should be stressed. Poetry must contain an attitude of high seriousness.[17] This characteristic of poetry is chiefly required for the growth of morality through poetry. He is sometimes considered as the first modern critic. His criticism is a notable example to Aristotelian criticism. He has greatly influenced J.M. Murry, T.S. Eliot, and F.R. Leavis as discussed in the later chapters.

John Ruskin, too, had a theory to satisfy the humane conventions of middle class morality.[18] According to him art is never irrelevant, it is a supreme creation and is close to morality. All the fine arts should be didactic and should teach nobility. For Carlyle, who was his contemporary, criticism stands like an interpreter between the inspired and the uninspired; between the prophet and those who hear the melody of his words and catch some glimpse of the material meaning, but understand not their deeper import. Thus, he gave to criticism the great task of spreading the views and communicating to mankind, the light of the enlightened few.

Walter Pater gave an entirely new view of literature. He said that literature was not to teach lessons or enforce rules, or stimulate us to noble ends. Instead it was to divert the mind for some time and fix such emotions in a man. This cannot be done in any other way. His theory was totally in the interest of poetry and he presented the aristocratic view of literature by emphasising merely the manner or the style. He is the father of the doctrine of "Art for Art's Sake". It is an expression that distinguishes a work of literature from the vast expanse of prose works. According to Walter Pater all beauty is only "fineness of truth, or what we call expression"; and again, all art "does but consist in the removal of surplus age". His theory of art has been adopted by the aestheticians of the twentieth century. Arthur Symons is closest to Pater. The Bloomsbury group with members like Lytton Strachey and Virginia Woolf too believed that delight is the primary objective of art.

Henry James, whose real interest lay in form, insisted that the main object of a novel is to represent life and not merely to entertain. Man, he said, is distinct from animal because he has a body as well as a mind and spirit. Hence, he has moral values.[19] A novelist who deals with the mind alone is superior to the one who deals with body alone.[20] James carried on the Emersonian doctrine according to which the beautiful is the highest and the imaginative writers of the first order have a kind of philosophy behind their work.[21] Thus he considered form as supreme and morality as a means of the formal end.

William Dean Howells, who carried the theory of Taine to America, is one of the well-known representatives of realism in fiction and criticism. He demanded that a work should be judged scientifically. "The perfect aesthetics", according to Howells, "results from the perfect ethics.... Where the artist and the moralist work together for righteousness, there is the true artist." A true critic will be:

> ...gentle, dispassionate scientific student of current literature, but realizes that it is a plant which springs from the nature of a people, and draws its forces from

> their life, that its root is in their character, and that it takes form from its will and taste.[22]

Anatole France, the most subjective of all critics, had a negative view about art. Skeptical he was for all values, beauty he thought was only an illusion. "Aesthetics is based on nothing solid", he said. "A good critic is one who relates the adventures of his soul among masterpieces". Thus he gives importance to the experience of the critic who is able to convey the actual experience of the artist. This idea was adopted by J.M. Murry in his criticism. In the section on Murry, this approach will be examined.

Henry Bergson is known to be a philosopher primarily. Artists, he thought, are those rare people who come nearest to perceiving, "...all things in their native purity, the form, colors, sounds of the physical world as well as the subtlest movements of the inner life."[23] He did not value idealism in art. Art, he says, has no other object than to, "...brush aside the utilitarian symbols, the conventional and socially accepted generalities...and bring face to face, with reality itself' .[24]

Benedetto Croce wrote *Poetry* (1936) after a long meditation. Its first part, "Poetry and Literature" deals with the nature of poetic expression and distinguishes it from other types of expressions often confused with it. Poetry shows obviously the quality of inspiration that appears in all human experience, because in poetry the relation of the individual to the universal from finite to the infinite is more evident than in the world of action. The second part "The Life Of Poetry" deals with the re-evocation of poetry. The last part deals with "Formation and Education of the Poet". It affirms the necessity for discipline but, still more asserts an artist's independence. The same aesthetic principles are applicable to all the arts. The judgement of poetry has only one aspect and that is of beauty. Beauty is the sole category of aesthetic judgement. In Croce's philosophy art is nothing but intuition or expression (within the mind) of impressions. The intuition becomes art when the spirit persists in it. The artist is a man who vividly observes. The vividness of his seeing is nothing but the vividness of expression. Life is the subject matter of art. Everything takes place within the mind of the artist. The impression of the inward aesthetic expression become beautiful when it unfolds itself successfully. The pleasure of art is to thrill which accompanies the self-liberation of successful expression. The work of art, the aesthetic work, is always internal, and that which is called external is no longer a work of art. The Crocean concept has been adopted by Jacques Maritan. Since poetry is a creative activity rooted in life, humanistic trend in his criticism is evident.

In the early years of the twentieth century, literary criticism was dominated by academicians like W.C. Browell, George Woodberry, and George Santayana in America; George Saintsbury, Sir Walter Raliegh and A.C. Bradley in England. On the whole all of them were carrying on the tradition of Matthew Arnold. They were, in general, considerate and fairminded but belonged to a group that was fast being replaced.

At the turn of the century there was vigorous experimentalism in art—imagism, expressionism, vorticism, Georgian poetry, etc. Imagism did not last long but it left its mark on poetry. In 1911, Randolf Bourne in his *Youth and Life* called for a vigorous re-examination of the past.[25] Van Wyck Brooks responded with his *America's Coming of Age* (1915) and was soon joined by others. In 1910, Jeol Spingran delivered his famous address, "The New Criticism", at Columbia University. He looks forward towards the later formalistic criticism of the thirties when he tells the critic to give importance to the form thoroughly.

At this time the main intellectual force was given by T.E. Hulme. The emphasis was on visual imagery. Simple language with appropriate vocabulary and freedom in the choice of subject matter was the chief characteristic. The technique was experimental and their chief emphasis lay on it.

T.E. Hulme in his essay on "Romanticism and Classicism" (Written in 1913 but not published until 1924), interprets romanticism in the general political sense of the French antiromantics endorsing, for example, the view that "...romanticism has made a revolution. They hate the revolution, so they hate romanticism".[26] Verse for the Romantics means a bringing in of some of the emotions that are grouped around the world. He went on to develop a view in which aesthetic, religious and political attitudes are carefully dealt with. Romanticism for him is "split religion". He favoured classicism, abstract art, religious attitude, belief in original sin, hard, clear and precise images, fancy, mediaeval age, discipline, and dictatorship or atleast royalism. He was against romanticism, naturalistic art, humanism, confidence in man, emotional attitude, imagination, self-expression and democracy. We can trace Eliot's views on classicism in literature, royalism in politics, and Anglocaoholicism in religion when we examine the ideology of theme.

After Matthew Arnold, aestheticism started overshadowing morality. Humanistic criticism is by nature serious and sincere. It has maturity and awareness. In the twentieth century the followers of this theory are known as Neo Humanistics.[27] They are concerned with the ends of literature as affecting man, with the place of literature in the life of man. The rejuvenators of humanism were Paul Elmer More and Irving Babbit in America. In the twenties they were joined by Norman Forester, Harry Hayden Clark, G.R. Elliott, Robert Shafer, Frank Jewett and many others, a good enough number to form a separate school. After the death of More and Babbit, Neo-Humanism evolved as Religious Humanism.

Our present conviction that poetry is an instrument of human betterment, and that it should not be overtly didactic is a legacy of the romantic period.[28] But as science strengthened and classicism flourished, romanticism started losing ground. In trying to return to older didacticism, Samuel Alexander gave the method of double or multiple valuation. Truth and beauty, as subject matter and form, are liable to be judged separately. This is a way of rejecting the works that are either deficient in form or in content. They can only survive if both form and content are in accordance with each other. John Dewey pushes to the background the dichotomy of form and content and brings to the forefront the moral and cognitive forces of literature. Art, he says, weds man and nature. At the heart of art lies the basic pattern of relations of the live creature to his environment. The richness of an aesthetic experience is a matter of form as well as of content. Form is an organized experience, valuable because it both reflects the tensions of the world, thereby mirroring its contradictory possibilities, and also gives them unity and totality. His closeness to Arnold is evident here.

T.S. Eliot was dissatisfied with impressionistic critics. He desired a scientific system of evaluation. He declared himself a classicist. Impersonality in poetry was a mark of excellence for him. The poet is great not because he puts his personality into his work but because he has a mind in which there are a variety of feelings which combine with each other to present a new combination. The greater the artist the lesser will he project his personality and impressions into his work. He shunned emotion at all levels.

Eliot and John Middleton Murry were contemporaries and antagonists in their critical approaches. A ten year long debate went on between them in which Murry was a supporter of romanticism and Eliot of classicism. While Eliot thought that every work should be governed rationally, Murry asserted that an "inner voice"[29] should govern a work of art. Murry's approach to literature was moralistic. He clearly states "The vital centre of our ethics is also the vital centre of our Art". He associated seriousness with morality and had a desire to discern and communicate the truth about life. In this he continues the tradition of Matthew Arnold and prepares the ground for F.R. Leavis, who has furthered this approach.

"New Critics" is a term given to a group of critics of the nineteen thirties and forties who had much in common. The publication of John Crowe Ransom's *The New Criticism* (1941) gave a permanent label to the critics of this group. The period of its greatest acceptance was after the Second World War. They gave primary importance to the text, "to the words on the page", the technique and the capacity of literature to exist autotelically. Some of the names which are associated with it are I.A. Richards, William Empson and F.R. Leavis (only partly) in England, Cleanth Brooks, Allen Tate, Robert Penn Warren, John Crowe Ranson and R.S. Crane in America.

The views of I.A. Richards on poetry, its nature and value are contained in and have been developed fully in his *The Principles of Literary Criticism* (1934). He has first constructed a general theory of value and has then shown how poetry was valuable in the light of that theory. His theory may be termed as "Psychological Utilitarianism". Poetry arises out of a balanced state in a poet to communicate to the reader. To expose this state of mind is the work of the critic. He also gives importance to communication.

I.A. Richards in his essay on "Poetry and Beliefs" says that a poet presents his attitudes in a poem but he does not assert that they are his own beliefs. In a play, attitudes presented may be merely a demand of the situation. For him the falsity of the poem is no defect, the truth no merit.[30] He says that we must free poetry from the entanglement of belief, and the arts are the store houses of recorded values. Yet he asserts that poetry is a supreme form of emotive language, thus deemphasizing its rational content. L.T. Lemon finds in this the greatest error of Richards. If poetry is a store house of recorded value, it must record experiences of humanity which is undoubtedly an intellectual pursuit. Here Richards shows affinity to the humanists.

With I.A. Richards begins once again the discussion of "Poetry and Belief". This issue has been further debated by T.S. Eliot, Middleton Murry and their successors. There are two aspects of this question of belief, as we shall see in the pages that follow. Firstly, does a poet believe what he says in his poetry? Is it the poet's belief that is presented in the works? Secondly, is it essentially the truth that is presented in the works? There is a slight difference between the two aspects, but the difference cannot be ignored. What interests us most here is, should the reader believe what the poet writes? As M.H. Abrams says, "The problem of belief, in one or another formulation, is no less ancient than criticism, and it has always been argued in terms of 'knowledge', 'truth', and 'reality', which are the cruxes of all philosophical disagreement."[31]

Undoubtedly, Plato was the first to discuss the problem of poetry and belief as for him poetry is twice removed from reality. But it is not possible here to begin the discussion from the very beginning and show its growth. It should be made clear once again that in poetry it is the intention of the poet and the effect that it has that matters most. Whatever the poet believes or seems to believe in poetry has a moral intention and his work should have a positive effect on the readers.

Tzvetan Todorov delivered the F.W. Bateson Memorial Lecture at Oxford in February 1988. In the lecture, he too dealt with the discussion of poetry and truth. Professor Todorov said that there have been various divergent views on the question of truth in poetry over the years. Nevertheless, these opinions have also something in common, namely the belief that literature is a discourse which allows a better understanding of the human world, and enables one to relate better to its particular values. Poetry must certainly please, but it must also instruct and, at the same time it must imitate nature. He further held that it was debatable as to how this instruction should be brought about. But however great these discussions may be, one conviction he insisted is shared by all, that is, "Literature has a dimension of truth and that it is connected with the world of values." He further added that instead of bringing a new answer to the old questions, they (the critics of 19th and 20th century) now claim that the questions themselves are futile or of no interest. I shall begin with the modern age in criticism, that is, with Arnold. To explain Arnold's position it would be better to give the views of J.S. Mill. Mill points out that poetry is a "representation of feeling". Further he states:

> [Science] addresses itself to the belief, (poetry) to the feelings. The one does its work by convincing or persuading, the other by moving. The one acts by presenting a proposition to the understanding, the other by offering interesting objects of contemplation to the sensibilities.[32]

Whereas, for Arnold, as Peter Allan Dale puts; it:

> Ideas, if not true scientifically, may be true emotionally, and it is this emotional truth that one experiences when ideas are expressed in poetry. In other words, the ideas in poetry, are for Arnold, beliefs that cannot be "scientifically" affirmed, but which are to be valued nonetheless because they produce certain emotional effects: they console, they elevate, they rejoice.[33]

Thus what cannot be proved factually may be a truth in the sense that it has a humanitarian basis. Poetic truth in this way differs from the factual truth of science. This is very close to Richard's "objectless beliefs", which though they may have lost their "truth" as far as science is concerned, still have important emotional value and accordingly account for some of the "most important and valuable effects which the acts produce." Elaborating this point Prof. Todorov says

> I wonder whether the solution to our enigma might not be found in the idea that critics have of the nature of knowledge. It is an idea which seems to have been profoundly influenced by the scientific model as we know it from the physical sciences to the point when the two terms have become interchangeable: there is no knowledge (no good, true, knowledge) that is not scientific. This is because people want all truth, to be expressed in the form of proposition of the kind that one meets in chemistry or biology books, and because people claim that truth has nothing to do with song (nor, according to some more radical views, with literary criticism itself, or even with history in general). If knowledge in the first instance is reduced to science (or to a certain model of science) there is no difficulty about going on to claim,—whether it be in order to welcome or to deplore the fact—that poetry has nothing to do with knowledge. This conception of poetry, far from being in conflict with the contemporary cult of science, is merely a side effect of it; and there is solidarity where one might have expected to see conflict.

To change this attitude and claim that poetry does have something to do with knowledge would imply that we were changing our views not only about poetry but also about knowledge itself.... Poetry is, or is also a search for truth and for values: there is no shame in acknowledging this and in seeking to understand how—in concrete terms—it comes about.[34]

Keeping this in view, I shall first begin with the early nineteenth century critic Jeremy Bentham, the mentor of J.S. Mill. According to Bentham, by standards of logical truth, poetic statements are falser "Indeed, between poetry and truth there is a natural opposition: flase morals, fictitious nature."[35] Therefore, the views of Bentham and Mill, in favour of Arnold's views are entirely unacceptable. I.A. Richards says that all language divides into two kinds. On the one side is "scientific statement", whose truth is ultimately a matter of correspondence, "with the fact to which it points". On the other side is "emotive utterance", including poetry, which is composed of "pseudostatements" whose function is not to assert truths but to organize our feelings and attitudes. And since we have learned to free the emotional efficacy of poetry from belief, poetry must take over the function of ordering our emotional life hitherto performed by the pseudo statements of religion.

M.H. Abrams, expressing his views on the subject, says:

> The poet must still win our imaginative consent to the aspects of human experience he presents, and to do so he cannot evade his responsibility to the beliefs and prepossessions of our common experience, common sense, and common moral consciousness.[36]

Before coming to some definite conclusion, another question that goes alongwith this must be analysed—How far does a poet's voice convey his beliefs? Eliot, as has been already noted earlier, along with Murry has reproached I.A. Richard's stand. He states that the extent to which poets write their poetry because of what they believe, and how far they believe a thing is merely because they see that they can make poetry out of it.

Nevertheless Eliot maintains that to entirely dissociate poetic beliefs from the beliefs of the poet is not possible.[37] In this he seems to agree with Murry's statement that a poet means what he says.[38] Eliot disapproving of Richards's statement says:

> A certain writer has affected a complete severance between his poetry and beliefs is to me incomprehensible. If you deny the theory that full poetic appreciation is possible without beliefs in what the poet believed, you deny the existence of poetry as well as criticism.[39]

He believes that if we preconceive that the poet does not present his own beliefs there is nothing to appreciate in a poem. For his own poetry he says, "I cannot wholly separate my poetic appreciation from my personal beliefs".[40] "To enjoy a work", he says, "we should have the pleasure of sharing the beliefs of the poet."[41]

Analyzing the different views of these critics it may be said that poetic truth must not be confused with scientific facts. Though the aim of science and poetry are almost identical as both have a humanitarian basis, the means to achieve this are entirely different. Science provides comfort to the body and it appeals to reason, while poetry aims at providing comfort to the mind, it appeals also to the emotions. Poetry has a wider perspective of comforting the body through the path of the mind. In poetry it is the intention of the poet and the effect that poetic belief has on the reader matters most. But to have a positive effect it is essential for the poet not to entirely dissociate his beliefs from that of the beliefs presented in the poem. There must be a relationship. So to say like Richards, "The truth of the poem is no merit and the falsity-no defect", cannot be accepted. Whatever the poet believes or seems to believe in his poetry must have a moral intention—his work should have a moral effect. Poetry, too, imparts knowledge, but this knowledge is different from that of science. Thus what is true for poetry may not be true for the science and poetic beliefs may not be scientific facts.

Returning to the historical perspective, the next critic to be discussed is F.R. Leavis. He has been called a New Critic by some but New Critics have very little in common with him. He saw imaginative literature as central to a culture and echoed Arnold's plea for propagating culture. He had immense faith in tradition. Tradition helps to transfer from one generation to the other generation those values of art that are vital to its existence. The values of cultural tradition must be consciously maintained in the modern world. Its aim was to expose the laxity of modern criticism and to give importance to the worthy writer. He considered those writers great who had originality, who presented a proper relationship between art and life and a vital capacity for experience and who presented an affirmation of life. In *The Great Tradition* (1948) Leavis has classified novelists according to their ability to affirm life, just as he has condemned poets in *Revaluation* (1936) and *New Bearings, In English Poetry* (1932), who have an empty content.

G. Wilson Knight was influenced by J.M. Murry.[42] He together with Herbert Read, is a confirmed romantic critic. Knight's importance lies in his pioneering work on Shakespeare that helps to read Shakespeare's plays in totality, which shows an inner evolution. His first interest he says "...the structure, the pattern, the body of the work in question almost irrespective of the exact language used".[43] Read laid emphasis on content and said that reason was essential in a work of art.

John Crowe Ransom, a New Critic has a slight tilt towards moralistic criticism.[44] He has discussed both pure and platonic poetry, first being the poetry of things, the second being the poetry of ideas. According to Ransom neither can exist in a pure state. Art exhibits minimum of reason and therefore the aesthetic quality of a poem can be judged with language alone. Yet the content of the poem plays an important role. He refers to form as something irrelevant which, he says, surrounds the core of content. The critic, he said, has to deal with the "irrelevancies" as this is what gives value to the poem. The core should not interest the aesthetic critic.

Allan Tate's conclusion that, "Poetry is one test of ideas; it is tested by experience, by the act of direct apprehension", is quite reasonable. A poem requires a wholeness a completeness in integrity of all components that make a full experience.[45] Nevertheless his statement that Emily Dickenson's inability to think improved her poetry shows that he does not give thought the value that a moralist generally gives. He maintains that ideas as such are not present in the poetry yet poetry affects as if ideas were present.

For E.M.W. Tillyard poetry expresses "great common places". Depending on how clearly the commonplace is expressed poetry is "direct" or "oblique".[46] For him the techniques of obliquity, wit, irony, etc. are not so valuable as the New Critics think them to be.

Irving Babbit is of the view that classist doctrine of imitation is a doctrine that suffered from the start from a "taint of formalism".[47] The attack on literature as mere self-expression which is implicit in Hulme and Eliot, is developed by Babbit.

According to W.K. Wimsatt pleasure in poetry arises from something more active than mere thought behind the words in a poem, because the reader himself has a point of view. Poetic value cannot be considered remote from the rest of human experience. He says:

> Poetry by its concreteness and dramatic presentation of value situations, whether it inclines to a right answer or to a wrong answer by the very fullness and hence imaginative power of its presentation has the meaning and being which makes it poetry.[48]

For A.C. Bradley, the "experience of poetry is an end in itself" and its poetic value is this intrinsic worth alone. Poetry has a world of its own, independent and complete, and to belong to it we must overlook our own values and beliefs and our world as such. Only then it is possible to achieve a unity in form and content.

Yvor Winters has done more to defend the importance of meaning in poetry than any other critic of his time. For him poetry is a statement in words about a human experience. The content of a work may communicate the emotion which is appropriate to make it rational. Man is a rational, emotional and a sensory animal living in a physical universe, hence poetry is a fusion of emotion and the motive. A reader cannot share the emotion of the poet unless he knows the motivation behind it.[49] Winters does not subordinate poetry to morality or philosophy, but he asserts that since poetry must deal with human experience it involves ethics. He does not judge a poem by its message alone. He realizes that the ornament and the meaning of a poet exist in unity.

Graham Hough is of the view that criticism may never be a means of promoting culture as Arnold and Leavis hoped, nevertheless it has its own share of duty towards it. Men, in future can turn back to the works of literature and identify themselves with it. Criticism should, in turn, establish or give an account of the relation of a work of art to its social order.[50] Thus Graham Hough, too believes in the subordination of form. Content should be the main tool of the critic.

Robert Weimann, a recent critic in his book: *Structure and Society in Literary History* (1976) observes that literature has two basic functions. One is of the imitation of reality and the other is that it carries a message. He says that these two functions keep changing with age.[51] What might be true for one age might not be true for another. Those works that are truly great have a message. Though the imitation of reality may not be relevant, the message is what gives importance to a work. This is the reason why Shakespeare even today remains great. We still find meaning in his works because of the message. Therefore, morality helps literature to remain alive in successive ages. Shakespeare is alive even today because the thought, the message that remains true even after such a long span of time.

Having traced the history of the most significant critics with a moralistic vision, I now proceed to examine three critics whose work centres round the moralistic stance and for whom literature and morality cannot be divorced from each other.

NOTES

1. R.A. Scott-James, "Walter Pater", *The Making of Literature* (1928; rpt. Delhi: Allied Publishers, 1963), p. 305.
2. H.W. Garrod, "Poetry and Life", *Poetry and the Criticism of Life: The Charles Eliot Norton Lectures for 1929-30* (1931; rpt. New York: Russell and Russell, 1963), p. 30.
3. Graham Hough, "Moral Theory", *An Essay in Criticism* (London: Gerald Duckworth and Co., 1966), p. 33.
4. Plato has been quoted by W.K. Wimsatt: "And so when we have annointed him with myrrh and set a garland of wool upon his head, we shall send him away to another city". W.K. Wimsatt, "Poetry and Morals", *The Verbal Icon: Studies in the Meaning of Poetry* (1954; rpt. London: Methuen and Company Ltd., 1970), p. 86.
5. S.H. Butcher, *Aristotle's Theory of Poetry and Fine Art* (1894; rpt. New York: Dover Publications, 1951), pp. 127-94.
6. E.G. Griffin, "Murry, Eliot and Style", *John Middleton Murry* (New York: Twayne Publishers, 1969), p. 53.
7. W.L. Guerin, E.G. Labor, L. Morgan, J.R. Willingham, "Prologue: The Precritical Response", *A Handbook of Critical Approaches to Literature* (New York: Harper and Row Publishers, 1979), p. 1.
8. *Ibid.*, "Traditional Approaches", p. 29.
9. William Wordsworth, "Preface to the Lyrical Ballads (1800-1802)", *Wordsworth's Literary Criticism*, ed. W.J.B. Owen (London: Routledge and Regan, 1974), p. 85.
10. C.W. Allen and H.H. Clark, eds., "Sainte Beuve", *Literary Criticism* (New York: American Book Company, 1941), pp. 468-78.
11. Matthew Arnold, *Unpublished Letters of Matthew Arnold*, ed., Arnold Whitridge (New Haven: Yale University Press, 1923), pp. 65-66.
12. Irwing Babbit, "Impressionist versus Judicial Criticism", *Publications of the Modern Language Associations*, NS, XIV, No. 3 (1906), pp. 687-705.
13. For H.A. Taine, "Introduction", *History of English Literature* (1863) trans. H. van Laun. See *Twentieth Century Criticism—The Major Statements*, ed. William J., Handy Max Westbrook (1974; rpt. Light Life Pub., 1976), p. 31.

14. Nietzsche: *The Birth of Tragedy* translated by Clifton Fadiman, Quoted in *Literary Criticism* eds. Allen and Clark (New York: American Book Company, 1941), p. 513.
15. *Ibid.*, p. 514.
16. Matthew Arnold, "The Study of Poetry", *Essays in Criticism,* II ed., S.R. Littlewood (New Delhi: Macmillan, 1938), p. 3 and Matthew Arnold, *The Complete Prose Works*, Vol. I, ed. R.H. Super, p. 2.
17. Matthew Arnold, *The Complete Prose Works*, Vol. XI, ed. R.H. Super, p. 331.
18. John Ruskin, *Arata Pentelici Lecture, IV* from R.A. Scott-James, p. 284.
19. Allen and Clark, "Henry James", *Literary Criticism*, p. 226.
20. *Ibid.*, for Henry James, *Partial Portraits* (1905), p. 227.
21. *Ibid.*, p. 285.
22. Howells, "Leo Tolstoy", *North American Review*, CIXXXVII, p. 847.
23. Allen and Clark, eds., "Henri Bergson", *Literary Criticism,* p. 611.
24. *Ibid.*, p. 616.
25. Wilber Scott, "The Background", *Five Approaches to Literary Criticism* (New York: The Macmillan Company, 1962), pp. 17-18.
26. T.E. Hulme, *Twentieth Century Literary Criticism* ed. David Lodge (1972; rpt. London: Longman Group, 1975), p. 94.
27. Graham Hough, "Criticism as a Humanistic Discipline", *Contemporary Criticism*, ed. Malcolm Bradbury and David Palmer (London: Edward Arnold Pubs, 1970), p. 41.
28. L.T. Lemon, "The Mirror of Morality: Edification Theories", *The Partial Critics* (New York: Oxford University Press, 1965), p. 47.
29. Middleton Murry, "The Cry in the Wilderness", *Aspects of Literature* (1920; rpt. London: Jonathan Cape, 1934), p. 185.
30. I.A. Richards, "Poetries, and Science", *A Reissue of Science and Poetry* (1926; reissued in 1935) (London: Routledge and Kegan Paul, 1970), pp. 51-61.

31. M.H. Abrams, "Belief and the Suspension of Disbelief", *Literary Criticism: Idea and the Act* (California: University of California Press, 1974), p. 149.
32. *Ibid.*, p. 167.
33. *Ibid.*
34. T. Todorov, "Poetic Truth: Three Interpretations", *Essays in Criticism*, XXXVIII, April 1988, Vol. 2, pp. 98-99.
35. M.H. Abrams, "Belief and the Suspension of Disbelief", *Literary Criticism Idea and the Act*, ed., W.K. Wimsatt, p. 168.
36. M.H. Abrams, "Belief and the Suspension of Disbelief", *Literary Criticism: Idea and the Act*, ed. W.K. Wimsatt (California: University of California Press, 1974), p. 168.
37. T.S. Eliot, "Dante", *Selected-Essays* (London: Faber and Faber, 1932), p. 231.
38. J.M. Murry, "Purgatory Blind", *Keats and Shakespeare*, pp. 55, 60.
39. T.S. Eliot, "Dante", *Selected-Essays*, p. 231.
40. *Ibid.*, p. 232.
41. *Ibid.*, p. 234.
42. S.G. Cassavant, "Spiritual Heroes", *John Middleton Murry: The Critic as Moralist* (Alabama: University of Alabama Press, 1982), p. 70.
43. G. Wilson Knight, "The New Interpretation", *Essays in Criticism*, 3 (1953), p. 384.
44. L.T. Lemon, "The Mirror of Morality: Edification Theories", *The Partial Critics*, p. 59.
45. Allen Tate, *Reactionary Essays* (New York: Charles Scribner's Sons, 1936), p. xi.
46. E.M. Tillyard, *Poetry Direct and Oblique* (London: Chatto and Windus, 1948), p. 48.
47. Irving Babbit, "Genius and Taste", quoted from *Five Approaches to Criticism* by Wilber Scott, p. 30.
48. W.K. Wimsatt, "Poetry and Morals—A Relation Reargued", *The Verbal Icon Studies in the Meaning of Poetry* (London: Methuen and Company Ltd., 1970, first pub. 1954), p. 96.
49. L.T. Lemon, *The Partial Critics*, pp. 64-65 and Rene Wellek, "A.C. Bradley", *A History of Modern Criticism*, pp. 28-41.

50. Graham Hough, "Criticism as a Humanist Discipline", *Contemporary Criticism*, ed. Malcolm Bradbury (1970; rpt., London: Edward Arnold Ltd., 1979), pp. 39-59.

51. Robert Weimann, "Past Significance and Present Meaning", *Structure and Society in Literary History Studies in the History and Theory of Historical Criticism* (Virginia: The University Press of Virginia, 1976), pp. 48-49.

2

Matthew Arnold

Matthew Arnold, a great poet and one of the greatest critics of his time has been an issue of controversy. Some consider him to be a great poet of his time but not a critic, while others consider him to be a great critic but just an ordinary poet. Still others feel that he was a poet at heart but turned to criticism. There are many reasons given by different critics for his transition from poetry to prose. What remains undisputed, however, is his image of a moralist. The concern here is to show how in literary criticism, he has adorned the topmost position as a moralist.

G.W.E. Russell established in 1903 that Arnold was not a great poet yet a true one. Arnold was for him a greater critic than a poet; he devoted twice as many years to criticism than to poetry. Arnold was a great critic because he wrote successfully on many subjects ranging from conduct, education, society, literature to politics and theology. This opinion is representative of Arnold's contemporary criticism. But over the years it has been established that he was a poet at heart. His literary criticism has confronted many attacks. Even in 1930 Garrod maintained that Matthew Arnold's religion was poetry and his connections with literary criticism were casual and intermittent, and that Matthew Arnold had to his credit, as far as literary criticism is concerned, only two books, "one good, one bad...besides the second series of *Essays in Criticism* (1888)."[1] Denying Arnold's critical achievements, he added:

> He was not a critic—he had written no criticism at all...but for the accident of the Oxford professorship, I am not sure that it was in his heart to be a literary critic at all.[2]

I strongly disagree with Garrod here. Poetry was the first love of Arnold but by staying with it alone he would not have achieved his exalted destination. To his age he sacrificed his Muse for a greater cause—the survival of literature as a means of achieving the cultural end. As time went on, critics realized Arnold's intentions. Almost within two decades after Garrod's remark, Matthew Arnold emerged as a literary critic of eminence. Basil Willey ranked Arnold as one of the better poets and one of the most important critics of the late nineteenth century. Joseph Carroll rightly says that in the last three decades Arnold has been consistently regarded as a critic of high repute. Tzvetan Todorov voices his opinion for an already established literary critic in the F.W. Bateson Memorial Lecture given in Oxford on 24 February 1988:

> ...he wants to put culture, of which literature is an essential component, in the place of religion and even philosophy. In Arnold and his successors poetry is entrusted with a mission that had previously been the preserve of religion; its task, quite simply, is to save us.[3]

Arnold's concept of religion remains a contentious debate even today. William Robbins, John Kent, Leslie Brisman, Nathan A. Scott Jr., Eric Tretheway, Ruth ap Roberts, James C., Livingston and Terry G. Harris are some names that have contributed to keeping alive this discussion even almost a century after Arnold. This will be dealt with later on in this chapter.

Arnold did not present his theory of literature and criticism in a single work. It is to be found in his essays on poets, dramatists and others, and to some extent also in his works on culture, society, and religion. His theory of literature is largely incidental. He usually does not write theory for its own sake. It is interspersed in his discussions of writers. The pages that follow will show that Arnold is a literary critic of a high order and his critical method and principles have been accepted and used by the great moralists of our own age.

Arnold's transition from poetry to prose has been variously interpreted. Howard Foster Lowry, after discussing this aspect of Arnold in detail, has summarised it thus:

> The conclusion I should draw is not that his poetic talent was constrained by the critical instinct, but that his output was sharply curtailed by the high standard he set himself.[4]

Among contributing causes Lowry lists the political interests which Arnold picked up at Landsdowne House, the later burden of the school inspectorship, heavy reading, and the poor reception that influenced Arnold's early poems. Lionel Trilling, however, stresses the uncongeniality of the age generally and the pressures of Arnold's critical intelligence,[5] while H.W. Garrod makes the Marguerite affair central to his transition from poetry to criticism.

Russell, as I have already mentioned believed that Arnold was always a critic and that he had strayed to poetry, "From first to the last he was a critic—a clam and impartial judge, a serene distributor to praise, and blame...."[6] But Arnold himself believes that it was all brought about by external pressures.[7] A quartrain which appeared as the epigraph to his last volume of poems indicates that his break with poetry was as desolating as it was involuntary:

> Though the the Muse be gone away,
> Though she move not earth today,
> Souls erewhile who caught the word,
> Ah! still harp on what they heard.[8]

Arnold himself was conscious of the departure of his "Muse". I believe, therefore, that Arnold's religion was poetry but the consciousness of his age made him move away from it to criticism or we may say, helped poetry to get back its consciousness to some extent.

Born in an age of utter dismay and disillusion, Arnold was preoccupied with the moral and cultural health of the society. The civilization of his time was for him decayed and diseased:

> ...for the world, which seems
> To lie before us like a land of dreams,
> So various, so beautiful, so new,
> Hath really neither joy, nor love, nor light,
> Nor certitude, nor peace, nor help for pain,
> Swept with confused alarms of struggle and flight,
> Where ignorant armies clash by night. (Dover Beach)

Arnold's letters to Clough show his responses to his environment. The 'Letters' show his resistance at times to the commercial, utilitarian ethos of his own middle class, at other times the moral strictures of his immediate circle, and at still other times the general confusion of thought arising from the contemporary European philosophy and theology. He thought his age to be unpoetical, "How deeply unpoetical the age and all one's surroundings are. Not unprofound, not ungrand, not unmoving—but unpoetical." The frustration of his age not only had its effect on his poetry but was also the chief reason behind his transit from poetry to prose. A few months later, in September 1849, he wrote to Clough:

> ...these are damned times—everything is against one—the height to which knowledge is come, spread of luxury, or physical enervation, the absence of great natures, the unavoidable contact with millions of small ones, newspapers, cities, light profligate friends, moral desperadoes like Carlyle, our ownselves....[9]

Then in 1852 he wrote again, in the air of the present times "...we deteriorate inspite of our struggles—like a gifted Roman falling on the invigorating atmosphere of the decline of the Empire."[10] Replying to and appreciating one of Clough's letters in 1853, he wrote, "Yes—congestion of brain is what we suffer from—I always feel it—and cry for air like my own Empedocles."[11]

The concept that poets can work at their highest pitch only when the "spiritual atmosphere" of the society is favourable, has been provided to posterity by Matthew Arnold. He gives the examples of Elizabethan England, the Germany of Goethe, and above all, the Greece of Sophocles. A body of poetry can be adequate to represent and interpret its society only when that society is adequate in its interpretation and representation of the nature of man. The society, as Arnold illustrates, provides ideas and also the medium. Burns could not attain the point of view, the elevated yet concerned detachment, which would lead to a "criticism of life" of the highest kind, in his kind of society.[12] G.H. Bantock states that Arnold finds the universe recalcitrant to his moral sense as also to his imagination.[13] Arnold himself, as has been noted earlier, was not satisfied with his age. He wanted to establish a society which could help the artists to write their works, rather than be a hindrance. One of Arnold's chief concerns was to establish and propagate human values in a world which did not interpret and represent human nature. F.R. Leavis, who was influenced by Arnold, states in *English Literature in Our Time and the University* (1969), that Arnold saw something new happening to humanity. Arnold saw and said that to preserve continuity of cultural consciousness a more conscious and deliberate use of intelligence was needed than in the past. Arnold was also aware, he says, of the fact that he was addressing to a large and immensely influential educated class. Arnold was "...too generous and fastidious" humanly to be satisfied, and moreover, with his eye on the inevitable coming of the economic, social and political transformations, he saw the dangers inherent in the ambiguity of the educated class— or educated classes.[14] Arnold was not preoccupied with a particular nation; he thought instead in terms of his age. Vincent Buckley rightly says that Arnold's provincialism is not of place but of time.[15] He further states that the attitude of Arnold arises from his intimate personal sense of complexity and the needs of his age. Eliot who opted for an impersonal approach was the opposite of Arnold in this aspect. Bilan however, thinks that Arnold and Eliot have similarities. Bilan obviously refers to a "human culture" as otherwise they cannot be compared and found similar.[16]

Arnold, as it is now clear, realised that his age was deeply "unpoetical" and therefore, tried his best to generate the poetical spirit. He felt that the function of poetry had been forgotten or at least there were some forces in the age that were hindering the growth of the type of poetry that was needed. His critical works reveal that poetry alone could enrich and enliven the cultural heritage and thus bring forth an age which would adjust well with the changing times.

Since religion was steadily being replaced by science and its disparaging effects like materialism were engulfing the world, Arnold took up the task of establishing order through literature. He had the faith that a belief in the aesthetic consciousness was capable of organizing and transfiguring the whole world of human experience. This view originated in Germany by a group of writers William Windelband, Katherine Gilbert, Helmut Kuhn, and Harold Hoffding.[17] At that time aesthetics seemed suddenly to open a new view according to which philosophy had, but occasional glimpse. Poetry was endowed with unprecedented power.

The preceding pages have made it clear that though Arnold had a lifelong conflict between his aptitude for poetry, on the one hand and on the other, his ethical sense of moral obligation as a Victorian citizen and his critical sense of duty as a member of the new intelligentia, he settled as a staunch moralist whose views on literature intend to expose its usefulness to society. Even today Arnold is a force to reckon with. My effort shall be to show why his position is secure even today and also to bring together some of Arnold's cardinal views which have greatly influenced the critics who have succeeded him.

The section that follows will throw light on Arnold's idea of poetry and shall also make clear his views on morality. He has been blamed for inconsistency. A close study reveals the reasons for it.

As a true representative of his age Arnold had an inner conflict. After a thorough examination of his critical works and poems, it seems that, there are three elements which are prominent in Arnold's work. He is (i) a poet of a basically romantic sensibility, (ii) a critic with a classical training, and (iii) he has a desire to reconstruct and this gives him the self-imposed role of a Victorian prophet. During his early years the third element was not obvious though there did appear traces of his consciousness, awareness about the society of his time. But as he grew up to be a mature critic this consciousness took a more concrete form. Some critics call this an inconsistency in Arnold's critical thought. For example, T.S. Eliot says:

> Arnold had little gift of consistency or for definition. Nor had he the power of connected reasoning at any length, his flights are either short flights or circular flights.[18]

Leon Gottferied[19] and Warren D. Anderson[20] have raised a similar dissatisfaction with Arnold's consistency. Geoffrey Tillotson criticizes Arnold's prose for the "lack of knowledge and grasp".[21] This is almost like saying that, if Arnold had knowledge and if he had grasp over his writings he would be consistent. F.R. Leavis in his essay on Arnold as critic deplores Eliot's view of Arnold's "The Study of Poetry", which Eliot so severely criticised. F.R. Leavis remarks that it cannot be proved that he was incapable of consistency and vigour of thought.[22] He further states that Arnold's intelligence was one that, even if not trained had its own discipline; an intelligence that is informed by mature and delicate sense of the human values and can manifest itself directly as a fine sensibility. William Robbins says that Arnold does not offer a complete and a coherent philosophy but he presents a set of humanistic ideals which stress the need for balance and sane perspective. In his book he deals particularly with the religious writings of Arnold and finds correlatives elsewhere in Arnold's works of the irreconcilables and tries to justify his religious position.[23]

William Madden maintains that Arnold was a lifelong atheist and his temperament was fixed early in life. He attempts to show that the main burden of Arnold's criticism is not a particular intellectual or moral gospel, but the exhibition and defence of this poetic temper and attitude:

> ...Arnold's criticism is consistently preoccupied with the nature and effects of the operation of the aesthetic consciousness, with explaining how art still had truth, why modern man could find refuge there, indeed, could find in the best poetry a new religion.[24]

John Holloway argues that Arnold inculcates not a set of ultimate beliefs—a "Life Philosophy"—but certain habits and a certain temper of mind.[25] But Holloway reviews his opinion about Arnold later and says that "...the willingness to speak out, and with decision, is the best thing in Arnold."[26] Let us see whether Arnold's criticism is largely consistent or not. Broadly speaking there are few explanations that are balanced and if they are analysed the answer evolves inevitably. A group of critics consider him to be a religious writer, another group regards him a cultural critic yet another group maintains that he lived and worked for the betterment of poetry.

Ruth ap Roberts argues in favour of Arnold's consistency and unity of thought.[27] According to her Arnold's chief concern was religion. This influenced all the works of Arnold—from early poetry to the final essays. She says that not only should *St. Paul and Protestantism* (1870), and *Literature and Dogma* (1873) be read in this light, but also works such as *Essays in Criticism* (1866 and 1888) and *Culture and Anarchy* (1869). J.C. Shairp and H.F. Bradley have charged Arnold with having an inadequate view of the relation of religion and culture ("the charge of aestheticism") and that—Arnold transmutes the Christian religion into subjective feeling. Livingston providing an answer to this says:

> Arnold helped Christian belief from a crude literalism and a morbid theologism. He saw how things were moving and perceived important religious exigencies in the period prior to the turn of the century. But more importantly, Arnold's insights on religious language, his perception or the need of an experimental beginning to any theological construction, his sagacious and subtle understanding of the interdependence of religion and culture, and his soundness in recognizing the moral dimension of the hermeneutical task as central and indispensable—all these remain as enduring contributions to religion and to the work of Christian criticism in the present time in the future.[28]

On the other side Joseph Carroll in an effort to unify the critical judgements of Arnold finds his individual perceptions and judgements having weight because they are not merely the expression of an amorphous sensibility, but rather formulations within a continuous effort, to give shape and definition to the whole range of human experience (XIII to XV). When Arnold comments on Keats, Goethe, or Voltaire, or when he judges Pope, Wordsworth, or merely set them within a hierarchy of literary excellence, his overriding concern is to situate them within a cultural system. William Madden, whose opinions have already been cited, says that the life which most deeply attracted Arnold was not moral but aesthetic; literature, he insists, was his real "meter", and throughout his career Arnold never ceased to identify his "true self" with his vocation of a poet (*CPW*, 192).

Arnold's works should be viewed with a wider perspective —religious, aesthetic or cultural explanations to his work reveal him but partially. To view him with a constricted point of view would, as has been observed above, result in a false distorted picture of Arnold's theory or a picture that is only partially true and not complete in itself. It is then that Arnold seems inconsistent. Arnold's works have a humanistic basis. Madden's opinion about him according to which he is an atheist cannot be considered just. His aesthetic leaning is a means to discover the powers of poetry and an effort to reconstruct society with the help of poetry.

As his awareness of the world around increased in dimension so did his concern for humanity. In religion Arnold saw the potential of saving humanity from being crippled under the pressure of doubt, despair, and the uncertainty of the age. But Arnold himself understood and realized that:

> ...at the present moment two things about the Christian religion must surely be clear to anybody with eyes in the head. One is that men cannot do without it; the other, that they cannot do with it, as it is. (*CPW*, 378)

In poetry he found a substitute for religion. Therefore to establish poetry as a saviour of humanity he worked endlessly. All through his career he worked for the same end—the reconstruction of society. As his vision of life matured and his interests gained firmer ground he became a critic from a poet and later on adorned himself with the self imposed role of Victorian prophet. Peter Allan Dale rightly points out that there is no doubt that the issues of poetry's relation to moral and religious ideas is one of the important critical problems that Arnold deals with.[29]

Matthew Arnold, throughout his career, maintained that poetry has the ability to edify and that criticism has to help in achieving this objective of poetry. Poetry was for him the "most satisfying form of human utterance". It should be noted here that all that Arnold desired of religion he also desired of poetry. Terry G. Harris in his essay on Matthew Arnold and his idea of religion says:

> As one reads his essays on religion, it is easy to recognize two separate but related principles informing his discussions: (1) the need for all elements of religion to be focused on improving conduct; and (2) the need to verify religion experimantally.[30]

Arnold aimed at bringing before the world the best poetry, poetry that had the power of sustaining, forming, and delighting us.[31] He desired that we conceive of poetry worthily and more highly than it had been the custom to conceive of it. It should be regarded as capable of higher uses and higher destinies. In a letter to Clough, Arnold declares that poetry must become:

> ...the complete *magister vitae* as the poetry of the ancients did by including as theirs did, religion with poetry, instead of existing as poetry only, and leaving religious wants to be supplied by Christian religion as a power of existing independent of the poetical power.[32]

Arnold discerned a power, a force in poetry. This is its great interpretative power. It helps to understand the mysteries of the world. He held that once we understand these mysteries with the help of poetry we no longer wonder and the senses become calm. Poetry alone can bring this about (*CPW* III, 32).

Poetry as Arnold understood it, is a balance of beauty and truth. Emotion too, plays an important role, "Poetry is moral ideas touched with beauty, heightened by emotion"

(*CPW* IX, 48). A poet is gifted, and it is this gift that helps him to understand life and convey the beauty and truth to the men. Poetic gift he says:

> ...is the faculty of being happily inspired by a certain order of ideas, presenting them in the most effective and attractive combinations,—making beautiful works with them in short. (*CPW* I, 261)

A poet for him, therefore, is a man with an extraordinary ability to understand human behaviour and present with beauty, the truth about life. Arnold gives equal importance to form and content, in his words:

> Truth and seriousness of subject and matter, felicity and perfection of diction and manner, as these are exhibited in the poets are what constitute a criticism of life made in conformity with laws of poetic truth and poetic beauty. (*CPW* I, 228)

This desire for balance has been more explicitly stated in a letter to Clough written in 1849:

> There are two offices, of poetry—one to add to one's thoughts—and feelings, another to compose and elevate the mind by a sustained tone, numerous allusions and a grand style.[33]

In both ways poetry can fulfil its function, according to Arnold. Poetry, he says, should not only be thought oriented: "An absolute propriety of form...is the sole necessity of poetry where as the greatest wealth and depth of matter is merely a superfluity in the poet as such."[34] This was the reason why Arnold showed dissatisfaction for Clough's works. It was full of thought content. Thought is essential but, a thought does not make poetry. Peter Allan Dale elaborating this point remarks that most important to him is what the poet does with that subject matter, how he shapes or structures it.[35]

The structure or the form of the poetry is of great importance. Arnold's position as discussed by Peter Allan Dale, is not merely of a moralist but also of a "...rather lonely English voice urging upon critics and poets alike the distinctly aesthetical, literary character of poetry".[36]

As has already been mentioned, there was a conflict between the aesthetic and the ethical within Arnold. This is clear in his works. Arnold did not believe in the dominance of the aesthetic quality but he emphasized the importance of a balance. Both thought and emotion, form and content, art and morality should be observed as a whole, rather than in parts. The Greeks, whom Arnold regards as great classical writers, are different from English writers in this aspect:

> ...with us attention is fixed mainly on the value of separate thoughts and images which occur in the treatment of an action. They regarded the whole; we regard the parts.... (*CPW* I, 5)

The morality of a work of art is, therefore, directly related to the wholeness. Edification should be the aim of all literary works. To edify, he says, is to raise the spirits, to heighten their moral sense and strengthen their religious faith (*CPW* I, 22).

The merely aesthetic work is as abhorable as the work with thought only. In a letter to Clough in 134.7, he writes:

> ...to solve the universe as you try to do is as irritating as Tennyson's dwadling with its painted shell is fatiguing for me to witness....[37]

"To solve the universe," here means to deal with the problems of the age directly and solely in poetry with the effort to overcome them. David J. Delaura explains, "Arnold's own 'poetic idea of the world' involves the attempt not to 'solve' but to 'reconstruct the universe'."[38] Arnold looks forward to a total change rather than to provide a solution to the problems of the world. Arnold criticized Keats's profusion of sensuous imagery in 1862. In a letter to Clough, he emphasized the importance of the "whole" work. The language, style and general proceeding of a poetry must be simple because in that age it had such an immense task to perform, "...it must not lose itself in parts and episodes and ornamental work, but must press forward, to the whole. It must be plain, direct and severe."[39]

Therefore, poetry must be moral in the sense that both form and content must unify and help in the edification of humanity. The poet himself has the poetic gift which helps to bring this about. The peculiar quality of poetry that makes poetry exalted is its interpretative power. It is moral precisely because it interprets life in two ways:

> ...it interprets by expressing with magical felicity the physiognomy and movement of the outward world, and it interprets by expressing, with inspired conviction, the ideas and laws of the inward world of man's moral and spiritual nature. In other words, poetry is, interpretative both by having natural magic and by having moral profundity. In both ways it illuminates man. (*CPW* I, 28)

Here Arnold delineates the primary function of poetry—to illuminate man. By illumination he means that poetry gives him a satisfying sense of reality, it reconciles him with himself and the universe.

For Arnold the morality of a work is its most important quality. For achieving this morality the creative works need to have some essential qualities. The next section will deal with those aspects of poetry which according to Arnold are essential to make it useful to humanity, which help in the illumination of man.

For Arnold, form and content should exist in unity in poetry. Whereas, content is important and helps to impart knowledge, form gives to poetry its identity. Both make poetry moral. The content chiefly refers to the subject and action of the poetry. There are two main aspects of the formalistic side of Arnold's criticism: "architectonic" and "grand style".

Arnold's views on form and content have both romantic and classical roots. Arnold himself confesses that he had turned to the classical poets because they seemed to offer him...amid "bewildering confusion of our times...the only sure guidance the only sure footing" (*CPW* I, 14).

From the very beginning of his critical career Arnold gave importance to subject. "All depends on the subject", he said, therefore excellent actions should be chosen. In the "Preface" to the first edition of poems he mainly discusses the cause behind deleting "Empedocles" from the collection of poems. It was one such poem in which everything was "to be endured, nothing to be done" (*CPW* I, 2). It can provide no pleasure and is "morbid" and "monstrous". The poem must give pleasure not only to the senses but also to the soul.

The "actions" that are considered excellent by Arnold are human actions, "...possessing an inherent interest in themselves, and which are to be communicated in an interesting manner by the art of the poet" (*CPW* I, 4). These actions must appeal to the "primary human affections; to those elementary feelings which subsist permanently in the race and which are independent of time" (*CPW* I, 2). Here Arnold lays emphasis on the universal element of the poem. Arnold says that the date of the action signifies nothing (*CPW* I, 4). A poem must have a "Truth" that is for all times, and all places. In this way a poem can communicate through emotions the "Truth" from one age to another and keep the work alive for all times. Alba H. Warren Jr. rightly observes that the "Preface" echoes the voice of Aristotle and this is what has made it "unique".

Further, Arnold states that "modernness" or "antiquity" of an action does not matter. The action should be interesting and to our passions, that which is great and passionate is "eternally interesting" (*CPW* I, 4). It should be noted here that emotions play an important role in Arnold's theory of poetry.

According to Arnold, the great and excellent actions constitute the main planks of the structure of a poem. The more convincingly they are delineated, the greater will be the structure of the poem. In a letter to Clough, he mentions that he, as a poet, was striving to "unite matter", rather than express it in all its uncontrolled variety. He used form as a means to make the content more effective. Rene Wellek, at the point of choosing the subject before hand, says that it is the "complement of the belief that there is a style independent of the subject matter."[40] This is not a disqualification, Arnold believed in the interdependence of subject and style. Poetry has an aim, according to him—it is not art for the sake of art. The form, as he said later in 1852, must be plain, direct and severe, it must not lose itself in parts, but must "press forward to the whole."[41] Peter Allan Dale, who has regarded Arnold as a reformer in poetical matters, says:

> The need for an architecturally ordered poem, the poem with all its parts reasonably "grouped" into a symmetrical whole is one that Arnold was never tired of pressing on his readers from the earliest letters to the last essays.[42]

I do not agree with Peter Allan Dale when he states that in the "Preface" (1853) the subject matter is not taken to be of primary importance: "...but the question of subject matter, though important to Arnold here, is not quite central."[43] Arnold enlists in the "Preface" (1853) ways and means to make the subject more effective. This is precisely the reason of his giving importance to the form.

Architectonice is what distinguishes the artist from the mere amateur. According to Goethe, "it is that power or execution, which creates, forms, and constitutes...not the profoundness of single thoughts, not the richness of imagery, not the abundance of illustration." Peter Allan Dale states that by architectonice Arnold means the "intellectual instinct at work in poetics. By intellect he means that principle in an artist which is responsible for producing the "...form, the method of evolution, the precision, the proportions, the relation of the parts to the whole" (*CPW* III, 283).

Arnold stresses on the need of "wholeness" in art. The classical writers, whom he admires, had wholeness in their art, that is, the thought and the form worked together in unity and looked forward to the action (*CPW* I, 5). To have this wholeness in the modern times, writers must have models. Imitation of the modern world which is in a state of "multitudinousness" and confusion would result in fragmentariness. The best models are the ancient French, Greek, and German writers. But if one has genius he can create works without models. The lack of critical ability has led to the great confusion in the present age. This critical ability is also needed to write great works. Shakespeare was a great artist because he had the critical ability and the genius. Literature on the whole is influenced by Shakespeare. But some artists who have accepted him as a model have failed to produce great works. The reason that Arnold gives is that Shakespeare emphasised "wholeness" which others often lack. Either they get involved with the subject or with the expression.

Arnold refers to several terms namely, "poetic action", "poetic art", "poetic genius", and "poetic duty". By "action" Arnold implies the spirit behind the work—the theme of the work. This is clear when we read his criticism about Keats. Arnold says that Keats is a disciple of Shakespeare. "Isabella" by Keats has the genius of expression but the action is not excellent. "Decameron" has the same story but it is more interesting as the poet subordinates expression to the content (*CPW* I, 8). Here "action" and "story" are not the same. An interesting work must have an excellent action, the story need not be interesting. The work, to be interesting, must necessarily have some objective. Excellent action appeals to the basic instincts of human feelings.

"Poetic art" refers to the language and imagery, form, and the expression of the work. Poetic genius is very close to architectonice as it also implies the ability or the intelligence of the artist to choose the action and present it in a way that "poetic duty" could be carried out:

> Creative literary genius does not principally show itself in discovering new ideas, that is the work rather the business of the philosopher. The grand work of literary genius is a work of synthesis and exposition not of analysis and discovery. (*CPW* I, 260-61)

Earlier he says:

> Genius is mainly an affair of energy, and poetry is mainly an affair of genius. (*CPW* III, 238)

Therefore, it is the genius that results in architectonice. Modern literature fails to achieve permanence because it lacks the capacity to assimilate ideas—it lacks the poetical action and art. Arnold remarks while writing about Marcaus Aurelius that spirit and vigour are close cousins of the "energy" of poetic genius. Poetic genius, art, and action should be in harmony. Sensibility, the most positive constituent of genius, brings this about. Sensibility is the soul of genius, it provides the material—the essential poetic insight, and creative emotion. Poetic genius alone has the ability to combine, the idea of beauty, harmony and complete human perfection.

According to William Madden the nature of "imaginative reason" was implicit in Arnold's discussion of genius.[44] Imaginative reason, as Arnold puts it, is the element by which the modern spirit, if it would live right, has chiefly to live. In the sense in which he first uses it, the term is contrasted both with "the senses and understanding" predominant in the late pagan world and also with the "heart and imagination", the qualities dominant in the medieval world. Arnold does not describe this term, he only gives it the adjective "well balanced". According to Madden, the word imaginative succeeds reason so the emphasis is on imagination.[45] This is an awkward preposition. The discussion on "poetry and reality" will deal with this. Here the chief concern is that he desires both imagination and reason, and in a balanced measure. A creative work, he intends to say, should be to the satisfaction of both the "thinking" and the "religious sense". The phrase "imaginative reason" might seem to mean the unification of two contrary elements in poetry.

According to Arnold, imaginative reason evolves from intelligence or the thinking power. In Sophocles, he says, the thinking-power a little overbalances the religious sense, whereas in Dante the religious sense overbalances the thinking power. When Arnold next uses the tern imaginative reason, he contrasts it to the religious sense:

> Where as Semitic genius placed its highest spiritual life in the religious sentiment, and made that the basis of its poetry—the Indo-European genius places its highest spiritual life in the imaginative reason, and makes that the basis of its poetry.[46]

As can be understood from the quotations given above, thinking power and religious sense are separable. For Arnold, imaginative reason is close to what can be called intelligence or thinking power. There is evidence that Arnold considered religious life the opposite of intellectual activity. In

"Democracy", he states that the qualities of intelligence, are the first of virtues which he says were openness and flexibility of mind (*CPW* II, 29). In "A French Eton", he remarks that modern societies increasingly tend to find their best life in a free heightened spiritual and intellectual activity. The religious life in contrast "...resides not in an incessant movement of ideas, but in a feeling which attaches itself to certain fixed objects," (*CPW* II, 67) such as stories and hymns. The usefulness of intelligence therefore is the chief characteristic of imaginative reason. Frederic E. Faverty puts forward a similar discussion and concludes on the basis of Arnold's ethnic and national characteristics that Arnold associates imaginative reason to intelligence.[47]

Arnold denies any significant degree of intelligence to English Literature (*CPW* III, 239). This is the reason of the lack of strength "in the poetic qualities, chaotic structure, and dubious intellectual content". It is from the intellectual quality that the elements of "high seriousness" and "criticism of life" evolve. What Arnold really implies by "criticism of life" is not stated by him. But whenever he refers to it, it is associated with the intellectual ability.

Arnold uses the term "criticism of life" for the first time keeping in mind the cultural perspective. If criticism is the means of seeing things as they are, if culture is that and more, if civilization is another word for culture then, "...the end and aim of all literature, if one considers it attentively is...a criticism of life" (*CPW* III, 209). The importance that he gives to "criticism of life" is clear when he writes about Byron—"The main end and aim of all our utterances whether in prose or in verse is surely a criticism of life."[48] Criticism of life serves a moral function. It involves not only the content but also the formal side of poetry:

> In poetry...the criticism of life has to be made conformably to the laws of poetic truth and poetic beauty. Truth and seriousness of subject and matter, felicity and perfection of diction and manner, as these are exhibited in the best poets, are what constitute a

> criticism of life, made in conformity of poetic truth and poetic beauty.[49]

The term "criticism of life" has been widely interpreted. F.R. Leavis calls it the application of ideas to life. Vincent Buckley says that Arnold throughout stresses that the ultimate value of poetry lies in its touching some profound truth of man. "Criticism", is a term by which Arnold means, "...interpretation and healing representation..." of life. For Arnold the question of life is in itself a moral question:

> If it is said that to call these ideas moral ideas is to introduce a strong and injurious limitation, I answer that it is to do nothing of the kind because moral ideas are really so main a part of human life. The question, how to live, is itself a moral idea: and it is the question, which most interests every man, and with which, in some way or other, he is perpetually occupied. A large sense is of course to be given to moral. Whatever bears the question how to live, comes under it.[50]

F.R. Leavis says, criticism of life, is evaluation of poetry. But poetry should evaluate life, if it has to fulfil higher destinies and must deal with "primary human affections." T.S. Eliot could not accept the Arnoldian concept of the criticism of life:

> It will not do to talk of "emotion recollected in tranquility", which is only one poet's account of his recollection of his own methods; or to call it "a criticism of life", than which no phrase can sound more frigid to anyone who has felt the full surprise and elevation of a new experience of poetry.[51]

Criticism of life, is a discussion of life. It may deal with the question of how to live and with the primary human affections. Life is for Arnold, the life of inner experience. It is in this that Arnold is in line with later critics such as Middleton Murry and F.R. Leavis. Poetry is the expression of this inner life. The poet's own views about life and his own experiences are communicated through the "criticism of life" to the readers. In this way the poet interprets life and we relate it to Arnold's earlier remark:

> Poetry interprets in two ways, it interprets by expressing with magical felicity the physiognomy and movement of the outward world, and it interprets by expressing, with inspired conviction, the ideas and laws of the inward world of man's moral and spiritual nature. (*CPW* III, 34)

Criticism of life is an interpretation of life and this gives to poetry the moral dimension. Discussing Arnold's criticism of life, Eliot says that "Art for Arts' Sake" is the "offspring" of Arnold's culture; and he insists that it is even a "perversion of Arnold's doctrine", because he finds it "vague and ambiguous". To this F.R. Leavis rightly says:

> At any rate, we can certainly not say that "Art for Art's sake" is the offspring of Arnold's "criticism of life"...it is an intention directly counter to the tendency that finds its consummation in "Art for Art's sake".[52]

Criticism of life is not the origin of aestheticism. It deals mainly with the subject, the consent. To some extent it deals with the presentation of the subject, in an effort to strengthen the subject and make it more effective.

"High seriousness" is another term that has not been explicitly explained by Arnold. Chaucer lacks "high seriousness", though in the Arnoldian sense his works deal with the criticism of life. He has allowed "high seriousness" to Gray, Shelley and Milton but not to Chaucer.

Before going further into "high-seriousness", Arnold's views on tragedy and comedy should be discussed. Though tragedy and comedy both can have seriousness, it is more difficult to achieve it in comedy. Seriousness is not seriousness of subject matter, "Tragedy breasts the pressure of life, comedy eludes it." But if comedy too breasts the pressure of life, Arnold would have no objection to it. In the "Preface" (1853), Arnold devalues comedy on the basis that it uses contemporary materials that are "too much mixed up with what is accidental and passing." It therefore, does not achieve classical grandeur. Though he disliked these shortcomings of comedy he did not regard the comical aspect, while criticizing poets, as a weakness. Writing about Aristophanes, he declares "...there is a comic side from which to regard humanity as well as a tragic one" (*CPW* I, 27). According to Joseph Carroll, high seriousness is synonymous with grand style, "The touchstone passages make it clear that high seriousness is basically the same as the 'grand style'."[53]

High seriousness is different from grand style; whereas seriousness is chiefly concerned with the subject, grand style is chiefly concerned with the formal end. Since style and subject are in a way an inseparable whole, seriousness also has some effect on style and grand style also has some effect on the subject. Both help to achieve morality. Arnold himself maintains that religion is the deepest thing in human life and art can attain high seriousness only by submitting itself to the "needs and motives" of religion.

Appreciating Gray's "Elegy" for its seriousness, Arnold says:

> "Elegy" is a beautiful poem, and in admiring it the public showed a true feeling for poetry. But it is true that the "Elegy" owed much of its success to its subject and that it has received a too unmeasured and unbound praise.[54]

Byron, he says, had "...perfect truth and seriousness of matter, but not in close alliance with perfect truth and felicity of manner" (*EC* II, 117). Therefore it can be said that seriousness is mainly concerned with the subject. Humour and seriousness can exist simultaneously as Gray had, "...with all this, strenuous seriousness, a pathetic sentiment, and an element, likewise, of sportive and a charming humour" (*EC* II, 50).

Seriousness is concerned with the subject, is has already been suggested. It is concerned with the thought, the ideas and also with the intention of the poet. Chaucer's work which is a criticism of life has been denied seriousness because it was composed in a light vein primarily for entertainment rather than to serve a moral purpose. The picture of life is true but not necessarily constructive. Whereas Shelley's grasp over the subject is weak but his ideology cannot be denied seriousness. This is the reason why Arnold found Chaucer lacking in seriousness and Shelley and Gray not devoid of it.

John Kerrigan points out that the sage in Arnold found increasingly compelling reasons for accepting seriousness as the primary requirement of literature.[55] Yet this cannot be evident in reading the early prose works of Arnold. It is only gradually that in the course of his career Arnold opted for seriousness. In the first important critical statement, the Preface of 1853, Arnold judged literature to be only incidentally "serious". Following Schiller he says, "All art is dedicated to Joy, and there is no higher and no more serious problem."[56] But as early as 1857, in his inaugural lecture at Oxford, he gave "seriousness", centrality. According to Kerrigan, Arnold does not here demand the humourless "high seriousness" which was to become his literary ideal in 1880s.[57] Gradually after 1860, Arnold started moving away from joy to seriousness. He wrote about "serious cheerfulness" and then about mingling of "wit and seriousness." His seriousness was tainted by laughter. And at about the same time he began to condescend to comedy. It was after 1860 that Arnold moved towards seriousness.

Arnold has stood for truth in poetry. The Keatsian idea of seeing things in their truth and beauty has also been emphasized by him. Poetry, according to him is the reality, philosophy is illusion because, "...to see things in their beauty, is to see things in their truth and Keats knew it" (*CPW* IV, 109).

Arnold had an extreme dislike for satire as satire was not truth. For Dryden and Pope, he says, that their poetry is eloquent and clever, but "...it does not take us much below the surface of things, it does not give us the emotion of seeing things in their truth and beauty" (*EC* II, 109). Genuine poetry has poetic truth. It has an object and the genuine poetic language is chosen likewise. In this sense, he says, Gray was a genuine poet.

Before discussing Arnold's view on "grand style", I shall discuss his "Touchstone Method", which could be described as a way of distinguishing good poetry from the ordinary. He says that an easy and a simple method is:

> ...to take recourse to concrete examples—to take specimens of poetry of the high, the very highest quality,

and to say: The characters of a high quality of poetry are what is expressed there. (*EC* II, 16)

Arnold presents passages from Homer, Dante, Shakespeare and Milton. John S. Eells has done a valuable study of Arnold's well-known touchstones showing that eight of the eleven express varying degrees of melancholy, and strong pathos. He also identifies these attitudes in Arnold's poetry and prose. David J. Delaura suggests that most of Arnold's touchstones are "formative" and "transforming" for human character because, in an unvictorian and surprisingly "existential" mood, they repudiate precisely the easier sorts of nineteenth century consolation, whether religious or rationalistic.[58] Fraser Neiman also finds the touchstones to be in some way moralistic. Touchstones exhibit, "simplicity and lucidity" of expression, but they almost, invariably recall a moment of pathos or a context in which a noble ethical attitude is exhibited either by some "stoical choice or by profoundly inward religious acquiescence".[59]

Thus the bulk of Arnold's "tonic" and "fortifying" touchstones whether of secular or the religious variety—that will do the work of religion, are in effect examples of "moral profundity". This, too, establishes the fact that above all things he desires only that poetry to be appreciated which has religious aim of fortification.

As has already been stated earlier, Arnold associates style with morality. In the process of illustrating his touchstones, he has made remarks on "Grand Style". Instead of attempting vain definitions, he quotes Scott and then Homer, Virgil, Dante, and Milton as he feels that grand style cannot be defined but can only be spiritually discerned. He says, "Grand style arises in poetry when a noble nature poetically gifted, treats with simplicity or severity a serious subject" (*CPW* IX, 188).

Arnold distinguishes two types of grandstyles—of Milton which he finds "grand style severe" and the other of Homer which he says is "grand style simple". Homer's style is more magical than Milton's style. Arnold's main emphasis is on the "...refining and elevation wrought in us by the high and rare excellence of the great style" (*CPW* XI, 188). That is, man's character can be moulded by the subject and also by the style. It is in this that the importance of style lies. Arnold believes that Milton's charm of diction and rhythm is felt intimately and profoundly by the countrymen. The emotions can also be transmuted through the style. This also reflects Arnold's belief that poetry is primarily for the communication of emotion through content as well as through form.

According to Arnold, every artist's style is influenced by his personality. Milton was, for him, inherently moral. Some amount of moral qualities are present in all human beings. These are transferred to the poetry both through content and form. The extent to which a man can develop and transfer it in poetry depends on the person's will and power. Milton admires the gift of the immense store of moral qualities in the style:

> Some moral qualities seem to be connected in a man with his power of style. Milton's power of style, for instance has for its great character elevation, and Milton's elevation clearly comes in the main from a moral quality in him—his pureness, ...In this elevated strain of moral pureness his life was really pitched, its strong immortal beauty, passed into the diction and rhythm of his poetry. (*CPW* VIII, 184)

According to Joseph Carroll, Arnold's assumption of the moral nature of the style may be linked with his assumption that the poet has "poetic gift". High seriousness, he says, is synonymous with grand style.[60] But, as has been discussed earlier, high seriousness is associated with the subject matter. Seriousness of style may give rise to the grand style. It can be said that there is some kind of seriousness by nature in every man. This seriousness can be associated with "poetic gift" or the "style" of the poet. This is not the high seriousness of subject matter. It is associated with the mode of presentation, the style, the manner. This seriousness in the style may be termed as the grand style. Its distinctive feature is that it communicates the moral qualities in a poet's nature to the reader.

For Arnold, the "meter" of poetry should be determined according to the subject of the poetry. The whole discussion in "On Translating Homer" reflects his views pertaining to the inherent fixed characteristics in special metrical forms. For the translation of Homer, he considers the ballad meter essentially inferior and argues that Homer must be translated in hexameters. The qualities of rapidity, plainness, and directness in thought, plainness and directness in substance, and nobility in Homer should be communicated. This is possible only if the hexameter is chosen.

Pointing out a difference between poetry and prose he says that in prose, the composer has to choose his vehicle; but in verse the composer has to accept the vehicle readymade. He further says that it is of vital importance on the part of the poet to choose the adequate form, so that the writer can convey the most. He insists that it was the sway of the French Alexandrine that hindered Moliere from being a tragic poet (*CPW* III, 230). Addison's compositions, he regards better than Pope's because Addison rightly chose prose in which his genius lay, while Pope's couplet did not suit his genius. Style, therefore for Arnold, is a superior means of communication. The poet must choose his style according to his genius so that he can convey to his readers all that he desires. It is, therefore, of primary importance.

Arnold, as has been earlier noted, differentiates between the style of poetry and prose. Language has a vital role to play in prose. In "The Literary Influence of Academies" he cites style as an index of intellectual conscience. He lays emphasis on the ethical influence of style in language and its relation with character (*CPW* III, 273). Therefore, like style, language too has ethical value. On being asked who the great men of letters were, he named—Cicero, Plato, Bacon, Pascal, Swift, and Voltaire. They had genius and an instinct for style. Their prose, he feels, is a "native necessity" (*CPW* X, 91). Thus, the style has importance because of its usefullness. In prose, style has importance as it is the mechanical arrangement of language and it also helps in the methodical arrangement of ideas. This is responsible for proper communication.

In prose works, according to Arnold, ideas and style are two major elements. The importance of literature, as is evident from Arnold's works, is that it presents ideas with the help of style so that the ideas may be communicated and may be understood by the reader.

Arnold ranks Swift and Voltaire higher than Goethe whose prose, he says, is loose, ill-knit and diffuse. Swift does not figure in Arnold's work until 1866; he has recorded in his note-books that he read *A Tale of a Tub* and also copies out a phrase from *The Battle of Books*—"Furnishing mankind with the two noblest of things, which are 'sweetness and light' (i.e. 'beauty and intelligence')."[61] Arnold has also named a chapter of *Culture and Anarchy* (1969) after the aforesaid phrase.

Arnold believes that intelligence can help to provide the right style. Beauty does not here mean style. He also says that Swift has abundance of light but lacks sweetness (*CPW* X, 174). By "beauty" he probably means "truth" as he appreciated the Keatsian concept of "Beauty is Truth".

The best prose style, according to Arnold, is that of Shakespeare, Moliere and Swift. There are two extremes in English prose: one having ideas only and lacking in style, the other having a good style but lacking in ideas. Lord Macaulay has a good style but lacks in ideas (*CPW* IX, 234). Addison, he says, has a "provincial oblivion" to disturbing ideas and so he is "somewhat bland and monotonous". Carlyle has ideas in abundance but both are marred by a "vehemence and turbulence that may be attributed to a provincial defect of perspective and proportion" (*CPW* VIII, 249). The best prose style, avoiding the two extremes, combines intensity of tone and fullness of substance with a lucid mastery of composition. In "Emerson" Arnold takes Swift as one of his touchstone writers—as a model of excellence. However passionate or choloric Swift may be, he controls his materials and so commands a respect that Arnold does not accord to Carlyle: "Shakespeare, Moliere, Swift—they too had, like Carlyle the devouring eye and the portraying hand" (*CPW* X, 174). But they are great literary masters, they are supreme writers, because they knew how to work into a literary composition their materials, and to subdue them to the purposes of literary effect. Carlyle is too vehement. The qualities of precision, authenticity and compositional mastery render Swift a true "prose classic". In "The Literary Influence of Academies", Arnold defines the true classicist as an author who is able to express new and profound ideas in a perfectly sound and classical style (*CPW* II, 248). Arnold throughout his career read Johnson. At many places he quotes his works. And as Joseph Carroll says:

> Among the four greatest English neoclassicists, Johnson's moral vision and his delight in the play of the mind set a comprehensive tonal framework for Arnold's own doctrinal range.[62]

Johnson's prose was for Arnold a model. He himself acknowledges the quality of Johnson's influence in the "Preface" to Johnson's *Lives* (1878). In his appreciation of Johnson he echoes the values of his father, Sir Thomas Arnold. In a letter to C.J. Vaugham, Sir Arnold wrote:

> Even their particular subjects, require to be read with constant watchfulness and suspicion, whereas, great men are always instructive even amidst much of error on particular points.[63]

Arnold similarly maintains that Johnson's neoclassical poetic resistibility and his political and religious conservatism set him at some distance from contemporary needs. Instruction, too, is a measure of greatness: "But he was a great man, and great men are always instructive." Contemporary needs that Arnold refers to, is the representative quality of Johnson. This together with other qualities has made him a great prose writer:

> The more we study him, the higher will be our esteem for the power of his mind, the width of his interests, the largeness of his knowledge, the freshness, and strength of his judgements. The higher too will be our esteem for his character. (*CPW* VIII, 319)

"Power of his mind", undoubtedly refers to Johnson's intellect, his reasoning ability. "The width of his interests", is the range of subject in his works. The "freshness" refers to originality.

Arnold considers Johnson a modern writer though his sentences are "long and pompous" and his diction was Latinate. The reason he gives is that he does not obscure the structure of his syntax, which is always "plain and modern". There were differences in the poetic doctrine of Arnold and Johnson, still Johnson's utterances are of a great and original man. Johnson, he says, is not a "satisfying critic of a poet like Milton", but his remarks on Milton because they are reflections of a very robust mind, are often thorough by sound.

Arnold's views on modernity are clearly stated. The modern age itself has its distinctive characteristics. It is full of systems of institutions, established facts, accredited dogmas, customs, rules, which have come to them from times not modern. This age does not progress by itself but has to be carried forward. But they have a sense that this system is not their creation and that it does not correspond with their demands. This reflects Arnold's dissatisfaction with his own age. He adds that the awakening of this spirit is the "Modern Spirit". It is due to this reason that the moral and the intellectual both deliverances are essential. Moral deliverance is a demand of all ages, of all individuals; intellectual deliverance is a necessity of the modern age. The cause of this demand is the confusion due to a "copious and complex" present with a "copious and complex" past.

According to Frazer Neiman, the modern element or spirit in an age is discernible in so far as the age seeks and achieves knowledge of itself. Such knowledge he calls "intellectual deliverance".[64] The intellectual deliverance as Arnold often emphasises, is most commonly expressed through the poetry of the age. This is the poetry that Arnold looks forward to. He believed that the representative quality can also make an artist great. The eternal greatness of the Greece of Pericles is that it is the adequate expression of a first class epoch. Shakespeare is an infinitely more than adequate expression of a second class epoch. It is the immence distinction of Voltaire and Goethe with all their shortcomings that they approach near to being adequate exponents, of a first class epoch.[65] This letter also reveals Arnold's view of the representative quality and the portrayal of reality in the great works. He praises Dante for presenting a picture of life that has or bears reality (*CPW* III, 4). He brought together as we may say—sweetness and light. Dante gave due importance to both poetry and reality—supplementing one by the other. Invention, that is imaginative ability, could further improve the work, makes it more interesting and effective. This, he says, should be done keeping in mind the positive effect of "invention":

> Dante saw the world and used in his poetry what he had seen for he was a born artist. But he was essentially aloof from the world, and complete in the life of the world for he was a born spiritualist. (*CPW* III, 4)

It is for this reason that Arnold refers to him as one of the greatest artists. Art abhors what is vague, hollow, and impalpable. Hence all that is depicted should either be from the world or it should look real. Dante, for example had a real Beatrice whom he had seen living and moving before him and for whom he had felt a passion. This basis of fact and reality Dante took from the external life—the life at the outward world. To be an artist in the real sense one should present reality together with imagination, if needed:

> Art requires a basis of fact, it also desires to treat this basis of fact with utmost freedom. (*CPW* III, 5)

The free handling of object becomes difficult when the object is too real or too near. Dante, he says, had met Beatrice only three or four times. Had it been more than this, there would have been a fear of his artistic nature being impeded.

The characteristics of the modern spirit as are given by Arnold are the "intellectual maturity" of man himself, the tendency to observe facts with a critical spirit, to search for their law not to wander among them at random, to judge by the rule of reason, not by the impulse of prejudice or caprice. Then manifestation of a critical spirit, the endeavour after a rational arrangement and appreciation of facts (*CPW* I, 20). Arnold here gives importance to the critical spirit. This shall be dealt with, in detail later in this chapter. Here it is notable that

Arnold does not give importance to art. But he does say that powerful thought and emotion, flowing in strongly marked channels, make a stronger impression. For this reason, the metrical form is a more effective vehicle for the writers of the modern age. In prose, he says, there is more freedom but the very limits give poetry a sense of precision, it helps to emphasize certain points in poetry. Modern spirit, therefore, has to be instilled in the people of the age to help them out of the prevalent confusion.

The modern spirit, according to Arnold, is important to make an epoch of literature memorable. In the nineteenth century this was lacking. There was neither the German wealth of ideas, nor the French enthusiasm for applying ideas. In the Shakespearean era the society was accessible to ideas. The ideas were powerfully upheld by the intellectual life of their nation, they were applied freely in the literature of the then modern ideas—the ideas of Renaissance and Reformation—hence there arose a unique greatness in English literature. In a letter Arnold remarked that in the eighteenth century the people were just like the people of Arnold's time while the Elizabethan's were not, but he also says that although the eighteenth century was interesting he himself would not like to have lived in it. The chief reason for his aversion is that the period suffered from a defective poetry and criticism of poetry. Writing about Byron and Shelley he says that they were geniuses because they were "born children of ideas". Keeping in view the social environment of the time, that is, viewing it in the social perspective, Arnold says that Byron and Shelley were aristocrats so they were courageous enough to "turn for the breaking bounds" (*CPW* VIII, 317). As a matter of fact the aristocrats had the confidence and the courage to write something which had not been attempted. They also had an easier way to success because they were heard. Their access to society was easier. They did not succeed due to their inadequacies. Yet, Arnold says, they will be remembered long after their inadequacies are fully realised. This is so because of their passionate, their "Titanic effort" to flow in the mainstream of modern literature. Wordsworth, Scott, and

Keats, he says, have left admirable works but they suffer from a defect. They do not apply modern ideas to life. They constitute, therefore, minor currents. It should here be noticed that Arnold considered the influence of the social environment when he analysed the works. Henrich Heine, who has been praised for his wonderful clearness, lightness and freedom, and with this the power of feeling, width and range, too had an inadequacy. He was great as he had the wit and the ardent spirit of France, the culture, the sentiment, the thought of Germany but he lacked the eternally useful moral deliverance. Morality is essential to any "true dignity of character". The phrase "true dignity of character" is not explained clearly. But we can understand its meaning from what he has stated about Heine. As Heine has been said to possess intellectual capability with also a fine style, he has plenty of "light". He also has "sweetness" but only to some extent. He depicts the culture, the sentiment, and thought but something more is needed for a "moral" work and that is "true dignity of character". This is therefore an interpretation of life, of human nature, of the truth about life which in the real sense is beauty. This may be understood to be a "criticism of life" with "high seriousness".

Heine's poetry, Arnold says, is modern. It is permeated with the ideas of the nineteenth century. His poetry is brilliant but not restful and is seldom edifying. Restful may here be taken to mean serious. Morality, as is clear from the views of Arnold on Heine, is a means of edification and can be achieved through high seriousness, criticism of life and intelligence; and intelligence helps to choose the right kind of style for the thought-content.

The debate regarding the relationship between poetry and religion is contentious ever today. Some critics consider Arnold's hope of replacing religion by poetry absurd, while others feel that it may materialize. Some of the recent critical works on Arnold have dealt with his religious works and consider religion as the master in whose service Arnold devoted his life and works. Arnold's poetical works as well as his prose writings reveal that he realised that religion had the potential of counteracting the doubt, despair, and uncertainty of his age and thus attaining order and stability in society. Writing in this respect Arnold says:

> But at the present moment two things about the Christian religion must surely be clear to anybody with eyes in his head. One is that man cannot do without it, the other that they cannot do with it as it is. (*CPW* VII, 378)

Arnold for this reason sought for an alternative to religion. In poetry, he found an adequate means as both religion and poetry have the same objective:

> The object of system of morality is to take possession of human life, to save it from being abandoned to passion or allowed to drift at hazard, to give it happiness by establishing it in the practice of virtue, and this object they seek to attain by prescribing to human life fixed principles of action, fixed rules of conduct.... (*CPW* III, 154)

Arnold clearly says that moral rules are rigorously followed laws. These are observed by sages, as they cannot be apprehended by others. The humanity, at large, which needs it desperately, is devoid of that force of intellect which can perceive them. They also lack the force of character to follow those laws. Thus, here he indicates that to make these laws apprehendable and easy to be followed by the common man poetry revolves round this basic and ultimate end. Beauty, high seriousness, criticism of life, and a style that helps to communicate the ideas make poetry more meaningful to man. Poetry should be in the interest of humanity. Arnold desires that poetry should have effect on its readers. "All fine poetry is moral," (*EC* II, 43) he says. While writing on Wordsworth, Arnold says that morals are often treated in a narrow and false manner. They are bound up with systems of thought. But this concept of morality, he finds, outdated. Thought alone is not essential for morality. Both the form and the content make poetry moral.

As has earlier been stated, morality according to Arnold deals with the question of life (*EC* II, 55). Wordsworth has a sense of a beneficient moral order. He deals with the deepest thing in human life. The noblest races are those, he says, who know how to make the most serious use of poetry. Shakespeare's works are more appreciated than *The Thirtynine Articles*. It is in this sense that he finds poetry religious. Poetry also successfully does the work of religion, that is, edification through the propagation of positive values. He states:

> The future of poetry is immense, because in poetry, where it is worthy of its high destinies, our race, as time goes on, will find an even surer and surer stay. (*CPW* IX, 234)

At a time when religion has been questioned by fact—science—poetry alone can save mankind as it does not depend on the fact but on idea. Arnold goes on to say:

> More and more mankind will discover that we have to turn to poetry to interpret life for us to sustain us. Without poetry, our science will appear incomplete and most of what now passes with us for religion and philosophy will be replaced by poetry. (*EC* II, 2)

There have been serious objections to his claim of poetry. T.S. Eliot writing about Arnold's views on religion says:

> They are tediously negative. But they are negative in a peculiar fashion; their aim is to affirm that the emotions of Christianity can and must be preserved without the belief. From this proposition two different types of men can extract two different types of conclusions: (i) that Religion is Morals, and (ii) that Religion is Art. The effect of Arnold's religious campaign is to divorce religion from thought.[66]

Buckley questions the accuracy of this statement. He says that Arnold's desire was to redefine religion in such a way that it is no longer a bond between God and man, a bond of which "doctrinal formulations are a necessary illumination and expression but a state of mind.... For Arnold religion can therefore be defined most nearly in terms of sentiment."[67]

Arnold worked to bring together the moral, religious and aesthetic sentiment. Poetry is the medium which can make it possible. His statement in the beginning of "The Study of

Poetry", where he hoped that poetry would one, day replace religion should not be misunderstood. Religion and science underwent a serious discussion in which fact emerged victorious. To bring back "faith" in the essential precepts of religion a new means was to be devised. Arnold through poetry tries to give to humanity a philosophy of life, to provide contemporary wisdom to the race and to help humanity to adjust to the new conditions. As for Arnold, religion is itself diffused in poetry. F.R. Leavis says, "Few now would care to endorse the unqualified intention of that passage...."[68] It is wrong, he says, to think that Arnold is no theologian or philosopher or that Arnold is incapable of consistency and vigour of thought. Leavis, says further, that many who do not agree with Arnold's concept of religion will agree that, as the other traditions relax and social forms disintegrate, it becomes correspondingly more important to preserve the literary tradition. When things are as they were in Arnold's time, they make necessary the kind of work that Arnold undertook for "Culture"—work that couldn't have been done by a theologian as such. William Robbins asserts that the sanity and catholicity of attitudes like his (Arnold's) are desperately needed in an age like ours. He declares that Arnold offers, "...not a rounded and coherent philosophy but rather a set of humanistic ideals which stress the need for balance and a sane perspective."[69]

Arnold's claims for poetry were moral. Buckley remarks that Arnold reveres poets who are in a sense "religious poets". They are the poets of an ethical—aesthetic sentiment, which is to Arnold's mind, the core of religion.

Ruth ap Roberts in her book *Arnold and God* (1933) asserts that religious thinking is the real vocation of Arnold. Writing about Arnold's interests in the literature of religions from the Greeks to the Celts, from Judicism to the *Bhagwat Gita*, she concludes:

> As school official, as social critic, as literary critic, he feels called to mediate to the people of the future their cultural heritage of the art—religion continuum and the cultural processes that maintain and develop their

> humanity, and these processes must now become less provincial and more cosmopolitan.[70]

She further says that for Arnold all dogma is vulnerable because it is presented as absolute. But what is "blessedly invulnerable is literature." Arnold then, she says, was not substituting poetry for religion, as some of his critics have claimed. Rather, for him, the best that has been thought and said in the world of human religious instinct is poetry.

As opposed to Ruth ap Roberts' view, William Madden says that poetry was in the true sense Arnold's religion. Being in an age in which he was, "...the life that most deeply attracted him was not moral but aesthetic."[71] Madden insists that literature was his chief concern and he is right in saying this:

> Literature, he more than once insisted, was his proper metier, and throughout his career he never ceased to identify his "true self" with his vocation as poet.[72]

Therefore Arnold's true vocation, as R.H. Super puts it, is to serve as a poet for he believes that literature could make things happen, that is, change people, it was the noble and profound application of ideas to life. And as Levine and Madden assert, even in his social criticism. Arnold was persistently driven towards aesthetic responses.[73] From this we should not conclude that his motive behind aesthetic response is not moral. In fact Arnold is basically a philosophical critic. For him the question of life itself is a moral question. He says, "the reign of religion, a morality touched with emotion, is indeed indestructible." And if this poetry assimilates religion it will have the power of transforming and governing religion. Here Arnold has used both the meanings of "religion". The first is "morality touched with emotion" that is the religion of mankind, while the second is religion that is dogmatic. It is this religion which poetry has to replace. He desires to make religion accessible to and acceptable by the common men who suffered from the dreaded disease of faithlessness. Literature, like religion, could change men by working upon all their powers—not intellectual merely, but aesthetic, moral, and social, and because it changed them it is, if one thought about it, not unlike religion.

Unlike his views on poetry, Arnold has given his views on criticism in well defined essays like "The Function of Criticism at the Present Time", "On the Modern Element in Literature", "The Bishop and the Philosopher", "A French Critic on Milton" and "A French Critic on Goethe". Besides this his views on criticism are scattered in his other writings.

Matthew Arnold gives to criticism more than the usual share of importance. According to Douglas Bush, Arnold considers it not only an educator and guardian of public opinion and taste but "an intellectual and philosophical discoverer of ideas, a necessary precursor of valuable creative activity."[74] R.H. Super discussing Arnold's objective of criticism concludes that the central core of Arnold's criticism is, then, his sense of value in supplying the "spiritual and intellectual" needs of the nineteenth century. This is not, as it shall be seen, an exaggeration of Arnold's views on criticism. But criticism is a process which acts as a catalyst in the spread of morality. Arnold has great reverence for "ideas" and they are a gift of criticism. A critical spirit free from prejudices is the chief requirement for the growth of good literature. And good literature helps in the propagation of healthy culture. To begin with, I propose to put forth the reasons of Arnold's immense faith in the critical spirit. Later in this chapter the relationship between culture and criticism shall be discussed.

As has already been pointed out, Arnold introduced us to the characteristics of the "modern spirit" and related it to the critical spirit. The critical spirit is required by both the poet as well as the critic. In "On the Modern Element", he says that "moral deliverance" is the demand of all ages, but "intellectual deliverance" is the peculiar demand of the modern ages. This demand for intellectual deliverance arises because the present age has around it a copious and complex past. At such a time, the objects of deepest interest to the modern age are:

> ...the literatures which have most successfully solved for their ages the problem which occupies ours, the

> literatures which in their days and for their own nation have adequately represented the spectacle before them.[75]

Writing about the modern age, Arnold states that the most characteristic outward feature of modern age, of an age of advanced civilization, is the banishment of ensigns of war and bloodshed from the intercourse of civil life. An important inward characteristic, again, is the growth of a tolerant spirit, that spirit which is the offering of an enlarged knowledge, a spirit patient of the diversities of habits and opinions. Other characteristic are the multiplication of the conveniences of life, the formation of the taste, the capacity of refined pursuits. And this leads to the supreme characteristics of all: the intellectual maturity of man himself, the tendency to observe facts with a critical spirit, to search for their law not to wander among them at random, to judge by the rule of reason, not by the impulse of prejudice or caprice. Thus arises the manifestation of a critical spirit, the effort towards a rational arrangement and appreciation of facts. Arnold left this essay unpublished for eleven years when finally it was published with a prefatory note deprecating both its content and form:

> No one feels the imperfection of this sketchy and generalizing mode of treatment more than I do; and not only is this mode of treatment less to my taste now than it was eleven years ago, but the style too, which is that of the doctor rather than the explorer is a style which I have long since learnt to abandon. (*CPW* VII, 20)

Despite the imperfections, "On the Modern Element in Literature", is not only one of the important works of Arnold but also one of the important works of English literature. Lionel Trilling remarks that at a time when the modern spirit was questioning both the validity of religion and the intelligence of those who desired still to accept it, Matthew Arnold came forward as a proponent of the modern spirit not only with his poems but also through his criticism, which was the embodiment of modern spirit. He emphasised that religion was good and necessary and must not be touched by the intellect.[76] This tribute makes it clear that Trilling finds negligible, if any difference between modern spirit and the critical spirit. In fact the critical spirit or the spirit to reason out and furnish solutions and ideas is an important feature of the modern age. According to Joseph Carroll the main achievement of "On The Modern Element" is that it has broadened the perspective of modernism so as to include within its limits any brilliant, complex civilization and it has also established for Arnold his own critical goal—the "comprehension of this present and past."[77] Sidney M.B. Coulling describes "On The Modern Element in Literature", as marking a significant turning point in Arnold's career, "...the development of an affirmative response to life." He ascribes this change to Arnold's tacit acceptance of the contemporary critiques of the "Preface". Arnold adopts the two main characteristics which he feels the critics should possess: a desire to face the world as it is and to give moral guidance to the people.

Arnold associates the critical spirit with the intellectual deliverance, that is, with reason. Emotion finds no place in the critical spirit. Moral deliverance and intellectual deliverance are different as in the latter reason has the vital role. The critical spirit has a moral purpose and can be achieved through intellect, through reason, not through emotions. Stating the importance of intellect, Arnold writes that the intellectual deliverance takes in account man's comprehension of the present and past. It can be perceived when the man is in possession of the general ideas which are the truths prevalent at his time. He says:

> It is perfect when we have acquired that harmonious acquiesance of mind which we feel is contemplating a grand spectacle that is intelligible to us, when we have lost that impatient irritation of mind which we feel in presence of an immense, moving, confused spectacle which perpetually baffles our comprehension. (*CPW* I, 19)

Thus impatient irritation of the mind is the result of emotionality whereas reason is the demand of the age and it can bring about the desired change. If criticism is touched by emotions the truth shall for ever remain concealed and at a time when people have to be pulled out of their ignorance emotions can further delay the process of awakening.

Arnold also aimed at attaining freedom. Both the deliverances are necessary for this. He says that in the "...enjoyment of both united consists man's true freedom." The absence of this in modern literature has made it comparatively poor, barren, and a shortlived affair. It is the society that has to be enriched with ideas and the critical spirit. According to Arnold, the periods of greatest creative achievement, in the England of Shakespeare, and the Greece of Sophocles:

> ...society was in the fullest measure, permeated by fresh thought, intelligent and alive, and this state of things is the true basis for the creative powers exercise. (*CPW* III, 381)

The English had neither the German wealth of ideas nor the French enthusiasm for applying them. They, therefore, failed in criticism. Though the English had imaginative powers, social attitudes and individual genius, it is this failure that excluded them from the mainstream of the modern culture.

Arnold analyses the conditions of different classes of society. This reflects the extent to which he is concerned with society. He finds a close relationship between the critical spirit and culture. He divides the society into four classes aristocracy, professional class, middle class and lower class. The middle class was acute and energetic yet "narrow minded, and ignoble." The English common people were according to him more raw, to say the very least, less enviable looking, further removed from civilized and humane life, than the common people almost everywhere. The members of the professional class to which Arnold himself belongs, had economically and socially a higher status and were aligned with the middle class, however, because they were educated at the aristocratic schools they were mainly identified in thought, feeling and manners with the aristocratic class. Aristocracy is by its very nature imperious to ideas. This is so because they attach value only to materialistic things. They are very slow in accepting influences impalpable, spiritual and viewless (*CPW* II, 11). If the best life of humanity, he says, resides in a heightened spiritual activity, the social predominance of an aristocracy limits not only its own members but, by the influence of its example, the rest of the society as well. Therefore, for the lower classes there is no adequate ideal. Though there had been revolutions in England, the social order remained unchanged. Their greater political stability has been purchased at the cost of an inadequate critical reason.

In *Culture and Anarchy* (1869) Arnold suggests two practical solutions for the socio-cultural problem: an improved public education for the middle class and the adoption of a more positive attitude towards the state as the agent of national well-being. The only absolute standard is the progress towards perfection. At an age like his own, Arnold believes criticism is more constructive, and essential than imaginative literature itself. He holds that the highest kind of criticism has a permanent value greater than that of any but "first rate" works of poetry and art (*CPW* III, 283).

Criticism, as Arnold maintains,

> ...is a disinterested endeavour to learn and propagate the best that is known and thought in the world and thus to establish a current of fresh and true ideas. (*CPW* III, 283)

Arnold desires that criticism should be devoid of "practical considerations", that is, personal prejudices that arise out of the self-centered nature of a practical man. A work should be reviewed objectively like the Greeks did. The considerations of politics or religion, or any other should not come in the way of criticism. Caprice, waywardness and provinciality should be eliminated. The critic should have knowledge of the best that is known and thought in the world. This pertains not only to concepts and their logical relations but also to "perceptions", given in experience. It is from this that the fresh and true ideas evolve. Thus a "rational" order of ideas includes a reasonable ordering of empirical reality—an arrangement of institutions, social practices, and publically established beliefs.[78] E.K. Brown gives the reason of Arnold's emphasis on criticism. He concludes that the task of the critic, as an exponent of reason is to free Europe from the bondage of an outmoded social and religious ethos and, at the same time fashion a new ethos that will nurture the instinct for development.[79] Lionel Trilling says that if we are to understand him we should understand the dual intention of his criticism and realize that his criticism is the reconciliation of the two traditions whose warfare had so disturbed his youth, namely rationalism and faith.[80] Arnold attempts a synthesis of these two aspects in all his works.

Broadly speaking, Trilling is right in saying this. But criticism is of great importance to Arnold, because it helps to propagate ideas and "...for poetry ideas is everything". Arnold observes that an age rich in critical spirit is followed by an age full of literary activity. Criticism establishes new ideas, while the modern element helps to achieve harmony of these ideas. These ideas are to a large extent true, yet true by comparison with that which it displaces, to make the best ideas prevail (*CPW* III, 261).

Ideas in poetry that evolve through criticism are true though they may not be scientifically true. Peter Allan Dale has analysed this extensively in his work. According to him, for Arnold the relation between poetry and belief centers on the status of those moral and intellectual ideas which he believes are essential for poetic excellence. The scientific truth of these ideas, Arnold feels, does not matter. All moral and intellectual ideas are subject to change and correction in time, therefore, the actual truth of any one idea is subject to serious question. —"there is not a creed that is not shaken, not an accredited dogma which is not shown to be questionable" (*EC* II, 1). Peter Allan Dale says:

> ...ideas in poetry are for Arnold beliefs that cannot be "scientifically" affirmed but which are to be valued nonetheless because they produce certain emotional effects, they console, they elevate, they rejoice.[81]

These "fresh" and true ideas reach the society and bring about a "stir and growth" which result in great creative epochs of literature.

According to Arnold, besides providing fresh and true ideas, the function of the critic is also to see that the best ideas prevail (*CPW* III, 265). The critic helps to establish those ideas that help in promoting good works of literature. He also differentiates the good works from those that are of no moral value, that are of no utility to humanity. Criticism prepares a ground for the future creative genius, such that the writers get knowledge of what is expected from them. Thus it indirectly helps to promote culture. Some critics are of the view that criticism is synonymous to culture. Basil Willey points out that in "The Function of Criticism", Arnold defines criticism in terms almost identical to those later applied to culture.[82] Douglas Bush, too, remarks that his definition of culture is virtually synonymous to his earlier definition of criticism, though it has an under-perspective and seeks to affect all people, in all areas of their lives.[83] R.H. Super, in the Preface to Book V, feels that "The Function of Criticism", is mainly written to promote culture He does not believe that criticism is a synonym of culture, but rightly believes that it is a means of strengthening culture, it recommends culture as the great means that can help men to overcome their difficulties, culture aims at total perfection by means of getting to know, on all the matters of our concern, the best which has been thought and said in the world; and through this knowledge a stream of fresh and free thoughts evolve which help to bring to an end the preconceived notions of the past ages. This, and this alone, is the scope of the following essay. And the culture they recommend is above all, "an inward operation".[84]

Arnold himself also acknowledges that there exists a close relationship between culture and criticism. According to him the most important function of literary criticism is to study books and find the influence they are calculated to have upon the general culture of single nations or with the world at large (*CPW* III, 43). He says that of this culture literacy criticism is the "appointed guardian". He further notes that all works of different subjects have a general literary criticism to undergo. They all are judged by one standard—their effect upon culture.

Thus for Arnold criticism is important because of its usefulness to society, because it serves the culture; and culture, he says, interests everyone. In *Culture and Anarchy*, he says that culture goes even beyond religion but it does not exclude religion.[85] Religious books come within the jurisdiction of literary criticism, so far as they affect general culture. This is the reason for his own deep interest in religious works (*CPW* III, 43). Arnold believes that religious works, whether through reason or sentiment, affect culture, "...enlighten directly or by softening, and purifying the way for enlightenment" (*CPW* III, 46). A religious work is useful when it attempts to enlighten the less instructed so as to sweep away their prejudices.

Arnold expects a lot from criticism and poetry. He points out, "The direct promotion of culture by intellectual power is the main interest of literary criticism." The great mass of human race has to be "...softened and humanized through their heart and imagination, before any soil can be found in them where knowledge may strike living roots" (*CPW* III, 43). Arnold believes that criticism can successfully do this as it provides ideas. Graham Hough says that Arnold wants criticism to be read as theology. He admits that the changed conditions of this age have restricted the scope of criticism:

> In this new cultural situation criticism can no longer expect to have the scope and authority that it once had claimed. Arnold's conception of a largely literary culture, refining and fertilizing the life of its time, may survive as a pious formula, but it only commands the allegiance of the past middle age. It has little to do with the pressure of the world as it is.[86]

William Robbins briefly surveys the present day turmoil of religious and secular attitudes, and concludes that in an age like ours "...the sanity and catholicity of attitudes like Arnold's are desperately needed."[87]

The extent to which Arnold's criticism is applicable cannot be understood. The importance of his criticism today lies in the fact that he opened a fresh ground for criticism—as a means of serving the cultural end.

NOTES

1. H.W. Garrod, "Matthew Arnold as Critic", *Poetry and the Criticism of Life: The Charles Eliot Norton Lectures for 1929-1930*, pp. 78-79.
2. *Ibid.*, p. 77.
3. Tzvetan Todorov, "Poetic Truth: Three Interpretations" trans. by Ann Jefferson, *Essays in Criticism*, Vol. XXXVIII, No. 2, April (1988), p. 105.
4. Howard Foster Lowry, ed., *The Letters of Matthew Arnold to Arthur Hugh Clough* (London: Oxford University Press, 1932), pp. 37-38.
5. Lionel Trilling, *Matthew Arnold* (1939; rpt. New York: Meridian Books, 1955), pp. 23-28.
6. G.W.E. Russell, *Matthew Arnold*, p. 20.
7. H.F. Lowry, ed., "Letter dated February, 1849", *The Letters of Matthew Arnold to Arthur Hugh Clough*, p. 99.
8. C.B. Tinker and H.F. Lowry, eds., *Poetical Works of Matthew Arnold* (New York: Oxford University Press, 1950), p. 227.
9. H.F. Lowry, ed., "Letter dated February, 1849", *The Letters of Matthew Arnold to Arthur Hugh Clough*, p. 111.
10. *Ibid.*, "Letter dated June 7, 1852", *The Letters of Matthew Arnold to Arthur Hugh Clough*, p. 123.
11. *Ibid.*, "Letter dated February, 1853", p. 130.
12. Matthew Arnold, "The Study of Poetry", *Essays in Criticism*, Series II, ed. S.R. Littlewood, pp. 21-31.
13. G.H. Bantock, *Scrutiny*, Vol. XVII, No. 1, pp. 39-40.
14. F.R. Leavis, "Literature and the University: The Wrong Question", *English Literature in Our Time and the University* (London: Chatto and Windus, 1963), p. 43.
15. Vincent Buckley, "Matthew Arnold: Poetry, Ideas and the Age", *Poetry and Morality: Studies on the Criticism of Matthew Arnold, T.S. Eliot and F.R. Leavis*, p. 55.
16. R.P. Bilan, "Society, Culture and Criticism: Language, Literature and Continuity", *The Literary Criticism of F.R. Leavis* (Great Britain: Cambridge University Press, 1979), p. 26.

17. William A. Madden, "Introduction", *Matthew Arnold: A Study of the Aesthetic Temperament in Victorian England* (1959; rpt. London: Indiana University Press, 1968), p. V.
18. T.S. Eliot, "Arnold and Pater", *Selected Essays* (1931; rpt., London: Faber and Faber, 1951), p. 431. A similar view has been given by T.S. Eliot in an earlier essay *The Use of Poetry and the Use of Criticism* (Cambridge: Harvard University Press, 1933), p. 111.
19. Leon Gottfried, *Matthew Arnold and the Romantics* (London: Routledge and Kegan Paul, 1963), p. 210.
20. Warren D. Anderson, *Matthew Arnold and the Classical Tradition* (1965; rpt. Ann Arbor: University of Michigan Press, 1971), p. 45.
21. Geoffery Tillotson, *Mid-Victorian Studies* (London: Atholone Press, 1965), p. 155.
22. F.R. Leavis, "Arnold as Critic", *Scrutiny*, VII (1938), p. 323.
23. William Robbins, *The Ethical Idealism of Matthew Arnold* (London: Heinemann, 1959).
24. William Madden, "Meta-Poems", *Matthew Arnold: A Study of the Aesthetic Temperament in Victorian England*. (Bloomington: Indiana University Press, 1967), p. 130. A similar view, though with a difference in the nature of Arnold's temperament, is put forward by R.H. Super in *The Time Spirit of Matthew Arnold* (Ann Arbor: University of Michigan Press, 1970), p. 90 and by Kenneth Allott in *Matthew Arnold* (London: Longman, 1962), p. 13.
25. John Holloway, *The Victorian Sage: Studies in Argument* (1953, rpt. London: Macmillan, 1962), p. 203.
26. *Ibid.*, "Matthew Arnold and the Modern Dilemma", *The Charted Mirror: Literary and Critical Essays* (London: Routledge and Kegan Paul, 1960), p. 161.
27. Ruth ap Roberts, *Arnold and God* (Berkeley: University of California Press, 1933).
28. James C. Livingston, *Matthew Arnold and Christianity: His Religious Prose Writings* (Columbia: University of South Carolina Press, 1986), p. 12.
29. Peter Allan Dale, "A Reformer in Poetical Matters", *The Victorian Critic and the Idea of History: Carlyle, Arnold, Pater* (Cambridge : Harvard University Press, 1977), p. 141.

30. Terry G. Harris, "Matthew Arnold, Bishop Joseph Buttler, and the Foundation of Religious Faith", *Victorian Studies* (Winter, 1988), p. 184.
31. Matthew Arnold, "The Study of Poetry", *Essays in Criticism*, Series II (1888; rpt. Delhi: Macmilian Company of India, 1980), p. 3.
32. *Ibid.*, "Dated October, 1952", *Letters to Clough* ed. H.W. Lowry, p. 124.
33. *Ibid.*, pp. 98-99.
34. *Ibid.*, p. 103.
35. Peter Allan Dale, "A Reformer in Poetical Matters", *The Victorian Critic and The Idea of History: Carlyle, Arnold, Pater* (Cambridge: Harvard University Press, 1977), p. 145.
36. *Ibid.*, pp. 143-44.
37. Matthew Arnold, "Dated December, 1847", *Letters to Clough*, ed. H.W. Lowry, p. 63.
38. David J. De Laura ed., "Arnold and Literary Criticism: Critical Ideas", *Matthew Arnold: A Collection of Critical Essays* (Englewood Cliffs, N.J.: Prentice Hall, 1973), p. 5.
39. Matthew Arnold, "Dated October 1952", *Letters to Clough*, ed. H.W. Lowry, p. 124.
40. Rene Wellek, "Matthew Arnold", *A History of Modern Criticism*, Vol. IV, p. 105.
41. H.W. Lowry, ed., "Dated October 1852", *Letters of Matthew Arnold to Arthur Hugh Clough*, p. 65.
42. Peter Allan Dale, "A Reformer in Poetical Matters", *The Victorian Critic and the Idea of History: Carlyle, Arnold, Pater* (Cambridge: Harvard University Press, 1977), p. 144.
43. *Ibid.*, p. 145.
44. *Ibid.*
45. William Madden, "Imaginative Reason: The Aesthetic Condition", *A Study of the Aesthetic Temperament in Victorian England*, p. 168.
46. R.H. Super, ed., "Pagan and Mediaeval Religious Sentiment", *The Complete Works of Matthew Arnold*, Vol. III, p. 231.
47. Frederic E. Faverty, *Matthew Arnold the Ethnologist* (Evanston, III: Northwestern University Press, 1951), pp. 54, 59, 61.

48. Matthew Arnold, "Byron", *Essays in Criticism,* Series II, ed. S.R. Littlewood (1938; rpt. Delhi; Macmillan India Ltd., 1980), p. 110.
49. *Ibid.*
50. *Ibid.*, "Wordsworth", *Essays in Criticism,* Series II, ed. S.R. Littlewood, p. 84.
51. T.S. Eliot, "Introduction", *The Sacred Wood: Essays on Poetry and Criticism* (1920; rpt. London: Methuen and Company, 1967), p. IX.
52. *Ibid.*, "Arnold and Pater", *Selected Essays*, see Buckley, *Poetry and Morality,* pp. 27-28.
53. Joseph Carroll, "The Style of Reason", *The Cultural Theory of Matthew Arnold*, p. 156.
54. Matthew Arnold, "Thomas Gray", *Essays in Criticism*, II ed. S.R. Littlewood, pp. 43-44.
55. John Kerrigan, "Arnold and Seriousness", *English* (Autumn, 1981), p. 263.
56. *Ibid.*, p. 266.
57. *Ibid.*, p. 267.
58. David J. De Laura, "Arnold and Literary Criticism: Critical Ideas", *Matthew Arnold: A Collection of Critical Essays* (1973; rpt. Englewood Cliffs: Prentice Hall, 1975), p. 130.
59. Fraser Neiman, "The Hideous Title of 'Professor'", *Matthew Arnold* (New York: Twayne Publishers, 1968), p. 90.
60. Joseph Carroll, "Poetry and Preservation", *The Cultural Theory of Matthew Arnold*, p. 120.
61. H.F. Lowry, Karl Young and W.H. Dunn, ed., *The Note Books of Matthew Arnold* (London: Oxford University Press, 1952), pp. 4, 580.
62. Joseph Carroll, *The Cultural Theory of Matthew Arnold*, p. 170.
63. Arthur P. Stanley, "Letter to C.J. Vaugham, Feb. 25, 1835", *Life and Correspondence of Thomas Arnold* (New York: Scrikner Armstrong, 1877), pp. 356-57.
64. Fraser Neiman, "The Hideous Title of Professor", *Matthew Arnold* (New York: Twayne Publishers, 1968), p. 84.
65. Robert Liddle Lowe, "Two Arnold Letters", *Modern Philosophy* (No. 62, 1955), p. 263.

66. Vincent Buckley, "Matthew Arnold: Poetry as Religion", *Poetry, and Morality: Studies on the Criticism of Matthew Arnold, T.S. Eliot, and F.R. Leavis* (London: Chatto and Windus, 1959), pp. 27-28.
67. *Ibid.*, p. 27.
68. F.R. Leavis, "Arnold as Critic", *Scrutiny*, VII (1938), p. 322.
69. William Robbins, "Introduction", *The Ethical Idealism of Matthew Arnold* (London: William Heinemann, 1959), p. ix.
70. Ruth ap Roberts, "The Parable of the Three Rings: Victorian Comparative Religion", *Arnold and God* (Berkeley: University of California Press, 1983), pp. 160-61.
71. William Maddan, "The Virgilian Learning", *Matthew Arnold: A Study of Aesthetic Temperament in Victorian England* (London: Indiana University Press, 1967), p. 192.
72. R.H. Super, "Arnold and Literary Criticism", p. 168.
73. George Levine and William Madden, ed., "Preface", *The Art of Victorian Prose* (New York: Oxford University Press, 1968), p. xiii.
74. Douglas Bush, *Matthew Arnold: A Survey of his Poetry and Prose* (New York: Macmillan, 1971), p. 5.
75. R.H. Super, ed., "On the Modern Element", *The Complete Prose Works of Matthew Arnold*, p. 19.
76. Lionel Trilling, "The Spirit of Criticism", *Matthew Arnold* (1939; rpt. New York: Meridian Books, 1955), p. 177.
77. Joseph Carroll, "An Intellectual Deliverance", *The Cultural Theory of Matthew Arnold*, p. 46.
78. Sidney M.B. Coulling, "Matthew Arnold's 1853 Preface: Its Origin and Aftermath", *Victorian Studies,* 7 (1964), p. 234.
79. E.K. Brown, *Matthew Arnold: A Study in Conflict* (Chicago: University of Chicago Press, 1944), Henry Ebel, in "Matthew Arnold and Classical Culture", *Arion,* 4 (1965), p. 207.
80. Lionel Trilling, "The Spirit of Criticism", *Matthew Arnold*, p. 177.
81. Peter Allan Dale; "A Reformer in Poetical Matters", *The Victorian Critic and Idea of History: Carlyle, Arnold, Pater* (Cambridge: Harvard University Press, 1977), p. 166.
82. Basil Willey, "Matthew Arnold", *Nineteenth Century Studies: Coleridge to Matthew Arnold* (New York: Columbia University Press, 1949), p. 258.

83. Douglas Bush, *Matthew Arnold: A Survey of his Poetry and Prose* (New York: Macmillan, 1971), p. 147.
84. R.H. Super, ed., "Preface", *The Complete Prose Works of Matthew Arnold*, p. vi.
85. Joseph Carroll, "The Shape of History", *The Cultural Theory of Matthew Arnold*, p. 213.
86. Graham Hough, "Criticism as a Humanistic Discipline", *Contemporary Criticism*, eds. Malcom Bradbury and David Palmer, p. 45.
87. William Robbins, *The Ethical Idealism of Matthew Arnold* (London: Heinemann, 1959), p. 359.

3

J. Middleton Murry

When writing about critics like Matthew Arnold and F.R. Leavis I did not have to prepare the reader for any controversies in which these critics might have been caught. But writing of Murry I must warn the reader that his reputation, which was at its peak in 1920s and 1930s began to suffer a decline in 1950s he was reduced to a mere "punching bag".[1] It, therefore, becomes necessary for me to refer the reader to certain works on Murry which place him in the right perspective. Ernest G. Griffin (1969), Sharron Greer Cassavant (1982) and L.R. Sharma (1986). In Sharma's work Murry's image is more than restored. His critical principles are elaborated and his influence brought to light.

Murry, who was regarded as a leading critic in the 1920s[2] and also one of the pioneers of modern criticism[3] soon became one of the most disliked and disturbed figures. F.A. Lea tells us in Murry's biography about his falling reputation in the 30s:

> Yet by the 30s, an opinion poll taken at Cambridge was to reveal Murry as the most despised literary figures of the time, and by the 50s he was either unmentionable or else forgotten.[4]

It is not the purpose of these chapters either to account for Murry's complicated relationships or his quixotic position in literary history. Both these aspects of Murry have been dealt with in detail in the works mentioned above. My chief concern is to show how Middleton Murry coming at the time when he did, carried the banner of the moralistic tradition of English literary criticism and handed it over to F.R. Leavis. It is ironical that Leavis who was considerably influenced by Murry chose to be indifferent and unappreciative towards him in the latter part of his career.[5] Cassavant who has studied Murry as a moralist says, "...in his qualities as a moralist he was a link between Matthew Arnold and F.R. Leavis."[6]

Middleton Murry considers poetry a means of communicating experience. Poetry helps to understand certain aspects of life which would remain incomprehensible if they were not felt through its medium. He appreciates those poets and prose writers who accept literature as a means of bringing to light the truth about life through the presentation of their own experiences. Literature is, according to him, an incomparable means of understanding truth. This truth that is conveyed through poetry cannot be conceptualised. He says, "The universals of poetry are not concepts, nor have they conceptualised equivalents."[7] Emotions that are otherwise inexplicable are translated into poetry. Poetry is a combination of emotion and thought. "It does reveal," as Murry puts it, "what cannot be uttered".[8] He also says that it is the result of an effort to bring unthinkable thoughts and unsayable sayings within the range of human minds and ears.[9] He considers Shakespeare to be the greatest poet. The nature of poetry, he says firmly, is Shakespeare's poetry.[10] Poets portray their perceptions. They do not have "ideas", therefore they are different from philosophers. It is for this reason that poetry has no equivalent. He did not have much faith in the communication of ideas through philosophy, but believed that, the distinctive feature of literature lay in communication of experience and the emotion that accompanied it.[11] It is for this reason that Murry's theory of poetry has a humanist basis.

Both Plato and Aristotle have influenced Murry just as Arnold has. Arnold's "Preface has its roots in Aristotle."[12] Aristotle's belief that poetry has higher truth and higher seriousness than history and philosophy, too, has influenced both Arnold and Murry.[13] Plato's influence on Arnold is perceptible when the latter reminds his audience of his

> ...observation to the effect that in our culture, the aim being to know ourselves and the world, we have, as the means to this end, to know the best which has been thought and said in the world.[14]

Murry, likewise, believes that literature alone has to its credit the means to serve this end.

But Murry's affinty with Aristotle and Plato does not end here. Derek Stanford states that from Plato, whom Murry had studied deeply at Oxford, he derived the notion that literature is, "...the creative revelation of the ideal activity at work in human life", and it is, he insists, the imitation of this "ideal activity" and not just random persons and events which Aristotle bids the poet undertake.[15] Contradicting Stanford, Cassavant insists that Murry found a link between Aristotle and Plato for in Greeks alone he found an integrated culture.[16] Murry is not as averse to Aristotle as Stanford has stated. In fact, his major premise is that art and life cannot be separated.[17] This is straight from the Greeks as Murry himself states, that their approach to life and their approach to art are the same, "...to them, and to them alone, life and art are one... in the Greek view, art is the consciousness of life".[18] Again, stating the closeness of poetry and life and delineating the relationship of poetry to other disciplines he writes that between belief and logic lies a third aspect, which the mystics and philosophers generally miss out. This is the kingdom of art, in which resides truth which may be even more authentic than them for some men.[19]

It shall be seen later that Murry's views even on metaphor are derived from Aristotle. Griffin says that he makes his Aristotle sound "idealistically 'Platonic'".[20] This is true as Murry reveals that the basis of Aristotle's criticism is a conception of art as a means of a good life. For Aristotle, according to Murry:

> ...criticism is a system of moral values derived from his contemplation of life.... The imitation of life in literature was for Aristotle, the creative revelation of the ideal actively at work in human life.[21]

Murry himself has been greatly influenced by Aristotle. He has practiced it in his criticism. These views have considerable closeness to Arnold, they have been adopted by Murry and have been assimilated in the criticism of F.R. Leavis. Murry, as has been seen, believes that art and life are inseparable. While writing about Dante, Arnold presents a similar view of art (*CPW* I, 2). Towards the end of his career Arnold still maintained that a true work of art needs to depict a picture of life. This is possible, as Arnold says, only by the author's "extraordinary fineness of perception"[22] and by "his sincere fidelity to it" (*CPW* I, 2). The writer must therefore present "fact", something he has seen happening. Similarly Murry writes:

> The active ideal of art is indeed to see life steadily and to see it whole...only he has a claim to the title of a great artist whose work manifests an incessant growth from; a merely personal immediacy to an inherent and all—comprehending attitude to life.[23]

Murry's concept of poetry is also close to Aristotle's. Poetry is "rooted in emotion, and it grows by the mastery of emotion, and its significance finally depends upon the quality and comprehensiveness of the emotion".[24] Arnold, too, believes that poetry should be about simple emotions[25] as has already been stated. According to Murry greater the artist is, the more completely is an event merged in his "inward Reaction to the event".[26] Not what happens to but happens in him, is the subject of our care.[27] Here he does not imply that the expression of emotion should be of an autobiographical order, nor that the artist should translate personal emotions and views directly. He aims at the wholeness of his expression and experience; a totality of response. As shall be seen later, it is this that attracted him to the nineteenth century writers of Russia. I shall discuss this later in the chapter.

Murry considered Shakespeare's poetry ideal. He appreciated the perfect semblance of thought and emotion. Emotion is transformed into a work of art. This emotion is a longing for things that are not like permanence amongst flux, security amidst unrest, stability amidst change, and eternity amongst morality. Therefore, poetry is the outcome of some longing or desire, be it romantic or classical. The difference is mainly of the approach. Shakespeare and Shelley both submitted to their emotions or desire of the mind but Shakespeare was "serene and secure" and Shelley had "the desire of the moth for the star" and was agitated. Thus poetry reflects the mind of the poet.[28]

In poetry "intellect and emotion, mind and heart, regain their lost unity within us". Pure emotion or pure thought do not result in the best kind of poetry. It stimulates the "organic entirety of the experience" in the poet. He gains integration at least "momentary union of thought and feeling" that is always joyful and beneficient.[29] It is for this reason that poetry has its importance. This is an Aristotalean concept.

The experience of a poet is communicated through poetry, that has been accepted by Arnold also but the experience is objectively conveyed. It proves to be "beneficient" because both the emotion and thought are harmonized. It is this balance that brings perfection. If the emotion is excessive it can prove detrimental. The thought tames the emotion and gives it a shape that has a healthy effect on the mind of the reader. Thus poetry conveys an experience through which "profounder intuitions of the poet can be realised and made communicable".[30]

Murry has great reverance for both Shakespeare and Keats. "Negative capability", a term which is close to Eliot's "impersonality" (though Murry has never used the term) is a characteristic of the poetry of both Shakespeare and Keats.[31] Arnold's concept of "disinterestedness" is also close to the Keatsian concept of "negative capability" which Murry idolizes. Murry believes that personal experiences should be presented objectively. This does not mean that the personality of the poet should not be reflected but it means that the poet should be disinterested, that is, the experiences should be presented in a manner that helps humanity rather than serving as an outlet of a poets frustations, likes and dislikes. Shakespeare and Shelley are two examples of this.[32] There is a natural submission of self to all experience. The poet must understand the mysteries of human life if he desires to achieve his purpose of serving humanity. For the poet the highest kind of poetry should be the vehicle of the highest kind of truth, and such that supreme benefit could be conferred upon humanity at large.[33]

Murry here remarks that to achieve "negative capability" a poet has to undergo suffering and make sacrifice. Otherwise the truth that is incomprehensible cannot be communicated. The poet alone can understand the mysteries of life and. Through his intuitive power communicate it.[34] Cassavant remarks that by means of negative capability man brings together and unifies all experience be it good or evil. He, therefore, accepts life completely as it is. Such wholeness in poetry Murry distinguishes in the poetry of Shakespeare, Keats and in the life of Jesus. Therefore he considers them unequalised masters of reality. They bore sufferings, faced them, accepted them and have proven adequate to great sufferings.[35] This stage is a spiritual state. It is acceptance of all experience—it is "...the forgiveness that forgives not only men but life itself, not only the pains which men inflict, but the pains which are knit up in the very nature of existence" (*Keats*, 201). This is the suffering that a poet has to undergo Murry further says, "Negative capability of the poet achieves its natural consummation in the humility of the Christian before the Cross" (*Keats*, 201). Griffin in an effort to trace the reason of Murry's placing Keats, Shakespeare and Christ on the same rung says that Murry tried to achieve negative capability in his criticism and his life, to be receptively open to all that was important to man. This was supremely manifested in Shakespeare for in his works there is a natural submission to all experiences. It is this philosophy that made Murry a good critic and an editor.[36]

Murry approves of poetry that is devoted to humanity. For this communication is as important as creation. The highest kind of poetry involves communication of the emotion of the poet, his experience. Reason has its limitations. All that cannot be stated is transferred through poetry (*Discoveries*, 26). Through the poetry of the greatest kind like Shakespeare's

"Phoenix and the Turtle" more can actually be felt than understood. Here Murry echoes the words of Arnold for whom poetry has importance because it can console and sustain us. Form and content both have effect on the audience, but it is form that makes the senses calm. Content mainly affects the intellect, the best poetry has thought and art in one. The absolute poetry according to Murry, is more self-satisfying. The personal element in it makes it obscure. In being too personal and mystical the "general ear" has nothing to gain. Thus poetry necessarily has to communicate a truth to the "general ear". A purely self-satisfying revelation snatches from poetry its value and identity (*Discoveries*, 26). This has been earlier stated. Poetry should have negative capability.

The communication of experience and emotion is made easy by the use of metaphor, symbol and image. A search into the genesis of metaphor would reveal the genesis of thought.[37] It helps to transform into words the feelings and the experience of the poet. Crystallization is linked directly with metaphor. It is a term that Murry used and originated in Stendhal's simile for falling in love in "De l'amour", in which the "writer's accumulation of emotional experience", forms itself about his character "like crystals about a string dipped into saturated solution". In metaphor the process of crystallization is in its most elaborate form; in the work of a very great poet it goes on continuously altering and transforming language (*Problem of Style*, 28).

The chief objective of crystallization is to communicate emotion. Whenever a poet tries to convey his emotion the result is a symbol, image, simile, metaphor or even plot. In a perfect work as in *King Lear* or *Antony and Cleopatra* crystallization is complete on every plane, in the first and fundamental creation of the plot, in the realization of the characters themselves, and in the language which they speak, or by which they are described. I have shown in a later chapter that F.R. Leavis's concept of language is close to Murry's crystallization.

According to Murry, metaphor helps to achieve concreteness in poetic expression. In his attempt to achieve precision a poet looks out for different forms of expression and gives a "physical turn to the spiritual, and the general effort of metaphor is in this direction" (*PS*, 97). Murry's concern for metaphor is explicit even in his practice of criticism. His effort is to show that emotions in search for concrete expression discover techniques which successfully illustrate them.

Murry praises the writer's use of metaphor, image and symbol but also warns him against their excessive use. In "Imagery and Imagination", he states that images should be spontaneous rather than preconceived. Giving Shakespeare's example, he says that in *Richard III* and *Richard II* there is an excessive use of intricate conceits. Realising the unnaturalness that this lent he later reduced the number of conceits. This, Murry says, may have been a development of diction alone but in fact it was an intellectual and spiritual development which brought this about. It was an "outward and visible" sign of an "inward and spiritual grace" (*PS*, 273). Thus the growth within the poet is communicated through the spontaneous use of conceits, and an excessive use only brings about unnaturalness. Besides this, a limited use of conceits also makes the characters more alive. Shakespeare's plays achieve naturalness by reduction in the conceits (*PS*, 278). This happens because he identifies his characters with himself. Their emotions and experiences were his own. This intense identification with the figures of his imagination provoked a spontaneity making the order of creation more real (*PS*, 279). It is for such statements that Murry has been criticised for mystical conclusions.[38] But it was typical of Murry to link the thought with the emotion, the psyche with the creation, and the man with his art. He tries to establish that, reality, the truth—has to be communicated through art, and the spiritual growth of an artist makes a work more natural, more real. Like Matthew Arnold, Murry too gives importance to style. For Arnold, form was a means of communication of thought. Similarly for Murry, as we shall see, form helped in conveying thought and emotion of a poet. Literature could alone do this as it has at its disposal both style and thought.

Style, for Murry, must communicate the individual mode of experience precisely, i.e., it should communicate individual thoughts and feelings or emotions. He identifies three types of styles:

(i) Style as personal idiosyncrasy of expression by which we recognise a writer,

(ii) Style as technique of expression,

(iii) Absolute style or the complete realisation of a universal significance in a personal and particular expression, which is the highest achievement of literature. (*PS*, 1-20)

Seymour Chatraan says that the word style should be reserved for the first meaning, that is, for the purely descriptive sense. Linguistics life to think of a writer's style as his pattern of choosable recurrents, the idiosyncratic selection of features he makes from the languages reservoir over and above the features it requires for its ordinary functioning.[39]

David Lodge accepts the first two categories as properly labelled style, but rejects the third, since it "implies the whole of modern poetics".[40] Louis Milic similarly concludes that Murry's book seems devoted more to literary criticism than to what is usually associated with discussions of style.[41] James R. Bennett agrees with Milic, "*The Problem of Style* is not a systematic manual on the elements of style", Bennett says that the definition divides complete realization in two parts: "universal significance" and "personal and particular expression".[42] Such diverse views on his concept of style show that the critics have failed to read the book in the spirit in which it was written. Murry regarded literature as a means to achieve the humanistic end. He believed that the poet is a man with heightened sensibility. The personal experiences that are communicated are on the universal plane. Style, therefore, is an expression of one's personal idiosyncracies raised to the level, where they become truths for humanity. Since it comes from the writer it reflects his personality and psyche such that he can be recognized by it. Murry himself regards the third type of style as the perfect one. The conclusion at which Murry arrives is:

> Style is organic—not the clothes a man wears, but the flesh, bones and blood of his body. Therefore it is impossible to consider style apart from the whole system of perceptions and feelings and thoughts that animate them. (*PS*, 122)

Murry does not regard language as a means to judge style. It is like judging a "man by his clothes". A good work of literature is a victory over language rather than a triumph of language. What the writer feels or thinks is more important. Giving examples of Massinger, he says, that his taste of language is good, but his style is generally bad. Webster on the other hand, had poor taste of language yet a positive style. But in writers like Shakespeare style and language coincide. By this Murry probably means that in Shakespeare's works "crystallization" was achieved. The highest style is, "...combination of maximum of personality with the maximum of impersonality". Style for Murry is a means of artist's communication. It is therefore an important aspect of literature. A good style is essential for enduring literature. Murry does not give importance to style for its making a work ornate. Neither does he consider images, metaphors, symbols as a means adding to the aesthetic value. In fact they give depth to the presentation of emotion and experience and therefore help in communication. Style is a quality of language which brings together emotions or thoughts or a system of emotions or thoughts peculiar to the author.

According to Griffin, the word emotion should not be taken in the sense in which it is generally used. Griffin points out that it is misleading to dismiss his theories easily as being based on emotion. First, he is in a long tradition in the use of the word, as an examination of the use of "movere" and derivatives which Renaissance criticism can demonstrate; and second, he expands, "...emotion to serve not just as the basis of a lyric but also of longer dramatic and narrative work".[43] "Emotion" is not merely an immediate feeling, but a "mode of experience" based upon a subtle interplay and development of original emotions. Moreover, with this increasingly complex development, there grows a progressively acute understanding of human situation in general. As the poet matures—has better understanding of human nature—his works accomplish the difficult task of giving to the particular the weight and force of the universal. Arnold also believed that simple emotions have universal significance and therefore in literature to universalize an event simple emotions should be presented. Emotion, for Murry is a means to present the truth more effectively. It can universalize the experience of the author. It is through emotion that a particular experience can be communicated to others (*PS*, 75). In fact in the process of communication, it is the emotion that is transferred. In this, too, Murry is in line with Arnold.

Murry voiced for a complete fusion of art and reality, Keats always attracted him as there was a fusion of "beauty and truth" in his works and it is this reality that Murry seeks to find in all works.[44] Before Murry, A.C. Bradley and Sidney Colvin had also discussed this aspect of Keats in their works. The relationship between truth and beauty is accepted fully in Keats's last great ode "To Autumn". Murry's theory of art is largely derived from it. "Beauty is truth, truth beauty", this is interpreted by Murry in several ways. It may imply that real is beautiful, still the fact remains that real is full of ugliness and agony. Murry gives an explanation which shows that "beauty" for Murry also is close to reality.[45] This beauty is lot easily evident. It is felt only when a state of mind is reached in which the person detaches himself from the "reality". Beyond this reality lies beauty. This is a state of mind that is attained with great difficulty. The disinterestedness of Arnold too aims at the state of mind where truth is supreme. To establish this truth is the work of the critic. According to Murry:

> When we love a Fact, it becomes Truth, when we attain that detachment from our passions whereby it becomes possible for us to love all Facts, then we have reached our Peace. If a Truth cannot be loved it is not truth but only Fact. But the Fact does not change in order to become Truth. All fact is beautiful; it is we who have regained our innocence to see its Beauty.[46]

Therefore, a work has to depict reality of life if it has to be beautiful. For this the writer has to reach a particular state of mind—a "true renunciation". He sets life as beautiful in all its colours and this beauty he expects to find in great works. When Truth is presented it essentially "awakens love", it is then that Truth becomes "Beautiful". To discern this Truth man has to pay its price. At moments of grevious suffering to experience beauty in truth man has to be grateful for and exalted by the privilege of experience. One has to be filled with love for the world of pains and troubles. These sorrows school an intelligence and make it a soul.

This is not where Murry stops. It is the communication of this idea of beauty that is important for him. Murry says:

> Beauty in all things, this was Keat's poetic intution, and revelation of this beauty the great human purpose to which he dedicated himself...for creative genius of the poet it means not only to have attained "high reasons", and the love of good and ill; but to have the purpose and the power to reveal to men that good and ill are to be loved; not only the faculty to see that the sum of things is supremely beautiful.[47]

The idea of beauty cannot be apprehended by ordinary men. A great writer, according to Murry, is conscious of this all pervading beauty and therefore is more aware, and has the ability to have full control over his emotions that is an ability to detach himself from his own sorrows and joys. He finds unity and harmony in the universe. This distinction of a man makes him a great writer only if he succeeds in communicating his perceived harmony to humanity. Early in his critical career Leavis lays out the characteristics of a poet which seem to be derived straight from Murry.

Murry's views on novel can also be traced back from Arnold's theory. He emphasized on the value of thought-content more than the form. He believes that a novel should instruct (*PS*, 85). Like Arnold, Murry differenciates between a story and a novel. He expects a writer to raise the story to the level of the novel (*Discoveries*, 13). A story is just a game which interests people, but a novel has to present something more—a significant aspect of life. Leavis, as we shall see later has, to a large extent, adopted Murry's views on the novel. This also reminds us of Arnold's "criticism of life". The story should in an easy way instruct the readers so that even the common man can easily understand it. It should make people know "notions of right and wrong", and should reveal "exacter and more subtle ideas of good and evil." Thus the novel should not be without a touch of morality. Arnold in the "Preface" to the first edition of poems says that the action should be great, the story behind it need not be interesting. Excellent action appeals to the basic instincts of human feelings. Leavis's affirmation of life drives its force from Murry's views on novel.

Murry gives importance to originality in a work of art. Besides that the story should be real and life-like and it should reflect one's own concept of life; one's own beliefs (*Discoveries*, 273). In this process it should reveal something new and fresh that there must be originality. In this also Murry is in line with Arnold as he too says that an artist should present one's own beliefs in a work of art. Leavis, as it shall be seen later, too followed Murry as he too believed that a work should be original, it must depict something more about life. Murry also believes, like Arnold, that whatever the artist writes should be real, something he has witnessed, or experienced (*CPW* III, 2). Only then can it be effective. Both agree that the artist must present something more—he must explain those aspects of life that are incomprehensible and illuminate men.

Like all other arts the novel has two important characteristics. It is interesting as well as something that appeals to the higher faculty—a higher and serious art (*Discoveries*, 133). This he found in Russian novelists—a "passionate synthesis of thought and life"—which is not discerned in the contemporary writers of England. In his essay, "The Honesty of Russia", he says that Tolstoy, Dostoevsky, and Chekhov, were those who despite the war crisis had a sense of connection between "all the great activities of human soul", who searched the potential of human behaviour and attacked the philosophical questions. This is what Murry valued highly. Literature was for him a search into the human soul.

> The Russian writer holds it instinctively as an axiom that a way of life to be truly satisfying must be based on a harmony of human faculties. Heart or mind must be one. There must be no piecemeal realization. If the claims of moral nature of man are in conflict with the claims of his intellectual nature, then the house is divided against itself and must fall. What is good, says the Russian, must be true.[48]

For both Leavis and Murry art and life must be in harmony. They both appreciated Tolstoy for bringing these aspects of literature together.[49] Flaubert, who seems to be quite the opposite of Tolstoy, has been condemned both by Leavis and Murry. According to Murry, Flaubert "hated" life hence was of the opinion that subject matter in a work of literature was of "no account".[50] As a result Flaubert's works lacked inner growth—"the root of the matter". Moreover, as Murry puts it,

> Literature was for him an ascetic revenge on life, not a culmination of it, he tore himself up by the roots and planted himself in the most-highly artificial atmosphere which a considerable writer has ever breathed. Under this unhealthy stimulation he evolved for himself the doctrine of the sovereign autonomy of art.[51]

Thus the chief objection to Flaubert's view of art was that he did not associate life with art in his works. Arnold's idea of morality also revolved around the question of life and Leavis's "affirmation of life" dominated, his theory of literature. It is this closeness between their views of art and life that makes us say that the criticism of life of Arnold finds its way through the works of Murry and forms the basis of Leavis' theory of art.

Murry in "Break-Up of the Novel", traces the history of the novel and gives reasons for its inadequate development in England. In this essay he also traces the growth of the novel and formulates his concept of the ideal novel and novelist. The tale-teller image of the novelist disappeared with the rise of the Romantic period. Towards the end of the 19th century the novelist was "the scribe and life dictated him". To make the novel fresh and interesting, original novelists like Flaubert and Henry James introduced, "intricate considerations of form". They made their works prestigious and mysterious by making novel-writing an extremely subtle craft. Then came the two great Russian novelists, Tolstoy and Dostoevsky, for whom content had more meaning than form. Murry's contempt for a mere presentation of "art" is obvious when he points out that the English novelists were involved in evolving a new concept of art while the Russians were way ahead in writing about life. He even praises Thomas Hardy for being the greatest amongst the western novelists as he was unique and did not give importance to form. Murry does not overrule, the importance of form but finds it much less important than content. In fact he says that the Russians, whom he praises, had a form of their own but their involvement with form was secondary, unlike James and Flaubert. The young and ignorant writers adopted this and poured volumes of diluted autobiography into the lap of the patient world. The greatest efforts only resulted in sentiments of nihilism and world weariness. After H.G. Wells, Joseph Conrad, and Arnold Bennett, only D.H. Lawrence was left amongst the novelists who could achieve harmony of life and art. France was left with Anatole France. The reason of his refusal to say much about this generation of novelists is that they did not consider the novel as a serious art which made novel writing a mere game in the hands of artists. Till the year 1913-94 nothing much happened in the sphere of the novel as art. Murry seemed to be extremely dissatisfied with the litterateurs of his age. He expected the novel to fulfil the demand of the age with its root in society. In this the novel was to perform a function which was very similar to that of poetry. On the other hand contemporary novelists who were significant for him were those who remained involved with revealing their consciousness. For Murry—this alone is true, this alone is valuable, "...the driving impulse is the demand of truth. A complete and fearless exploration of the self reduces the chance of self deception to the minimum" (104). Even in *Heaven—and Earth* (1938) he maintains that in self exploration lies the exploration of the world around, and this is how the truth is revealed.

Murry believes that the novel survived because it presented a consciousness of life. He almost demanded the abolition of story because it distorts reality. Like Arnold, Murry shows an extreme dislike for moving away from truth—from fact. But if the story is close to reality and life, like the stories of Russians, he has no objections. According to Murry:

> Life does not shape itself into stories, much less does an individual and unique consciousness lend itself to complete expression by means of an invented plot.... All that we can know is our own experience, the nearer shall we be to the truth.[52]

This is almost Arnold paraphrased. Writing about Dante, Arnold says that in a work of art "fact" should be the basis. It should be combined with imagination to give it a fresh meaning (*CPW* Vol. III, 2). Thus as in poetry, if a novelist presents his own experiences he is closer to reality and therefore to life. He desires that some aspect of life must be discussed in literature. In the same essay, Murry also hints that a novelist is no ordinary being but one who understands human nature, universalizes his experience and communicates it with intensity and depth to humanity at large. Thus, he approves of the subjective element as it helps in presenting a consciousness of life. Leavis, too, never disapproves of the autobiographical element but believes that it ought to be universalized.[53]

In Tchehov, Murry finds a different kind of a writer; one who reconciles personality with impersonality. Murry has written about Tchehov in *Discoveries* and *Aspects of Literature*. He finds Tchehov and Katherine Mansfield (Tchehov being Katherine Mansfield's mentor) quite similar. In art it is as though "an intense beam of peculiar light were cast upon a fragment of reality". By matching the objects revealed by it, we can tell the colour of the light far more easily than we could if the colour was described to us because,

> we are made sensitive of the light at the moment when it is, or is felt by the writer, to be more illuminating than the ordinary light. (*Discoveries*, 144)

Thus in their works, as Murry says, art helps to communicate fully the experiences. This is precisely what both Arnold and Leavis also expected from art. The "intense beam of peculiar light" is art which by falling on the "fragments of reality", helps to reveal fully the experiences of life.

Murry did not find Tchehov as great as Shakespeare or Tolstoy or Dickens, yet there was something in him that brought him close to the reader. This was so because "we feel him so near to us that we refuse him the name".[54] The world with which he dealt is the world in front of us. Yet there was still something mysterious. This "mysterious simplicity" often figured in his criticism. It also reminds us of Arnold's views on the subject matter of poetry. He says that poetry should have a grand interpretative power which must help to understand the mysteries of life. It must also deal with simple human emotions and interpret life in such away that we are no longer bewildered by its mysteries. He is in line with Arnold as we can see that he too wants to discuss the question of 'how to live' in a literary work. Writing about Tchehov he states that he not only understood life but also knew what it must ideally be. His words are so "enchanting" that even they help us to feel, to understand life. It even imparts such knowledge which is otherwise impossible. Further, he states:

> We do not know what is happening in ourselves, we are overwhelmed by a single feeling when we try to hold it before our eyes, splinters like light through a crystal into contradictory emotions, laughter, tears, pity, love and one knows not what infinite and unfamiliar tenderness from our depth. Yet these are blended and made one by a kind of sacramental solemnity; we have been partakers of a mystery. And Tchehov works this magic on our souls again and again and again. (*Discoveries*, 101)

Murry here describes the effect that Tchehov's works have on readers. What he seems to point out is that their content has an effect on the emotions of the readers and thus helps in the communication of experience. It reminds us of Aristotle's "Catharsis". Here tragedy is replaced by "mysterious simplicity" and has an effect on the 'soul' of the reader. Murry finds Tchehov's works simple and subtly communicative of the morality in his plays. Therefore, Murry accepts Tchehov's art as an art which he calls "pure". It is obvious that simplicity and subtlety in expression is commended by Murry because it affects the soul of men. This is the "Prerogative of the finest art". This type of art Murry appreciates as it helps in communication. He feels that, "illumination is so steady and so unemphatic that at first it escapes us altogether" (*AL*, 78). According to Murry it is a deliberate way employed by Tchehov. Flaubert's art is not acceptable to him because it does not help in understanding the mysteries of life:

> I do not wish to be understood as saying that Tchehov is a manifestation of "art pour art", because in any commonly accepted sense of the phrase, he is not. Still, he might be considered as ah exemplification of what the phrase might be made to mean. (*AL*, 78)

Murry finds a particular unity in the work of Tchehov. This is what distinguishes him from minor artists and raises him to the level of a pure artist and a genius. There is no contradiction or conflict, in his works, he is true to himself, "As is the work, so is the man" (*Discoveries*, 78). Murry finds a harmony between the artist and his work. The unity in the works of Tchehov is indicative of the unity of mind and heart. Therefore, he fully communicates the consciousness of his soul. Ultimately literature to Murry is exploration of soul and communication of experience.

Murry finds a difference between the unity of Tchehov and that of the few other great writers of his rank. It is "far more nakedly aesthetic" than those before him. He reconciled the greatest possible "diversity of content" with the greatest possible "unity of aesthetic impression" (*AL*, 78). Once again it is obvious that Leavis's roots lie close to Murry. Both repeatedly consider pure art to be inseparable from morality.

When Murry writes about the maturity of Tchehov, it reminds us of the maturity that Leavis so often uses as a criterion of a great work in *The Great Tradition* Tchehov's maturity was accompanied by "personal freedom". By "personal freedom", Murry probably means that Tchehov's works did no deal with his problems, that is they were free from his own problems, but his own experiences were universalized. In other words he had what Murry termed negative capability. Such individuals are, according to Murry, pioneers of humanity and it is on them that the future of true civilization depends. Maturity, as Murry understands it, is derived from a close study of humanity. For Leavis also, this is true. Leavis has classified the works of George Eliot into two categories, the mature and the immature. The criterion is impersonality. It must be kept in mind that for Leavis a work of art ought to serve humanity and he primarily thinks that the portions that are over-emotional tend to inhibit the objective of a work of art as they tend to make a work obscure, hence, they are immature. A study of life that is communicated to the readers such as to have its fullest effect on them is mature.

Murry believes that even in subjective works truth should be expressed. In modern fiction there are two subjective methods. There is the presentation of consciousness or the presentation of vivid moments of consciousness. But the idea behind both is to express truth. The second kind of literary pieces can be understood with ease as they speak a universal language. Nevertheless, Murry says, that an objective writer interests the readers more than the subjective. Ulysses is a work of genius, because in it both the subjective and the objective modes coexist. He says that a work is communicated only if the consciousness is "...crystallised about some foreign object to have an intelligible shape" (*Discoveries*, 145). Here he again gives great importance to communication. It is a quality of genius that the objective and subjective are intelligently mingled, so that "the reality becomes the symbol of profoundest certainties" (*Discoveries*, 146). Presentation of a complicated consciousness needs little effort. In simplifying it, so that it is readily communicated and achieves greatness, lies the artist's genius. This needs, as he puts it, great effort:

> And this toil, this labour, is vital to literature. Only when it has been faced and accomplished does a book possess the mysterious quality in virtue of which we pronounce it is masterpiece, namely that gives delight at

> every level of apprehension. A truly great novel is a tale to the simple, a parable to the wise, and a direct revelation of reality in the light of a unique consciousness to the man who had made it part of his being. (*Discoveries*, 148)

Murry here reveals that simplicity is a great achievement. In this he is like Arnold who supported simple subject matter. Arnold's emphasis on "simplicity" is also in the interest of humanity—he wanted readers to understand the mysteries of life with ease.

Murry, in the ultimate analysis, does favour the "story". The question that arises is, did he over wholly rule out the story? His initial disparagement may be explained as a measure to warn the writer—to make him realize that the story is not all, even without it the best works can be written and that besides a story, a novel calls for more. This "more", as Murry himself illustrates, is the communication of the consciousness of life and the experiences of a man who has great awareness and a heightened sensibility.

Like Matthew Arnold, Middleton Hurry believes that philosophers and scientists have the "knowledge of reality". They may disagree with the poet's claims to know reality or the readers claim to attain through the poet's work—a knowledge of reality.[55] This "real" according to Murry, is neither the "real" of science, nor that of philosophy. It is not the reality of the specialist of any sort, but this reality seeks to make ordinary human beings more aware of themselves and of their society. This reality is directly concerned with the life of men:

> To know that reality as it is may not be "knowledge" for the philosopher, or for the scientist; it is knowledge for us, and it is the only knowledge we greatly care about.[56]

Therefore, he says, reading a Shakespearean play gives more pleasure than knowing a secret of the universe. There is truer and more complete experience of reality, which brings joy and serenity. What needs to be noted here is that Arnold too desired "serenity and joy" through literature. This, he also says, could be brought by the communication of reality. This reality is very different from the reality of the scientific truth. We are here reminded of Peter Allan Dale's statement that what is emotionally true may not be scientifically true.[57]

Murry's views on morality can be discerned from his views on poetry, his approach to literature, and his criticism of the poets and novelists. Besides this, he has also stated his views in short essays in *Pencillings* (1923). Murry's biographer, F.A. Lea, tells us that Murry learnt certain aspects of his approach from Bergson. Lea says that in the essay called "Art and Philosophy" Murry acknowledges certain debts to Bergson:

> Life, it tells us, proceeds by "unending creations", of which the artists' are the type and continuation. Since no analysis of the old will suffice to predict the new reason, in order to apprehend life, must be transformed into intuition. That point, as it were, at which the reason becomes itself and by its own heightened working conquers the crude opposition of subject and object from which at a lower level it cannot become free by the same token—this being the artists prerogative—philosophy must be transformed into a recognition of the rational supremacy of art.[58]

In another place, Lea tells us that for Murry art expresses a new wholeness of the personality, a unity to which the intellect is merely instrumental. Here the implicit has become explicit.

Again in the Arnoldian tradition, Murry considers great poetry to be almost religious. H.C. Duffin poinds out:

> All great poets, said Middleton Murry, must be religious, but most poets great and lesser, have been religious only in the sense, of being in vital contact with the universal spirit, which in all religions based on the numinous is called God.[59]

In the book entitled *Pencillings*, Murry has written a number of very short essays. Some of these contain his views on morality. Murry judges a work on the basis of its morality and tries to discern its moral intention. His view of morality differs from the widely prevalent view. In short, a work that is moral must necessarily benefit humanity. "A desire to discern and to communicate the truth about life" is a moral intention. The intention can be dissociated from the action. People always confuse between the morality of the behaviour of the writer's character with the morality of his work. Even a non-moral creation like Falstaff serves a moral function, therefore he is a moral creation. According to Murry, every character that we feel to be typical, to be in his individual existence "symbolic" of one of the great forces which we vaguely discern at work in human life, is a moral creation. The work of every writer who can create such a character has morality.[60] Leavis, like Murry, also believes in producing characters which are representatives of their age or their types. Murry considers Dickens moral because he created Micawber, not because he drowned Steerforth. But he has simultaneously warned the writers not to violate the morality of his time. Great writers, he says, always depict their age and come to terms with their age:

> They express their morality in manners that are tolerable to their countrymen. (*Pencillings*, 114)

Thus a great writer feels the pulse of his age, and creates literature accordingly. That is, the writer not only has the ability to understand the age, but also to furnish works according to the need of the hour, he is alive in his time and so are his works. Murry says that if a work has to last it must have "morality", because morality means:

> ...the power to engage the highest attention of man with feelings and thoughts derived from the faithful contemplation of human life. To avoid morality is not to be bold, or advanced, or artistic; it is simply in the long run to be uninteresting. (*Pencillings*, 118)

Therefore, for Murry, a work has to be close to contemporary life to be interesting. His innate desire is that works of art be interesting as only then will they be read by men. Works which are for the sake of art, or which are away from "life", are of little or no use as they do not interest men. Such works are thus not moral. An interesting work, that is, a work close to life, is essentially moral. This reminds us of Leavis's assumption that "lively characterization is a major strength of art".[61] It means, as we shall see, the same as what Murry implies by "interesting". For Murry, as for Arnold and Leavis, form and content of a work should be in harmony to develop morality in a work of art. While Arnold's views on art and morality have been discussed in the previous section, Leavis's views shall be stated in the section that follows.

Murry's views on art are scattered all through his works. In *Pencillings* he discusses the relationship between art and morality. Pater, he says, the master of "art for art's sake" distinguishes between "qualities of mind" and "qualities of soul". The qualities of mind are, in the real sense, qualities of technique. Murry, elaborating this, says:

> They find expression in formal beauty, in coherent structure, in economy of language; they are sign of the constructive intelligence without which a complete and perfect expression of the writer's apprehension of life is impossible. Qualities of soul, on the other hand, are qualities of the apprehension itself, rendering it sympathetic' to some, alien to others. They are the cause of those devisive reactions of our temperament towards an author's work which are swift and unshakable. (*Pencillings*, 123)

According to Murry, in doing this we are judging the man by his clothes. We judge the qualities of his soul by moral standards. True impersonality has a "closer correspondence between expression and apprehension" and therefore it "provides us with still more certain evidence of the quality of soul". It is a state where "the last disguise is fallen from the writer's habit of thought and feeling". Therefore, like Arnold, he also believes that both form and technique add to the morality of a work.

Murry thought it necessary for all good writers to regard the significance of both form and content. In their works both qualities are aligned. Pater, he says, had no doubt about it. A work is great when:

> human destinies are squarely faced: that the author's soul; was responsive to the deepest human doubts and bewilderments, and that his vision included the beauty

> and the joy and the ugliness and the sorrow of human life, glorify nothing. (*Pencillings*, 126)

In great works of literature he demands perfection of art integrity of the writer's soul and comprehensiveness in his attitude. Of these, three qualities are moral. Middleton Murry's main concern was with the content of a literary piece. Like Matthew Arnold, he believed that high seriousness should accompany a work of art so that literature can accomplish its purpose. He says, "Matthew Arnold set the fashion originally, and he picked it up from Aristotle."[62] Seriousness in a work of literature shows that it is moral, and that the writer is seriously communicating the "profoundest truth" that he feels about human life. Like Arnold, he believes that both tragedy and comedy can have high seriousness. Literature must illuminate our human experience, he says. Arnold also is of the opinion that the picture of life that is presented in literature must be constructive only then can it be said to have high seriousness. Since both tragedy and comedy have the potential to illuminate both can have high seriousness. He is unlike T.S. Eliot who fails to give due weightage to seriousness in *The Sacred Wood*. Eliot considers George Eliot a more serious novelist than Dickens because George Eliot was a writer of tragic situations and Dickens of comic ones. Seriousness should not be confused with "tragedy or solemnity". It is, according to Murry, a vital quality of enduring literature. It is "the seriousness in content" rather than that of style which matters. Dickens may be more careless than George Eliot in style but still remains a serious writer (Leavis later also accepted Dickens as a serious writer). Flaubert cannot be called serious though his style is perfect. Such style is of minor virtue. Thus it is seriousness of content that makes a work moral as it communicates the profoundest truth about life. It is from Arnold that Murry has derived these views. As will be seen later, F.R. Leavis's views on the subject too are similar to that of Murry and Arnold.

For Murry, art was never a positive quality. Writing in defence of Murry, Sharma says that Leavis misreads Murry. Lawrence, he adds, was a great artist.[63] But for Murry, being an artist was not all that important as in all the three major works on Lawrence *Son of Woman* (1931). *Reminiscences of D.H. Lawrence* (1933) and *Love, Freedom and Society* (1957), Murry repeatedly insists that Lawrence's aim was not to produce art. He had the potential but he did not do it purposely. Further quoting from *Son of Woman* and *Love, Freedom and Society*, he states:

> Murry did not fail to see artistic possibilities in Lawrence. On the contrary, he was trying to defend him against the earlier critics who were accusing Lawrence of lacking in artistic abilities. In fact, Murry places Lawrence above all his contemporaries. Due to Murry's mystical and visionary approach to literature, Lawrence appeared to him to be "beyond art", he had, as it were, transcended the realms of art and reached the domains of the prophet. But Lawrence could come back to art, if he so desired and as he does in *The Plumed Serpent*. Why F.R. Leavis could not understand Murry's intentions and abilities as a critic of Lawrence, remains dubious. Either the reason was that the standards of judgment in both critics were different; the term "art" had a different meaning for both. But a more plausible reason could be that Leavis was, like most others, blindly following Aldous Huxley's comment on Murry's *Son of Woman*....[64]

Murry had great regard for Dickens but writing about him in *Pencillings* he calls him "an artist in parts". This does not indicate that for Murry Dickens was not great in the true sense but it shows, that being an artist really did not make a novelist great.

Writing, about Flaubert in his article "Flaubert and Flaubart", Murry criticizes the modern artist who is "positively swollen headed; ...when nobody, believes you are anything, the instinctive reply is to believe you are everything" (*Discoveries*, 144). Against a society which has a function for the artist only in so far as he is a manufacturer of a profitable merchandise, it is scarcely surprising that the artist retorts that his is, in fact, the supreme function, and his position so exalted that it is invincible to the naked eye.

Murry says that the modern artist cannot be understood by the people in general. The modern artist also fails to perform his duty towards the society. This lack of ability is because in being original he becomes obscure. The recording of consciousness by Proust, Joyce and Dorothy Richardson, according to Murry has not proved to have a damaging effect on the novel. A true artist, he says is one:

> Whose work manifests an incessant growth from a merely personal immediacy to a coherent and all comprehending attitude of life.[66]

Middleton Murry has presented his theory of criticism in several essays, namely, "The function of Criticism", "The Cry in the Wilderness", "Poetry and Criticism", "Reason and Criticism", "A Critical Credo" and "The Courage of Criticism". Besides these, his views on criticism are interspersed in all his works. *The Problem of Style* (1922) has more practical criticism and some theoretical concepts. In the above mentioned essays and works, Murry deals with the nature of art, the function of criticism, and the method that critics should apply to perform that function.

Murry's chief aim was to help literature out of the existing turmoil so that it could be of use to humanity. In a formalistic time, as Kaufmann says, he exercised:

> ...the Arnoldian option, asserting that criticism "should openly accept the fact that its deepest judgments are moral" (*Countries of the Mind*), and that "art is the consciousness of life" (*Aspects of Literature*).[67]

Murry believes that poetry and criticism are similar in some ways, "True criticism is in itself an organic part of the whole activity of art." Murry drew a system of values by which a work ought to be judged. Like the Greeks, the approach to life and art must be the same, and the standard with which life and art ought to be judged must be the same—"As art is the consciousness of life, criticism is the consciousness of art". The chief objective of "true criticism" is the harmonious control of art by art. The critic must justify literature. In other words, criticism must bring out the ideal of life implied literature.[68] For this reason a hierarchy of values is required. Murry insists that it is only the aesthetic capability that helps to establish the values of life. Art, according to Murry, reveals to us the principles of its own governance. Criticism has to apply these values to literature. To this Cassavant says that there is a difference between a poet and a critic in their use of an "aesthetic system".[69] The literary critic should apply a "conscious aesthetic system", while the artist's aesthetic system could possibly be unconscious. For this reason, says Cassavant, Eliot believed that a good literary critic should essentially be a creative writer:

> The lines drawn between Eliots artist-as-critic and Murry's creative critic mark the fundamental distance between them, even in, his early period of mutual appreciation and encouragement.[70]

There is a remarkable similarity between Arnold and Murry when Murry says that—a critic should judge a work of art with the help of some prescribed values.[71] The purpose of Arnold's touchstones was precisely to provide prescribed values. F.R. Leavis too, it will be seen later, adopted this approach in his criticism.

According to Murry, a true literary critic must have a humanistic philosophy. This philosophy should share its value with art. He must have some values, so that he can judge a work of art according to how completely it "...manifests an incessant growth from a merely personal immediacy to a coherent and all comprehending attitude to life."[72] The philosophy of art and life should be the same, that is, humanistic. It is only then that truly great criticism can be achieved.

Another Arnoldian feature of Murry's theory of criticism is that for him too the function of criticism involves the establishment of an "ideal". A critic should establish a hierarchy among the great artists of the past and the present. The hierarchy of the past helps to test the creative ability of the present day artists. Sharma gives a fitting conclusion to Murry's function of criticism:

> At the superficial plane criticism performs two functions. First, it gives some kind of direction to the numerous

young writers of a time. Second, if a genius were to suddenly appear, criticism should recognize that genius.[73]

Arnold's influence is evident here. Murry while presenting his views on some critics finds Coleridge's concept of criticism as close to his own because, in him, too, there is a strict and mutually fertilizing relation between the moral and aesthetic values. Murry is surprised at Eliot's rating Dryden superior to Aristotle and Coleridge.

Murry's concern with culture is evident in his theory of criticism, just as it is in his works other than literary criticism. Elaborating the concept of art in criticism, Murry has written another essay, "The Cry in the Wilderness". He disapproves of the use of psychology in criticism as the critics in his time did not do justice to the psychological processes. Morality has to be the basis of psychological criticism. But in the criticism of his time, he finds discussion of psychology without its concern for the soul of the artist; that is without considering his experiences in the moral perspective:

> ...vital centre of our ethics is also the vital centre of our art. Moral nihilism, which can be obscured only temporarily by an insistence upon technical perfection as in itself a supreme good. Neither the art of religion nor the religion of art is an adequate statement of the possibilities and purpose of art but there is no doubt that the religion of art is by far the more vacuous of the two. (185)

In "A Critical Credo", Murry brings to light once again the similarity between criticism and creation, just as he defines the function of criticism:

> The function of criticism is, therefore, primarily the function of literature itself, to provide a means of self expression for the critic. (*Countries of the Mind*, 183)

The difference lies in the fact that literature is the literary critic's subject. He too has to promote certain values of life and provide some fresh ideas. Arnold's concept of criticism, too, is very similar to this. Criticism is, Murry says, an "art of literature". It must interest humanity or else it will not be read.

Criticism is, according to Murry, different from reviewing. Both are in a sense equal in importance. They both should emphasize "law-making", rather than personal impressions. This "law-making", seems to have been derived from Arnold and could have influenced the thinking of Leavis, who also adopted it. This system of laws is helpful to the writers of the age and is also a record of all the past impressions and reactions of critic. What is of vital importance to Murry is that these should be his own impressions and they should not be affected by the temporary disturbances in the sensibility. The critic should avoid "momentary enthusiasms and passing disgusts". Once again we are reminded of Arnold's "disinterestedness" which means almost what Murry states in the lines given above. The critic, according to Murry, may be a historian like Sainte Beuve, a moralist like Matthew Arnold, or a technician like Robert Bridges. But the best critic is one who would combine all these "predispositions" in proper parts. Murry has given a stepwise illustration of the method to be adopted in criticism and thus to successfully establish laws—values of life. First, the critic should try his best to convey the whole effect of the work he is criticizing, its "peculiar uniqueness". Next, a critic must "work back" and "define the unique-quality of the sensibility" which helped to bring forth this sensibility (Here the relevant circumstances of the writer's life have their proper place). Only after this he must analyse the means by which this sensibility was given "expression"; in other words, to conduct a technical examination into the style. Fifth, a still closer examination of a characteristic passage, that is, a passage in which the author's sensibility is completely expressed. This fifth and final step is really a return to the first, but with the important difference that the relevant material has been ordered and placed before the readers.

In "Reason and Criticism", Murry states that reason plays a vital part in the process of criticism. Like Arnold he realizes the importance of intelligence. Reason results from a continuous conflict between heart and mind, feeling and intelligence. In the process of criticism, reason rather than intelligence and feeling should be applied. If the critic is emotionally involved with the work of art the criticism cannot be disinterested. If only intellectually a work of art is viewed, the criticism will result in philosophy that may be difficult to understand. Therefore he is right when he says, "Reason is the understanding of life".[74]

Murry's chief interest was to serve humanity. For this he believed that an artist has to understand human nature. By understanding the individual, he believed, it is possible to understand the society. And it is, therefore, pertinent to note that not only in his theory of poetry and novel do we find him desperately finding ways and means of understanding the individual's "soul", but even in his approach to the different poets and prose writers we find him understanding the man behind the work—the individual who is more aware than most men, a representative man of his time. Besides this, in *Heaven—and Earth* (1938) and in several other essays scattered all through his works we find him struggling for the cause of the "individual". It is for this reason that he is a cultural critic and for this reason *Heaven—and Earth* is widely read in universities as a book covering the "culture course" and as Griffin says, his books "...help to articulate the consciousness of the age and to suggest paths for future literary and cultural development."[75] Cassavant agrees with Griffin. According to her, Murry's continuous effort was to work for "cultural issues".[76]

Murry might be accused for "narrow nationalism", but his life long effort was to become a "normal Englishman". He himself says in *Community Farm* (1952), "England's first duty to the world society is to be England as it is France's to be France."[77] Leavis, as we shall see later, also aimed at understanding the cultural tradition of England before that of other countries. Yet, like Arnold, he had great regard for Greek, Latin and French literature. This helped him to place English writers in their true positions. Kaufmann understood his efforts for making a better society and culture. He says that Murry's aim was to "clean" his whole country: "Literature was his instrument, the broom he wielded against the disorder of his time."[78] His political involvement was also an effort unto this end. Murry partly accepted Marxism. Christians of England distrusted a thinker who proclaimed himself a believer in the theories of Marx. He was also shunned by Marxists as he did not come to terms with Marx's materialism. Yet he did not withdraw from, active political life. From the dark days of the First World War, he was determined to devote himself to the realization of ideals—to the avoidance of another war and achievement of a just and a more humane society. His morality, therefore, was rooted in freeing humanity from the bonds of skepticism. Murry, too, was conscious of his own intense morality. He went to the extent of feeling that he was not working for literature but for morality alone:

> I have a feeling that I have been completely outside the mainstream of literature: that I don't "belong" and indeed never have belonged. My concern has been that of a moralist, and I have never been sufficient of an artist to be diverted from it.[79]

Nevertheless his sincerity has made him today an important critic of the moralistic tradition. Cassavant has summarized Murry's objective thus:

> All limitations considered, he produced a considerable body of illuminating criticism, and he made literature accessible to unsophisticated readers.... The principles that underlay his judgements—that a great literary work must demonstrate a comprehensive moral vision which universalizes experience, that such works must be placed in a hierarchy according to the profundity of that vision, that art and life must not be held separate—are principles most great critics have held.[80]

For Murry literature is important because life is. He therefore uses the biographical approach to a very large extent. Every book or essay of Murry shows his interest in the life of the author under consideration. It is due to this reason that Murry places much importance in belief in literature and in the truth of poetry. In *Keats and Shakespeare* Murry tells us that the poet only says what he means and hence statements in poetry are very relevant. Murry often goes to extreme limits to prove his author right or wrong. It is for this reason that he is subject to much criticism. In trying to prove that in "To Autumn" Keats was attempting to say that "Ripeness is all",[81] Murry invited much critical disgust.[82] But if we approve of Arnold's dictum that poetry is at bottom the criticism of life then Murry's statement seems to be the logical continuation in the same direction. Only in Murry the Arnoldian quest, and what one thinks is perhaps a subtler version, finds a continuation.

Murry incorporates into his critical fold an idea from Wittgenstein's theory that what can be shown cannot be stated. Hence poetry must exhibit a criticism of life and criticism should be concealed in the form and not in glaring existence. It is for this reason that Murry discusses poetic form with so much concentration that he is sometimes confused with a New Critic. For example, Lawrence Lerner erroneously regards him to be a New Critic.[83] Perhaps the truth of Murry's critical vision lies in the fact that when he appreciates a text his sensibility takes into account the author, his universe and above all the words on the page. His biographer, F.A. Lea, says:

> To front experience on behalf of mankind; that was Murry's ideal; and it was as much an ethical ideal as an aesthetic: "Vital centre of our ethics is also the vital centre of our art". Eliot first shocked him and then illuminated him by calling him primarily a "moralist". His criticism from the outset was a quest for values a determination of what was good for man. Hence his objection to l 'art' pour l 'art', and his insistence on the necessity of establishing a hierarchy that art was the best in kind which expressed and communicated a comprehension of life most completely. This was the standard by which he set head and top of the 20th century writers Tchehov and Thomas Hardy.[84]

Murry considered Lawrence to be the greatest mind of the 20th century and hailed him as a prophet in all his major writings on Lawrence:

(a) *Son of Woman* (1931)

(b) *Reminiscences of D.H. Lawrence* (1933)

(c) *Adam and Eve* (1944)

(d) *Love, Freedom and Society* (1957)

It is interesting to note that whereas Murry tried to liberate D.H. Lawrence from the harsh remarks against him (Lawrence) by several of his contemporaries, he is today considered to be a critic who maligned him.[85] Murry is interested in the prophetic rather than the artistic creations of Lawrence. Murry shares Arnold's views on the nature of art and Leavis misunderstands Murry's approach to Lawrence in not being able to appreciate the latter's artistic ability.

Murry points out the autobiographical nature of Lawrence's novels, short stories, poems and essays, following the psychoanalytical approach, which happenis to be the chief tool of most biographical critics, he says that ail the heroes of Lawrence suffer from the same problem which he (Lawrence) himself faced.[86] They appear to be unfulfilled in their relationship with women and men. Murry is above all concerned with the message and prophecy which Lawrence has for his audience.[87] As Griffin points out:

> The title, *Son of Woman*, indicates what Murry thinks caused Lawrence to deny his calling. From evidence in the novels and in other writings, such as *Fantasia of the Unconscious*, Murry shows convincingly enough, that Lawrence's mother-fixation largely shaped Lawrence's future associations with women. Whether Murry should go on to say that his mother's love made him incapable of wholeheartedly giving his love to another woman may be more doubtful, but here again he can quote Lawrence's own words in support. His thesis is that Lawrence determined to escape his true destiny of spiritual awareness by transforming it into love, of women of which he was not capable. Even sexually, Murry maintains Lawrence was weak, certainly, he remained childless.

> Having failed with women, Lawrence wanted a perfect relationship with man—not physically on the homosexual level, but on a level of sex communion beyond the phalic, although still not purely spiritual. He sought a "sexuality of touch", a Blutbruders chaft deeper than consciousness, in the mindless, premental sphere. This search also failed, so that Lawrence was thwarted in achieving the communion he wanted, or imagined he wanted with both woman and man. When he determined to escape altogether the sterile intellectual consciousness of modern man, he tried to lose himself in admiration of a primitive and soulless people—which, says Murry, he also could not do.[88]

An interesting feature of *Adam and Eve* is that Murry makes an effort to relate his graplings with Lawrence to a theory of civilization by taking Lawrence and Aldous Huxley as representatives of the division forced by historical Christianity:

> Both were driven to an individual and personal mysticism, Lawrence to a mysticism of the flesh, Huxley to a mysticism of spirit. These mysticisms were complementary, but irreconcilable, as it were, thesis and antithesis of which the synthesis was adumbrated only by Lawrence. The emergence of this thesis and antithesis was the reemergence after four centuries of a specious solution by protestantism, of a fundamental conflict between the religious—ascetic and the secular-sexual which had divided historical Christianity from the time it became the religion of a civilization.[89]

From the above quotation Murry's concern for civilization and society (the moral concern) is evident. Murry's interest in Lawrence's religion of sex in *Son of Woman* and in other places is also an example of his moral concern.

One of Murry's most successful books is *Keats and Shakespeare* (1926). His response to Keats has been widely aplauded. One of his chief achievements in the analysis of Keats's poetry is his discovery of Keats's poetic thought.[90] Today Keats is considered to be a great thinker. Before Murry wrote Keats's thought was not so well known. Richard Harter Fogle has brought out this point very effectively. He says, and rightly, that Murry is the critic who first influenced people in taking him "seriously as a thinker". Commenting on Murry in relation to *Keats and Shakespeare*, Fogle says:

> His actual achievement is very substantial indeed in *Keats and Shakespeare* he succeeds in conceiving a unique and autonomous poetic mode of thought.[91]

John Carswell points out this trait of Murry's criticism when he says:

> We believe there is no such thing, there is science, and there is Literature but true literature and true science are always in a sense philosophical. They are occupied with reality. In this *The Adelphi* also will be philosophical.[92]

Murry seemed to be always on the look out for the truth. He seemed to be discovering life through literature and he was a mystic of some repute. It was therefore natural for him to study the author's life as well as his works. In doing so he did not look at any literary piece in isolation. On the contrary he saw it as a part of a larger whole which was made up of the author, his works, and his universe. To explain this aspect of Murry's criticism, I propose to consider the example of Murry's approach to John Keats.

Murry wrote several books and articles on Keats throughout his life. Keats happened to be the kind of poet who could become a spiritual hero for Murry. The chief reason being that he fell in line with that poetic mode of thought which characterized his model poet—Shakespeare.[93] Even though some critics have regarded Murry's approach to Shakespeare more successful than his approach to Keats his treatment of Keats is even more characteristic of him because he followed the biographical approach and much more was known of Keats's life than of Shakespeare's. Murry's intuitive grasp of an author was undoubtedly very great. T.S. Eliot in his *Selected Essays* took Murry to task for his (Murry's) "Inner Voice" and hence what could have been a virtue of Murry's criticism became a vice. Mrs. Middleton Murry in her letter to L.R. Sharma, dated 10th June, 1980, says that when writing of

Keats Murry behaved as if he was Keats himself.[94] This could be seen as a ridiculous act as well as an act of profound sincerity towards the author. Murry had a great reverence for his text and tried to annihilate himself in order to share the experience of the man behind the literary work. In doing this Murry was actually following the advice of Keats himself who considered negative capability to be the greatest achievement in an artist.

> As to the poetical character itself (I mean that sort of which, if I am anything, I am a Member; that sort distinguished from the Wordsworthian or egoistical sublime; which is a thing per se and stands alone) it is not itself—it has no self—it is everything and nothing—it has no character.... It has as much delight in conceiving an Iago as an Imogen. What shocks the virtuous philosopher, delights the "Camelion" poet.... A poet... has no Identity.[95]

Being greatly involved with his poet, Murry was able to write criticism with an immediate appeal *Keats and Shakespeare* is not merely a book on Keats's poetry but it brings the reader in close contact with John Keats, the man and his work. To read the book is to experience an exploration of Keats's universe. Even though several contemporary books on Keats do not acknowledge their debt to Murry's *Keats and Shakespeare*, it still remains perhaps the best introduction to Keats.

The letters of Keats naturally become very significant for Murry's understanding of the poet. He emphasizes that the best study of Keats's mind is derived through his letters. Murry follows the development of Keats's mind. At every stage the letters are read and interpreted with a gusto which shows a very close contact with the poet. In *Keats and Shakespeare* (1926) as well as in *Keats* (1955) much importance is given to Keats's personal relationships and particularly to his very personal relationships. Throughout he gives us an indication of how certain concepts in Keats's poetry emerge from his relationships.

In his enthusiasm for his discoveries and explorations, Murry sometimes makes exaggerated claims and sweeping statements. An example of this can be seen in his statement that if Keats had been six inches taller, the history of 19th century poetry would be different. In making such a claim Murry is obviously using the psychological approach in studying Keats's mind. By now it is a well-known fact of literary theory that most artists create due to their abnormalities. But when Murry wrote of Keats's creativity so much had not been formulated theoretically. It was not because of his knowledge of psychology but his closeness to Keats that he could make such a claim (*Keats*, 162).

Murry believed that great poets always mean what they say. Hence he tried to get to the meaning of what was said in great poetry. The experience of the poet is given great value and perhaps Murry felt that a poet speaks from experience. In *Countries of the Mind* Murry tells us that a poet's consciousness can be known from the metaphors he uses. In studying the metaphor and imagery of a poet one can get to the poet's consciousness. The best example of this is to be seen in Murry's treatment of Keats's in "On First Looking into Chapman's Homer". In this analysis, Murry shows how certain symbols and images reveal Keat's thought process:

> So the poet's mind has been accumulating through successive acts of sense perception a series of images which can be assimilated into the main process of his thought and act as surrogates for it. And the condition of this assimilation is an emotional and qualitative correspondence. His perception of the moon is a delighted discovery so is his perception of the ocean—in both the hidden loveliness of an unknown reality is revealed to him, therefore both in the qualities discovered and in the emotion awakened in discovery of the nature of poetry. With his senses he discovers nature, with his thoughts he discovers the nature of poetry.
>
> His two crowning sense discoveries were those of the moon and the sea, and these are instantly pressed into the service of his thought, the images of the moon and

> ocean can serve at well to embody the objects of thought. And he is able to think more exactly concerning the nature of poetry because sensuous images of moon and ocean have become true symbols of the reality about which he is thinking. So that in the process of unconscious elaboration the continually progressing thought is given ever fresh definition and substance by the images it is able to assimilate, and on the other hand, the images acquire a thought—content. The thought steadily gains focus and intensity the images significance. (*Keats*, 163)

From the above extract Murry's ability to extract thought content from poetic images is exemplified.

An interesting explanation of Keats's "Grecian Urn" has been given by Murry in *Keats*. Summarizing the critical judgements of the last two lines, he says:

> For Doctor Bridges the final lines redeemed a poor poem, to Mr. Eliot they spoil a good one, for Sir Arthur Quiller Couch they are ignorant and uneducated, for Mr. Richards that still ambiguous unity he calls "a pseudo-statement". (*Keats*, 163)

Murry finds these approaches as based on a mental analysis. To understand the process by which Keats arrived at such a statement a critic has to intuitively identify with it. The critic should not be satisfied with the meaning alone. He should understand what the image or the symbol meant to the poet at the time he wrote it and thus get to the root of the experience that has been presented. Murry goes deeper into the words and subjectively arrives at an explanation as he finds no other method to understand it. Words which convey peace and were written in moments when Keats' mind was in turmoil may seem easy but are in fact difficult to understand. Such a message is in the words: "Not my will, but thine be done". It is a meaning of this kind that we should seek in "Beauty is truth, truth beauty" if we are really desirous to understand what the words truly meant to Keats and what Keats meant by them. Elaborating on this point Murry justifies his opponent's charges against him saying that the truth, the true truth, is such that it gives rise to love and such truth is beautiful. He later says that what Keats is saying is profoundly true, it would not have been so if it was not profoundly beautiful (*Keats*, 299).

E.C. Pettet notices Murry's concern for Keats's thought-content in "Ode on Melancholy", and in "Ode to a Nightingale".[96] The former Ode, according to Murry, expresses profound and experienced thought in the final stanza and therefore is of the highest significance as poetic philosophy.

Murry has much to say about Keats's negative capability, his spontaneous and efforted poetry,[97] his sensation and his thought. Murry maintains that Keats was proving upon his pulses, being convinced in his nerves, that life was a contradiction. On the one hand he was conscious of its beauty on the other he felt, its pain. Murry has said much about Keats's disinterestedness and in this he is truly an Arnoldian critic (*Keats*, 307).

Middleton Murry like Arnold, regarded Shakespeare as the ideal poet. *Keats and Shakespeare* and *Shakespeare* reveal the reasons behind his admiration for Shakespeare. *Shakespeare* is quite representative of Murry's criticism. He most often employs the biographical approach to criticism. Stating the reason behind this, Murry says, in *Keats and Shakespeare*:

> Great poetry is the utterance of that to which the human soul responds of that to which the human soul endorses so that history of the souls of the greab poots is the most essential history of the human soul itself. (146)

Murry, like Arnold and Leavis, regards poets as people who are more aware than others. It is important to get to the meaning of a literary work as through it the "soul" of its author can be understood. Since he utters truths and helps to understand the mysteries of life, a poet is one who ought to be understood well. Without this literature would have no meaning. Murry even insists that poets create works of art so that their "soul should be known". Besides, the works of art have the potential to improve men. Precisely it is in the process of understanding the poet's soul that men have a better understanding of truth and life. This brings about the change in them. Whatever the poet says is a reflection of his soul. These ideas of the poet have an effect on the men. Like Arnold, Murry can therefore be said to believe firmly in the affectivist theory of poetic value according to which poetic enjoyment does not depend upon the literal truth of what the poet says, only upon the psychological effect of what it is saying and how it is saying it.[98] Besides, the above view of Murry has a striking similarity with Arnold's theory of poetry being a criticism of life.

C.G. Thayer is of the view that the psychobiographical approach is not to write the biography but to know a great writer better.[99] Murry wishes to make Shakespeare more real and immediate to the reader's imagination. Defending the psychobiographical approach Sharma says:

> To understand the work and art of a writer, one should take the help of his life because work and life are interrelated. The critic should place himself in the place of the writer and try to feel his experience.[100]

Shakespeare, about whom much is still unknown, is treated with a unique intuitive perceptiveness in Murry's *Shakespeare*. For example, after reading the elaborate simile of house building in the Falstaff plays, Murry believes that it emerged out of some vivid personal experience. Either Shakespeare was building a house for himself or thinking about building one. Trying to place himself in Shakespeare's position Murry feels that it must have been a tremendous task for "a penniless professional man of letters". This was proved true by later research. Griffin remarks that Murry's intuitive insights often proved to be correct. In 1958, while writing the Falstaff plays he was actually building and renovating an abandoned home for himself.[101] By sketching out the incidents of Shakespeare's life, Murry perhaps tries to make men understand his plays more fully for he believes that some incidents of a writer's life are retold in his works. But there are others which are indirectly expressed through the images. Therefore as already stated imagery has considerable value for him. Though both Thayer and Griffin regard this approach as dangerous, a reviewer of *The Times Literary Supplement*, says that this helps the plain man to see more of "beauty and meaning" in his plays.[102] Murry's him behind reconstruction of the author's life through his works was to make the works more interesting for the readers and also was an effort to bring the readers so close to the author that the actual feeling or emotion of the author is communicated, thus making the most of the work.

Murry relates Shakespeare's works to England's history and to his contemporary England. Murry finds that the history plays of Shakespeare are a deep study into the question of an ideal king illustrating what an ideal king should be. It is the study of the theme of order in relation to the doctrine of divine right of kings, and the deep study of the kings from Richard II through Henry V is an evolution towards a character who can embody ideal kingship. That king is king indeed who utters the soul of people (*Shakespeare*, 149).

Heaven—and Earth also deals with the theme of the establishment of order. At the vortex he places the ideal Englishman. This ideal Englishman is the subject of "The Shakespeare Man". Murry regards Hamlet as the only "Shakespeare man" amongst the characters of Shakespeare's plays. Murry's works, as rightly stated by Cassavant, are for the laymen.[103] By presenting his views of the king, he is making the laymen aware of what is right and what is wrong. He presents Shakespeare's philosophy of life through his works in such a way that even the inexpert reader can understand it.

Murry finds Shakespeare's plays more spontaneous after *Richard II* and *Richard III*. This he attributes to Shakespeare's control over language. In this chapter Murry also presents his views on language (*Shakespeare*, 149). For him language evolves from within the man. Shakespeare, he says, most have felt that the kind of unusual language he was giving to his characters in moments of nominally tense emotion was unnatural. This might have been the reason of his slowly becoming more natural with less hyperboles. Though he feels this might have been merely a development in diction but in fact it was an intellectual and spiritual development which brought this about—"It was an outward and visible sign of an inward and spiritual grace" (*Shakespeare*, 149). This made his characters more alive. Murry attributes this to the fact that Shakespeare started identifying his character with himself. They were no longer outside but in him. Their emotions and experiences were his own. This brought about naturalness and spontaneity together with strong emotion. This makes Shakespeare one of the greatest dramatists according to Murry. Thus Murry desires that the dramatists should present a work in which there is a fusion of thought and emotion and the identification of self with the characters in such a way that there is spontaneity in the work.

Murry refers to Shakespeare's dramatic method as "humanization of melodrama" (*Shakespeare*, 228). Shakespeare did as much as he could to make his characters credible human beings to himself and to others. With the situation before him, the characters derive their first rudimentary life from the situation. This is the reason why the characters are humanized. Murry uses *The Merchant of Venice* as an example of humanization of melodrama. He observes that mere than other plays of Shakespeare this is "a matter-of-fact fairy tale," a true folk story converted into a drama; and it makes its appeal to human consciousness from where folk-tales took their origin. Shylock's hatred for Antonio is a fairy tale hatred, one between good and evil. He accepted an ultimate fact of the moral, universe, the opposition between good and evil. The hatred of the villains lies deeper than their consciousness. Man was the center of Murry's critical works.

On going through *Blake* (1935) a work that has been variously criticised, the thing that strikes most is Murry's incessant effort to establish certain values for which he himself has great regard. Murry tries to simplify Blake to make him comprehensible. It is the thought-content of Blake rather than his artistic capabilities that Murry respects. S.G. Cassavant summarizes Murry's interpretation of Blake's teachings:

> Eternity is a continuing potentiality of the Now, When man liberates his Identity (the true unconscious being) from the prison of the self (the self-conscious ego) he is Free to know Eternity, to become God. The contraries of corporeal life are redeemed, the duality of estranged

> body and soul are resolved, by Annihilation of the Self and rebirth to original Identity. The man who possesses his Identity passes beyond good and evil to acknowledge of oneness, a universe in which each part contains the whole.[104]

Murry appreciates the self annihilation in Blake's philosophy. He himself has been influenced by it. Even in Keats's works he appreciates the selfless attitude and compares Jesus and Keats. It is a growth that gradually brings the man close to God and the end is thus attainment of "spirituality". Spirituality is an experience which is immediately recognized by those to whom it comes as being an intrinsic quality. Whether it comes,

> ...mediately through the creation of art, immediately in a timeless instant of pure contemplation, is two fold in character. It reveals the world without and it reveals the within. (*Blake*, 149)

Marry calls Blake an "imaginative artist". Blake was one, Murry says, who was inspired by Eternal Imagination. A man is inspired by Eternal Imagination when the selfhood is in abeyance (*Blake*, 149). Pure spontaneity results in unconscious "self abeyance". The other self-abeyance is deliberate and for humanity and spiritual in the true sense. Thus, for Murry a spiritual act is humane in nature. Spontaneity means "selfless obedience to that which is beyond the ego". Therefore, the activities of the artist, whose work has true significance, may proceed from either of these orders of self abeyance, but they must proceed from them. Murry refers to Blake as an imaginative artist because he devoices all his powers to figurative and symbolical images of the knowledge of Eternity. Murry does not approve of an excessive use of images and symbols. The effect, he says, on humanity should be creative. Murry associates Blake's imagery to his philosophy of life. Blake's philosophy of five senses is turned "outwards", that is, away from Eternity, the road to which for Blake, lies "inwards", inward not in the psychological sense, but in the spiritual sense as it is said the "kingdom of Heaven is within you" (*Blake*, 149). While the sensory images are presented the senses should be kept wide open. The five senses, he says are "in reality a gate leading on to Eternity". This is the reason why Murry calls Blake an "imaginative artist". It is here that we find Murry appreciating the art of a poet. True "Art", he says, has to be imaginative and also symbolical of the "Eternal Imaginative". For Murry, Blake is not a mystical or religious artist but in the true sense an imaginative artist.

In Murry's critical texts his links with culture are evident quite often. "Whitman: Poet-Prophet of Democracy", is one such essay where Murry shows his dissatisfaction with the contemporary age and also desires a change in the society. Murry upholds the virtues of democracy and voices his opinion against Russia which made a "monstrous claim" to democracy.[105] The real meaning of democracy, he says, is contained in Whitman's *Democratic Vistas* and this work also looks forward to the famous *Leaves of Grass* by Whitman. But, Murry says, the glory of this great work remained unaung by the Americans of Whitman's time as they were "...too engrossed in the material mastering of a continent to have time to pause and take their spiritual hearings...."[106] Whereas in England the work was received with enthusiasm. The reason for such a difference in the response lay in the fact that England at that time was groomed by the "best minds". Carlyle, Ruskin, Arnold and Morris were the influences which made the minds receptive to Whitman. We should remember that Arnold also regarded literature as having the potential of making minds more aware and making an age rich in creative works. Leavis, too, explicitly says this in *New Bearings in English Poetry* (1932; p. 19).

Democracy in the true sense of the word, according to Murry, aims at the validity of the individual. The society is "self governing" with responsible Individuals, in a democracy. "It is a compelling vision of the society towards which humanity must stumble on." In a democracy infinite worth is attached to the individual and he is accepted as supreme with all his imperfections. The society is ruled by law of love. Therefore, Murry believes that democracy is almost religious. It develops out of an existing society and is "entirely new" and therefore its religion incorporates all that is valid in the religion of the preceding society. Since its major premise offers eminence to common man it is in the true sense the voice of Jesus Christ as he too proclaimed the equality of souls. The worth of the individual lies in the fact that he is a part of the universal One. The body and the soul of the individual in a democracy are One—"an individual One." This individual One is a part of the universal One. In this he finds Keats comparable to Whitman. This seems to be a "religious-ethical" basis of democracy. Whitman, he says is a "prophetic-man", because he is:

> ...in part, the attractive image of the citizen of the new completely human society of which the crude integument is what we call Democracy; he is, in a yet more important part, the tongue-tied soul in travail of the idea of which he is the instinctive vehicle.[107]

Therefore, according to Murry, Whitman's greatness lay in his exploiting the individual's potential to make the world a better place.

Middleton Murry's chief concern, as has been earlier suggested, was with humanity and which in a wider perspective delineates his interest in culture. Throughout his critical career he has prescribed directly or indirectly ways and means of edification of mind kind as a measure of strengthening culture. Whereas in *Keats and Shakespeare*, *Shakespeare*, *The Problem of Style*, and *Aspects of Literature* he has suggested repeatedly, the importance of experience and the ways of communicating it more effectively, in *Heaven—and Earth* his endeavour is to show how great writers have actually brought this about by universalizing their experiences. There is a considerable change in the approach to the writers. This is because he tries to relate their significance in the history—their achievements and how they brought this about. His approach is not psychobiographical while analysing writers there are portions which give a clear view of his dedication to the cause of culture. According to Cassavant, "It contains the fullest, most satisfying statement of Murry's theory of modern civilization."[108] Most of the "heroes" of his work are established propounders of democracy. He is concerned over the widespread totalitarianism and argues in favour of the strength of the individual. According to Murry, with the decline of the Renaissance, came the end of individualism, as civilization faced a death blow from the rising forces of Protestant doctrine of individuality.[109] From this evolved political liberty, nationalism, imperialism, exploration and invention and the fast developing "machine age" that devoured the potentialities of the individual and thus brought an "...end in a living death to the individuals, and universal catastrophe to mankind". Such a world can be redeemed by love. The objective of the book is to commemorate the heroes of thought, the philosophers of "heaven and earth", who have, striven to regenerate the world by the "...divine vision in the spirit of selfless love." Giving an optimistic view of this state of perfection, he says:

> A clear vision of distinct and unattainable perfection does not lead, as some believe, to despair. That condition cannot be desperate, to which all men know they are condemned by the nature of existence. It gives man true unity instead of false, for one thing. Men who are united by the common knowledge that their imperfection is such that it can be redeemed only by an act of divine mercy, are united indeed Unity is born of humility not pride. The modern world is proud, proud unto death; and perhaps it is only when it has been trodden under in the mire of its own spiritual degradation, and has endured a terrible universal humiliation, that unity among men will be a reality again.... The earth will be solid for us again, when we are sure of our distance from heaven. (*Heaven—and Earth*, 25)

In Chaucer, Murry saw the first great poet of England for he alone echoes the voice of his time. He observes that order for which Shakespeare craved so desperately had in Chaucer's world "a divine organ". Its great social unit was the village community seen at its best with the poor Christ-like parson. But there were the hunting monks, the money—grabbling friars, the corrupt somnours and pardoners which the Church allowed to be parasitic. For this reason the Church lost the "compulsive power" of universal spiritual authority which Murry considers essential. E.G. Griffin remarks that we can not go back to an old form; but we can learn, and Murry suggests useful lessons based on the misconduct of the landed peasant, and the moral rights involved in "holding" and "owning" land.[110]

In Cromwell's speeches Murry finds a literary quality. The growth of individualism that brought about the English Civil War was in the initial stages nurtured by Cromwell's ideas. He understood the necessity of order of the medieval Catholic Church. Murry depicts Cromwell as the demiurge of the modern world, upon whose massive shoulders the private and the individual man "...was heaved into the center of European history, for weal or woe."[111] Murry compares Cromwell with Milton and finds Cromwell greater as "...he could be tender to the weakness of men." Milton's works, says Murry, may be works of art but Cromwell's are "...Prophecy wherein the artist forgets himself and speaks at once for God and a People."[112]

Rousseau is the next democrat to whom Murry was attracted. He has written about Rousseau in *Heaven—and Earth* (1938) and in *Aspects of Literature* (1920). Murry believed that Rousseau's mind never strayed from the simple and permanent problems of humanity for to be a completely "ethical man" one should become a conscious political thinker.[113] This is precisely the reason for Murry's own involvement with politics. Rousseau's mind never wandered far from the simple, profound and permanent problems of humanity.... Murry was impressed by Rousseau's disinterested attitude with which he viewed contemporary society, and his dominant, concern afterwards remained to establish a society in which a good man could live without being repressed by his environment. Murry himself was involved with this most permanent concern of human kind. Rousseau's effort was to make men understand themselves and society, because only when they understood themselves could they understand society. He warned men against the "fatal" moral consequences, the "fatal" human consequences, of that civilization which remained in his day merely a progress of moral decadence. Murry saw Rousseau's works as the force behind the French Revolution.

Goethe, who was influenced by Shakespeare and Spinoza, says Murry, had a profound historical sense, with his reverence for individual greatness, he combined in him a splendid awareness of the world process. Murry finds in Goethe the "daemonic man", that is, he is a man who believes that the "...creative power of Nature manifest on the specifically, human level."[114] Goethe is the prophet of this power of nature becoming manifest in human history, which Murry sees as a process of which the consummation will be an order governed by Christian love.

In Montaigne originated the theory of individualism. His book is "...one long and infinitely various act of self discovery, self objectification, made possible only by self forgetfulness." Since Murry later revealed that in understanding oneself, man understands society, he probably found Montaigne's contribution to the culture considerable.

Marx, who brought a revolutionary change in the modern world, through his ideas, failed to impress Murry as in his demand for economic equality he overlooked the demand of political liberty. He even moves away from Murry's belief that every great, creative revolution which begins from feudal society needs to reassert all that was positively asserted by previous revolutions that began from the same point. Besides Marx's salvation was based on despair for him Rousseau's idea of progress was an illusion, and he deemphasized the moral and political evolution of society and it suffered from "...a constantly operative unconscious tendency to minimise the efficacy and the necessity of moral motive in history" (344). What troubled Murry most was that Marx could not be understood by a simple mind and therefore the ultimate aim of proper communication was not possible, Murry, it should be remembered, always kept in mind that the works should be easily comprehensible by common man for only then could they be an effective means of strengthening culture.

William Morris, like Murry, saw art as the expression of social life (372); he had the "genius of experiencing", and therefore he looked back to, and wrote about the time when he felt, "...the religious communion and natural community were in harmony" (375). Cassavant says that Morris was Murry's "...socialist hero, an organicist whose economic precepts are joined with ethical vision."[115] Morris preached Murry's belief that "...socialism begins, and can only begin, in a devolution in the heart and the mind of man."[116] Morris, also linked social renewal to the integration of life and work—one of Murry's central themes.

That Murry's literary criticism is regarded to have much less significance than Arnolds and Leavis is quite evident. But one of the contentions of this thesis is that he largely preserved the values and concepts of Matthew Arnold. His position in the history of English literary criticism must not be undermined. Unfortunately this has happened. It is likely that if he did not play the role, that he did, in shaping moderns literary criticism in the 1920s, English criticism could have developed differently. F.R. Leavis, particularly in the early part of his career learned much from Murry.[117] The largely neglected debate between Murry and T.S. Eliot is likely to have had a great impact on the mind of Leavis. Leavis has noted the remarkable influence Murry's criticism and his journalism had on the intellectuals of that time.[118] Surprisingly scholars have noted the influence of Eliot on Leavis but the influence of Murry on him has been scarcely noticed. Murry's views on nature of literary language, the thought-content, impersonality, crystallization, and so on have had a considerable impact on Leavis. The chief contribution of Murry to the moralistic school of criticism is one of handing over the tradition from Arnold to Leavis. It is this aspect of his criticism that has been missed and it is this that this thesis largely concerns itself with.

NOTES

1. Keith Kushman, "Review of F.A. Lea's, Lawrence and Murry: A Twofold Vision", *The D.H. Lawrence Review,* Vol. 19, No. 1 (Spring, 1987), p. 45.

2. Jersme Meckier, "Huxley's Lawrentian Interlude", *Aldous Huxley: Satire and Structure* (London: Chatto and Windus, 1969), pp. 119-21.
3. Frank Kermode, "On the Frontiers of Criticism", *Manchester Guardian* (10 June 1960), p. 8.
4. F.A. Lea, "John Middleton Murry", *Voices in the Wilderness* (New Delhi: Heritage Publisher's, 1977), pp. 168-69.
5. L.R. Sharma, "Murry's Influence on Leavis", *In Defence of J. Middleton Murry* (Allahabad: Dikshit Publishing House, 1986), p. 141.
6. Sharron Greer Cassavant, "Vices and Virtues of an Autobiographical Critic", *John Middleton Murry: The Critic as Moralist* (Albama: The University of Albama Press, 1982), p. 129.
7. J.M. Murry, "Pure Poetry", *The Countries of the Mind*, Vol. II (London: Oxford University Press, 1931), p. 55.
8. J.M. Murry, *To the Unknown God: Essays towards a Religion* (London: Cape, 1924), p. 265.
9. Rene Wellek, "The New Romantics: J. Middleton Murry", *A History of Modern Criticism*, Vol. V, p. 93.
10. J.M. Murry, "English Poetry in the Eighteenth Century", *Discoveries* (1924; rpt. London: Cape, 1930), p. 159.
11. Rene Wellek, "The New Romantics: J. Middleton Murry", *A History of Modern Criticism*, Vol. V, p. 93.
12. Frazer Neiman, "The Defence of Poetry", *Matthew Arnold* (New York: Twayne Publishers, 1968), p. 76.
13. *Ibid.*, "A Far-Set Goal", p. 158.
14. Matthew Arnold, "The Function of Criticism at the Present Time", *The Complete Prose Works of Matthew Arnold*, Vol. III, p. 275.
15. Derek Stanford, "Middleton Murry as Literary Critic", *Essays in Criticism*, Vol. VIII (1958), p. 61.
16. S.G. Cassavant, "Critical Perspectives", *John Middleton Murry: The Critic as Moralist*, p. 44.
17. L.R. Sharma, "The Critical Method Middleton Murry", *In Defence of J. Middleton Murry*, p. 58.
18. J.M. Murry, "The Function of Criticism", *Aspects of Literature*, p. 10.

19. *Ibid.*, "The Poetry of Mr. Hardy", *Aspects of Literature*, p. 132.
20. E.G. Griffin, "Murry, Eliot and Style", *John Middleton Murry*, p. 51.
21. *Ibid.*, p. 52.
22. Matthew Arnold "Count Leo Tolstoy", *Essays is Criticism*, Series II, ed. S.R. Littlewood, p. 152.
23. J.M. Murry, "The Function of Criticism", *Aspects of Criticism*, p. 14.
24. Murry, "There was a Little Man", *Between Two Worlds* (London: Jonathan Cape, 1935), pp. 368-69.
25. Chapter II Section on Matthew Arnold of this book.
26. Murry, *Discoveries*, pp. 232-33.
27. *Ibid.*
28. Murry, "The Nature of Poetry", *Discoveries*, p. 22.
29. *Ibid.*, p. 26.
30. Murry, "The Meaning of Style", *The Problem of Style*, p. 26.
31. *Ibid.*, "Purgatory Blind", *Keats and Shakespeare*, p. 58.
32. *Ibid.*, "The Nature of Poetry", *Discoveries*, p. 22.
33. *Ibid.*, p. 26.
34. S.G. Cassavant, "Spiritual Heroes", *John Middleton Murry: The Critic as Moralist*, p. 57.
35. *Ibid.*
36. Griffin, "The Keatsian Critic", *John Middleton Murry*, p. 84.
37. Murry, "Metaphor", *J. Middleton Murry, Selected Criticism 1916-1957*, ed. Richard Rees, p. 66.
38. Cassavant, "Spiritual Heroes", *John Middleton Murry: The Critic as Moralist*, p. 77.
39. James R. Bennett, "The Problem of Style", *The D.H. Lawrence Review* (Spring, 1969), p. 33.
40. David Lodge, *The Language of Fiction* (New York: Columbia University Press, 1967), pp. 50-51.
41. Louis Milic, "A Quantitative Approach to the Style of Jonathan Swift", *The Hague* (1967), pp. 50-51.
42. James R. Bennett, "The Problem of Style", *The D.H. Lawrence Review* (Spring, 1969), p. 32.

43. E.G. Griffin, "Murry, Eliot, and Style", *John Middleton Murry*, pp. 53-54.
44. Richard Harter Fogle, "Beauty and Truth: John Middleton Murry on Keats", *The D.H. Lawrence Review* (Spring, 1969), p. 69.
45. J.M. Murry, *Mysteries of Keats* (London: Peter Nevill Ltd., 1949), p. 174.
46. *Ibid.*
47. *Ibid.*, p. 177.
48. J.M. Murry, "The Honesty of Russia", *The Evolution of an Intellectual* (1920; rpt. London: Cape, 1927), pp. 16-29.
49. F.R. Leavis, "The Great Tradition", *The Great Tradition* (London: Chatto and Windus, 1948), p. 15.
50. J.M. Murry, "Gustave Flaubert 1821-80", *Countries of the Mind*, pp. 206-07.
51. *Ibid.*, p. 206.
52. J.M. Murry, "Break-Up of the Novel", *Discoveries*, p. 140.
53. F.R. Leavis, "The Great Tradition", *The Great Tradition*, p. 15.
54. J.M. Murry, "Thoughts of Tchehov", *Aspects of Literature*, p. 91.
55. Richard Rees, ed., "Reply to I.A. Richards", *John Middleton Murry: Selected Criticism 1916-1957*, p. 210.
56. *Ibid.*, p. 213.
57. Peter Allan Dale, "A Reformer in Political Matters", *Victorian Critic and the Idea of History*, p. 166.
58. F.A. Lea, *Voices in the Wilderness*, p. 22.
59. H.C. Duffin, "Of Poetry and Matthew Arnold", *Arnold: The Poet* (1962; rpt. Delhi: OUP, 1964), p. 144.
60. J.M. Murry, "Morality", *Pencillings*, p. 110.
61. F.R. Leavis, *Anna Karenina and Other Essays*, p. 43.
62. Richard Rees, ed., "Seriousness", *John Middleton Murry: Selected Criticism 1916-1957*, p. 59.
63. L.R. Sharma, "Murry's Theory of Literature", *In Defence of J. Middleton Murry*, p. 115.
64. *Ibid.*, pp. 29-30.

65. J.M. Murry, "The Function of Criticism", *Aspects of Literature*, p. 26.
66. R.J. Kaufmann, "On Using an Obsessed Critics: John Middleton Murry", *The Graduate: Student of English*, 3 (Winter, 1960), p. 5.
67. J.M. Murry: "The Function of Criticism", *Aspects of Literature* (1920; rpt. London: Jonathan Cape, 1934), p. 11.
68. *Ibid.*, "The Cry in the Wilderness", *Aspects of Literature* (1920; rpt. London: Jonathan Cape, 1934), p. 180.
69. Sharron Greer Cassavant, "Critical Perspectives", *John Middleton Murry: The Critic as Moralist* (Alabama: The University of Alabama Press, 1982), p. 44.
70. *Ibid.*
71. Richard Rees, ed., "The Function of Criticism", *John Middleton Murry: Selected Criticism 1916-1957*, p. 4.
72. *Ibid.*
73. L.R. Sharma, "Murry's Theory of Literature", *In Defence of John Middleton Murry*, p. 132.
74. Richard Rees, ed., "Reason and Criticism", *Selected Criticism 1916-1957*, p. 93.
75. E.G. Griffin, "Murry, Eliot and Style", *John Middleton Murry*, p. 42.
76. S.G. Cassavant, "Introduction", *John Middleton Murry: The Critic as Moralist*, p. 1.
77. E.G. Griffin, "The Englishness of Murry", *John Middleton Murry*, p. 99.
78. Kaufmann, "On Using an Obssessed Critic", *The Graduate Student of English*, 3 (Winter, 1960), p. 6.
79. R.J. Kaufman, "On Using an Obsessed Critic: John Middleton Murry", *Graduate Student of English*, 3 (Winter, 1960), p. 6.
80. S.G. Cassavant, "Introduction", *John Middleton Murry: The Critic as Moralist*, pp. 4-5.
81. Leavis, "Keats", *Revaluation*, p. 245.
82. F.R. Leavis, "Keats", *Revaluation* (1936; rpt. Harmondsworth: Pelican, 1972), pp. 245, 253. D.G. James, "Purgatory Blind", *The Romantic Comedy* (London: OUP, 1948), p. 116. Arnold Daxanport, "A Note on to Autumn",

English Romantic Poets, ed., M.H. Abrams (London: OUP, 1975), p. 446.

83. Lawrence Lerner, "Introduction", *Shakespeare's Tragedies* (Harmondsworth: Penguine Book, 1963), p. 11.
84. F.A. Lea, "The Anthenaeum", *Voices in the Wilderness* (New Delhi: Heritage Publishers, 1977), pp. 70-71.
85. L.R. Sharma, "Artist-Hero Critic-Admirer", *In Defence of J. Middleton Murry*, pp. 22-31.
86. H.V. Routh, "The Twentieth Century and After", *The Tear's Work in English Studies,* 1932, p. 303.
87. L.R. Sharma, "Artist-Hero Critic-Admirer", *In Defence of J. Middleton Murry*, p. 29.
88. E.G. Griffin, "The Meaning of Lawrence", *John Middleton Murry* (New York: Twayne Publishers, 1969), p. 129.
89. J.M. Murry, *Adam and Eve: An Essay Towards a New and Better Society*, p. 136.
90. Richard Harter Fogle, "Beauty and Truth", *The D.H. Lawrence Review* (Spring, 1969), pp. 68-69.
91. *Ibid.*
92. John Carswell, "The Adelphi", *Lives and Letters* (London: Faber and Faber, 1978), p. 198.
93. S.G. Cassavant, "Spiritual Heroes", *John Middleton Murry: The Critic as Moralist*, p. 81.
94. L.R. Sharma, "Artist-Hero Critic-Admirer", *In Defence of J. Middleton Murry*, p. 30.
95. John Keats, "Letter to Richard Woodhouse Tuesday, 27 October, 1818", *The Letters of John Keats,* ed. by M.B. Forman (London: OUP, 1931), pp. 226-27.
96. E.C. Pettet, *On the Poetry of Keats* (Cambridge Cambridge University Press, 1957), pp. 309-10.
97. J.M. Murry, *Keats and Shakespeare*, pp. 23, 29, 122, 169, 214.
98. Peter Allan Dale, "A Reformer in Poetical Matters", *Victorian Critic and the Idea of History: Carlyle Arnold and Pater*, p. 165.
99. C.G. Thayer, "Murry's Shakespeare", *D.H. Lawrence Review* (Spring, 1969), p. 50.

100. L.R. Sharma, "The Critical Method of Middleton Murry", *In Defence of J. Middleton Murry*, p. 43.
101. Griffin, "The Englishness of Murry", *John Middleton Murry*, p. 109.
102. S.G. Cassavant, "Spiritual Heroes", *John Middleton Murry: The Critic as Moralist*, p. 72.
103. *Ibid.*, "Introduction", *John Middleton Murry: The Critic as Moralist*, p. 4.
104. *Ibid.*, "Spiritual Heroes", *John Middleton Murry: The Critic as Moralist*, pp. 66-67.
105. J.M. Murry, "Whitman: Poet-Prophet of Democracy", *J. Middleton Murry: Selected Criticism 1917-1957*, ed. Richard Rees (London: Oxford University Press, 1960), p. 270.
106. *Ibid.*, p. 271.
107. *Ibid.*, p. 288.
108. S.G. Cassavant, "Vices and Virtures of an Autobiographical Critic", *J. Middleton Murry: The Critic as Moralist*, p. 119.
109. J.M. Murry, *Heaven—and Earth*, pp. 2-3.
110. Griffin, "The Keatsian Critic", *John Middleton Murry*, pp. 100-01.
111. J.M. Murry, *Heaven—and Earth* (London: Cape, 1938), p. 106.
112. *Ibid.*, p. 170.
113. Murry, "Rousseau", *John Middleton Murry: Selected Criticism 1916-1957*, ed. Rees (London: Oxford University Press, 1960), p. 224.
114. J.M. Murry, "Goethe", *Heaven—and Earth* (London: Cape, 1938), p. 249.
115. S.G. Cassavant, "Vices and Virtues of an Autobiographical Critic", *John Middleton Murry: The Critic as Moralist*, p. 120.
116. J.M. Murry, "William Morris", *Heaven—and Earth*, p. 367.
117. L.R. Sharma, "Murry's Influence on F.R. Leavis", *In Defence of J. Middleton Murry*, pp. 141-44.
118. F.R. Leavis, "Hardy: The Poet", (*Southern Review*, VI Summer, 1940), pp. 97-98.

4

F.R. Leavis

F.R. Leavis has established himself as a major critic of the twentieth century. He had been working to elevate English to its place as a central subject in the education of humanities. He lays emphasis on the study of criticism and on cultural history rather than on academicism and the vagaries of taste. As early as 1949 Leavis was recognized as a critic of first importance and a critic with a characteristically moral sensibility not only in the sense that he happily affirmed the value of common morality but also in the sense that, having felt life to be of a certain weight and pressure, he desired that art should be able to relieve mankind of its pressure by reacting to experience with a proportionate counter thrust of endurance and intelligence. His critical writings have undoubtedly proved effective and have changed the course of our thinking about literature. It has very often been remarked that his works form a major and the most influential portion of the English criticism since Arnold. Whether this is true we shall see in the last chapter but his greatness as a critic is unquestioned. The fact that "Leavisians" have come into being is proof enough. The major works that contain his literary criticism are *New Bearings in English Poetry* (1932), *Revaluation* (1936), *The Great Tradition* (1948), *The Common Pursuit* (1952), *D.H. Lawrence: Novelist* (1955), *Anna Karenina and Other Essays* (1967), *The Living Principle* (1975) and *Scrutiny*, a journal that he published between the years 1932 and 1953.

As Victorian complacency led Arnold to hold a moralistic view of literature, a similar response to the Industrial Revolution and post-war depression might have stirred Leavis to seek to work for the cause of literature. The war engulfed life and in its sway wiped out vestiges indicative of links between the changing times, civilization was crippled as traditions were threatened. Leavis has never been averse to change but has desired a concomitant change in literature. Leavis says:

> What we have lost is the organic community with the living culture it embodied; folk songs, folk dances, Cotswold cottages and handicraft products are signs and expressions of something more on art and life, a way of living, ordered and patterned....[1]

To make up for this loss, he feels, cultural continuity is to be maintained. The organic community, he argues, existed till the late nineteenth century despite the inroads of Industrial Revolution and local variations. This made possible Shakespeare and Bunyan. With its disintegration started the weakening of the cultural root. As has been suggested by Kaufmann:

> It has been his delusion that the world's change can be prevented, his mission has been the vitally direct one of preservation and practical continuity.[2]

From the beginning of his career Leavis stressed on the need of literature as a means to cultural unity. Even towards the end of his career Leavis was concerned with the ways in which our civilization "thwarts and imperils" creativity.[3] Creativity gives civilization and its variants validity. *For Continuity* (1933) deals with this problem. *Nor Shall My Sword* (1972) has an essay "'English', Unrest and Continuity" which ends with a similar desire for cultural continuity. In another essay "'Literarism' versus 'Scientism'", he concludes:

> Looking round at this beautiful university, I have said to myself, "Surely here the creative battle to maintain our living cultural heritage—a continuity of profoundly human creative life—must seem worth fighting, must be seen as a battle that shall not be lost."[4]

From this we can conclude that to the educated minority Leavis entrusted the work of cultural continuity. Before discussing the reason for his choosing literature as a means to achieve "cultural continuity", let us examine what he implies by the term.

F.R. Leavis gives immense importance to culture. He is close to Arnold when he says that there is a "human culture" to be aimed at and that it must be cultivated by a certain "autonomy of spirit", but he wants something more.[5] This he even accepts. Leavis, according to R.P. Bilan, is concerned with the "...defining and bringing into focus the English culture represented by English literature."[6] Arnold aims at alleviation of British provinciality by the growth of intellectual culture of the continent, while Leavis finds English literature efficient enough to serve the purpose. Rene Wellek charging Leavis with provinciality says that besides English and American he seems to have no interest in any other literature.[7] But this should not be understood to be provinciality or narrowness of views. Instead Leavis feels that it is good to write about one's own land and its people because we know them well. Without understanding the people of another country it is improper to write about them. He says:

> Better then be provincial than cosmopolitan, for to be cosmopolitan in these matters is to be at home nowhere and he who is at home nowhere can make little of any literature—the more he knows, the larger is his ignorance.[8]

The reason for Leavis's looking forward to English literature as a means, rather than to other intellectual pursuits, is that he considers language to be the center of culture:

> Largely conveyed in language there is our spiritual, moral and emotional tradition, which preserves the picked experience of the ages regarding the finer issues of life.[9]

Since literature focuses on preserving language, it is the means of preserving culture.

Leavis nowhere defines the word "culture", instead he seems to avoid it; but he suggests what he implies by it at many places. In *For Continuity* (1933) he says that the language that he finds suitable for the growth of culture is not just ordinary language. The educated minority, which is aware and sensitive, is capable of not only appreciating great creative writers of the past but of recognizing their latest successors who constitute the consciousness of the race (or of a branch of it) at a given time. For such capacity does not belong merely to an isolated aesthetic realm, it implies responsiveness to theory as well as to art, to science and philosophy in so far as these may affect the sense of the human situation and of the nature of life. Such is the educated minority that can preserve tradition. It is their language that Leavis writes about. It is a language that preserves in it the human experiences of the ages and spirit of the age:

> I mean by "culture" the use of such, language. I do not suppose myself to have produced a tight definition, but the account. I think, will be recognized as adequate by anyone who is likely to read this pamphlet.[10]

But as R.P. Bilan rightly says, his definition of culture is loose.[11] In *Anna Karenina and Other Essays,* Leavis remarks that the more one thinks about language the more difficult a concept it turns out to be. Awareness of one's language denotes awareness of one's culture.[12] Awareness of language of ancient times or of a foreign place is possible only after an awareness of one's own language. If we substitute language with culture, as Leavis implies, this statement means that to understand foreign culture one should understand one's own culture. This together with his statement quoted earlier, "There is a human culture to be aimed at",[13] shows that Leavis has in mind humanity as a whole. But in achieving "cultural continuity" first comes the awareness of one's own culture.[14] Raymond Williams finds Leavis' idea of language denoting culture a new development of the idea of culture. He finds it difficult to understand Leavis' idea of culture because it continuously increases in its meaning and finally "becomes almost" identical with our whole common life."[15] This difficulty resolves if the culture is taken in a wide perspective. In fact it is in this that the real meaning of Leavis' culture lies. As has earlier been stated, culture is associated with the growth of an "organic community".[16] This means that the growth in culture means the development of the organic community. Thus he desires something more than the development of language alone. But it is through the development of language (the sense in which Leavis uses it) that cultural continuity can be maintained.

Leavis chooses literature as a means to promote culture because it is in literature that language is preserved and grows. Poetry can communicate the actual quality of experience with subtlety and precision unapproached by any other means.[17] He insists on the English language and literature and feels that the focus of cultural continuity can only be in English. This might contradict a remark made earlier that Leavis is not in the strict sense 'provincial'. But it should be noted that he believes in first having a knowledge of one's own language. Perhaps here English means the study of English literature:

> English literature, magnificent and matchless in diversity and range, and so full and profound in its registration of changing life, gives us a continuity that is not yet dead.[18]

This is true for other literatures as much as it is true for English literature. He insists that first one's own language should be studied, and has given great stress on English. Since he is here talking about the importance of study of language in English universities, he talks about English literature. This should not be understood as his slighting other languages or as his being provincial. W.J. Keith says that Leavis' importance derives from the fact that he insisted on seeing English studies not as "a private cult" but as a "discipline of thought", a subject that mattered and was worth fighting for.[19] Robert Boyers also agrees with Keith as he shows that Leavis makes poetry a "mode of thought".[20] This is the reason for Leavis' high expectations from English studies. Kaufmann rightly says that Leavis dealt with the practical use of literature. Leavis, he says, is a critical thinker whose subject matter is moral use of literature and he gives equal importance to both "moral" and "literature".[21] But all his efforts aim at cultural continuity. To set up a university or to establish literature as a major subject, is not his ultimate aim "...it is the answer to a present extremely urgent need to civilization". The need is to discover a way to save cultural continuity, the continuous collaborative renewal which keeps the "heritage" of perception, judgement, responsibility and spiritual awareness living, responsive to change and authoritative for future guidance.[22]

The importance of literature also lies in the fact that he feels the other traditional continuities have completely disintegrated, yet he is of the view that we still have a positive cultural tradition.[23] In earliar times all the creative arts helped to promote culture. Now, he feels, only literary tradition can keep culture alive. Leavis's view of literary tradition will be discussed after his views on literature.

Like Arnold and Murry, Leavis believes in the closeness of art and life in literature. According to Rajnath, a great critical achievement of Leavis is that he combines "technical excellence" together with moral value.[24] He discusses how Leavis in his early phase was preoccupied with technique, but later on as he moved towards Lawrence, he deviated from this:

> Great literature, Leavis has told us with considerable emphasis, is not a matter of technique alone: it is vitally linked with life and moral values. In the novelists that Leavis places in the great tradition, especially D.H. Lawrence, Leavis finds a balance of technical virtuosity and moral concerns.[25]

Lionel Trilling states that Leavis has done one of the most useful jobs that a critic can possibly accomplish—he has established a coherent tradition and in so doing has constituted a large body of work.[26] Besides emphasis on thought-content Leavis puts "marked moral intensity" on the form of the novel. Rene Wellek finds "life" and "art" so completely blended together in Leavis's concept of literature that "life" for Leavis is first of all simply realist art Eliseo Vivas criticizes Leavis severely for not explicitly pointing out how he achieved this.[27] He says that it is evident that Leavis's guiding principle is moral. Vivas says that Leavis is interested in discovering whether art ministers life directly, or whether it does so indirectly, as a means of exploring imaginatively the consequences of actions. On inquiring how Lawrence achieved morality, he said "...by the presentment of life or reality truthfully and with sincerity."[28] But beyond this Leavis does not go. Leavis, says Vivas, leaves us in dark as to the measures taken by Lawrence to achieve his moral end while remaining an artist. This charge may be correct to some extent, as Leavis has not stated the means of achieving the fusion of art with life. But by going through his critical works we do come across some aspects of literature that he greatly values. Harmony of art and life is possible only if these aspects are present in creative works. My effort is to bring together these qualities that he considers favourable for the growth of morality which is possible only when art and life are in synthesis.

Leavis finds literature a means of maintaining cultural continuity because it is close to a language in which cultural tradition is preserved. Thomas L. Jeffers rightly says that though Leavis was staunchly agnostic about Christianity he nevertheless affirmed that any culture worth having must foster a religious sense, by which he meant what Blake and Lawrence had meant—"a belief in the creative imagination as a power of deriving from something not ourselves".[29] But in his own time he found literature not quite effective because contemporary intelligence had little to do with poetry. Moreover there were many poets, but none of them were outstanding. This, he says, was due to three major shortcomings—there was no standard current, no live tradition of poetry and no public capable of informed and serious interest (*New Bearings*, 11). Since these are the things lacking, precisely these are the lines which need improvement. For this literature must have a serious concern with life, it must affirm life, that is, give a positive view of life, it must be representative, original and must have the ability to communicate. Intelligence has a great role to play. Without intelligence the other aspects of literature that he so much valued could never have been achieved.

After going through the works of Leavis it is evident that he lays great emphasis on seriousness. He writes about "serious interest", "sustained seriousness" and "moral seriousness"

(*The Great Tradition*, 40). Leavis does not define the word "seriousness". This lends a flexibility to the word. The discussion that follows is an effort to understand what Leavis meant by seriousness. Both Arnold and Murry also regard it as an important characteristic of great literature. William Walsh says, that if a novel has to survive it has to present new feelings in a new way. A novel is "serious" when there is a deep apprehension of reality and when its construction is "in terms of art".[30] But seriousness implies something more.

Writing about Conrad, he first refers to the deficiencies of his own age. He suffered from a lack of serious interest in humanity. The "words on the page" had no roots (*GT*, 38). This hints at the weakness in Conrad's approach. He then gives the example of Conrad, who chose literature for its "distinctive qualities". These 'qualities' refer to the ability of literature to fill the gap between man and culture.[31] Conrad's concern with art, like Jane Austen, George Eliot and Henry James "is the servant of a profoundly serious interest in life" (*GT*, 30). Here Leavis emphasises that all of them are innovators in form and method. This means that his concern with "serious interest in life" is related to form and method that is seriousness cannot be achieved without seriousness in form and method. It also implies that interest in life is related to interest in form. Hence if the content alone is serious, has concern with life, the work of art cannot be serious. It needs an adequate form that can help to communicate an experience. To have strength in the words on the page, there must be a serious interest in life, which implies a serious interest in form as well as in content.

Leavis does not include Dickens in the great tradition because he lacked seriousness, that is, he represented life but since his genius was that of a great entertainer he did not fulfil the profounder responsibility of a creative artist. The nature of his art is not serious. His interest primarily lies in entertainment not in the upliftment of mankind. The interest in humanity is secondary. A work that has entertainment value alone cannot be called serious. Because he lacks a genuine concern for mankind, he is not in the great tradition. But *Hard Times* is one work which is unique amongst Dickens' novels as it has "sustained seriousness" that is characteristic of a perfect work of art (*GT*, 30). The key characteristics of Victorian civilization had clearly come home to him with overwhelming force. The themes were rich and were tightly knitted in their variety. Had the other novels of Dickens given primary value to humanity, that is, given a fuller representation of society without 'loose inclusiveness' and had given secondary importance to entertainment, his work would have fulfilled, according to Leavis, the responsibility of a creative artist. He might then have been included in the great tradition. This argument contained in *The Great Tradition* (1948) was at a time considered the greatest flaw in the book. From the year it was published to the time when Leavis wrote *Dickens: The Novelist* (1970) he received repeated disapproval for it.[32] In 1949 Trilling wrote an article which raised Leavis to the level of a pioneer moral thinker but he states with amazement that there are occasions when the relation between Leavis's intelligence and his moral sense is not maintained. Steiner wrote in 1967 that the limitations proposed by Trilling always seemed to him restrictive of Leavis, not of Dickens.[33] Steiner finds the preference of *Hard Times* over such manifestly ampler achievements of *Bleak House* or *Great Expectations* as illuminating. Leavis has seriousness of committed feeling, of vehement imaginative enactment. It is this which Dickens possesses and that makes of him, after Shakespeare, "...the Principal creator of remembered life in English literature" Reportedly Leavis was working upon a full-scale critical study over Dickens. He did revise his opinion about Dickens, and as William Walsh has stated the purpose of the work: was to demonstrate the creativity, the artistry and intelligence of Dickens, to cancel finally the reputation of Dickens merely as "a popular entertainer of genius".[34] But though this passage of Leavis was received indifferently by the critics it still seems to have significance. The passage undoubtedly is objectionable but it does make it very clear that Leavis measures the richness of art by its usefulness to society. He is not against humour but he places it after seriousness and genuine interest in mankind. It should not be an end in itself, but a means to an end. As

Hard Times is an attack on the culture of utilitarianism, he finds it apt to the need of his time.

George Eliot would not have been as great as she is known to be today if she did not have moral seriousness (*GT*, 42). What is moral seriousness? Leavis associates seriousness with a genuine interest in life. Flaubert, he says, has good form but lacks moral preoccupation, lacks range and depth in his interest in humanity and greater interest in moral preoccupation. It should here be recalled that Murry has similar views about Flaubert. His reasons for disapproving Flaubert's art are the same as Leavis's. It must be remembered that for Leavis art cannot be separated from life, and formal cannot be separated from moral.[35] An interest in life is a moral preoccupation. David Lodge insists that the moral preoccupation of *Emma* can be appreciated in terms of 'the formal perfection' of the novel. This is true because his meaning of moral fable shows that art cannot be separated from life and morality. In a moral fable each character has to be assessed, judged, evaluated. No figure or situation must be irrelevant. There should be a well thought out scheme. Hence moral seriousness refers to genuine interest in life which includes the formal perfection. Buckley says that for him, the whole poem is "moral". In great poets as in great novelists, the interest in "form" is all of a piece with the interest in "human centrality" (*GT*, 23).

F.R. Leavis stresses the fact that seriousness is the first condition of any kind of real intelligence, and interest in human nature. This means that if there is real intelligence and interest in human nature, and there is lack of seriousness, the first two are of no importance. By "interest" Leavis means a profound concern having the urgency of personal problems—more than personal in significance. To compel art out of contemporary plight is needed the seriousness, the spiritual and moral intensity and resolute intelligence. Hence seriousness means genuine interest in humanity. Seriousness is both of form and content. When a work of art has seriousness it is highly representative, that is, it is aware of its time and has the spirit of its age, has human issues with insight into human behaviour, with range and depth. The form must not be loose and repetitive instead it should be closely knit. Leavis desires seriousness both of form and content. As Leavis's criticism progressed his concept of seriousness merged with the concept of life. His "affirmation of life" later evolved into a major premise which also incorporated "seriousness".

According to Kaufmann, F.R. Leavis does three closely-related things, he affirms the use of intelligence, indicates important ways to use it, and shows those who have it just how intelligence in process works.[36] The *Times Literary Supplement* wrote rightly:

> Leavis's ultimate distinction as a critic lies in his unerring sense of how—in what forms and with what limitations —the pressure of creative intelligence shows itself in the writers he admires.[37]

This is a fact that cannot be deemed insignificant. But what again can be asked is his meaning of intelligence. He affirms the use of intelligence but writing about Conrad he says that Conrad achieved a wholeness in art because he was a novelist and a seaman and not novelist and a high level 'intellectual' (*GT*, 44). He seems to contradict his own statement. But here he uses 'intellect' as opposed to life, as opposed to emotion. Leavis has a derogatory attitude towards intellect that goes to the extent of ignoring life. In "Daughters of Vicar" he sees the emotional characters as superior to high class characters that are opposed to life. Intellect that is restricted to books, has no concern with life, ignores life and lacks emotions, is derogatory.[38] All the writers he praises for their intellect have a genuine concern for life and emotions. They present their raw experiences which are a part of their life. This intellect is incomplete without emotion. Therefore, Leavis's views on "intellect" are derived at least in part, from the Murry-Eliot debate which is discussed by Ernest Griffin (43-51). Murry's views on intelligence and intellect are contained in "Concerning Intelligence" *The Criterion* (Vol. VI, 524-33). Leavis says that a poet must be intelligent and sensitive. If the poetry and the intelligence of the age lose touch with each other, poetry will cease to matter much and the age will be lacking in finer awareness.[39]

Thus a poet must be intelligent in the sense that he should be aware of the needs of the age. This idea figures in Murry's essay (528). He should be sensitive enough to experience and be stimulated by the slightest change, to perceive the human experiences and be intelligent enough to understand the potentialities of human experience.

Throwing light on the way a poet has to make use of his intelligence Leavis says that the age of a poet has an effect on him. Each age has its own "preoccupations and assumptions" as far as poetry is concerned. Each age, therefore, has its own subject, material and modes. It differs in content and form. It is the tendency of poetry to confine itself to ideas "essentially poetical" which, when the conditions which gave rise to them have changed except the poet's most valuable material, the material that is most significant to sensitive minds, are barred out of poetry. The poet has to be intelligent to choose the right subject and to change with the demand of time. The poet's being more aware, conscious, and sensitive is also a sign of his intelligence. The distinctive quality of a poet is that he is at the most "conscious" point of the race. He has the capacity to experience and communicate. Above all, he has the ability to reflect in his poetry his experience totally—his experience is not separable from his interest in words. But Leavis's own age lacked this and therefore poetry ceased to matter. The Romantic age was behind the Victorians. But as the problems faced by men changed, it became impossible for them to endure the "day dream" habit of poetry. Hence the tragedy of the lack of intelligence was that the age was devoid of awareness. The result of this was that there was no seriousness in the creative works. In his own time the "adult sensitive mind" wanted poetry that would deal with the contemporary problems directly and completely. The poet was not one with his age. Tennyson tried his best and had scientific allusions in his work. Though he was representative but his poetry was truly of the palace. It lacked concern for the masses and seriousness. It withdrew from the plight of humanity. Leavis finds in this withdrawal the cause of the despicable condition of poetry in his age. There was genius but it was not innovatory, so it was not qualified to give poetry a new direction. Tennyson, Arnold, Browning, and Meredith, no one succeeded. A poetry that was adequate to the changing time was needed. Resurgence of poetry was the reply to such a situation. Only a man with exceptional intelligence could bring about this, as for a total transformation, new techniques, a new language, and a new subject was required. Originality that emerges from intelligence was heeded to provide a start. Poetry to survive needs development and growth. It was T.S. Eliot who gave poetry all it needed. He made a new start and established new bearings. But for him the modern age would not have achieved its glory.

There is a movement in Leavis from Eliot to Lawrence. It is said that in the first phase of his criticism he is influenced by Eliot and in the second phase by Lawrence.[40] His views on some aspects of literature change accordingly. He gave importance to intelligence in both phases. Eliot's mind was "unquestionably of a rare distinction" (*New Bearings*, 25). Lawrence, he claims, possesses the true intelligence that is the agent of the whole being, while Eliot being a divided man lacks fullness of life.[41] While in the first phase Leavis does not associate emotion with intelligence in the later years for him, emotion was essential for true intelligence. Buckley says that emotional and spiritual wholeness inevitably go together. Intelligence goes alongside when it is the, "agent of this wholeness". Leavis here implies, according to Buckley, that poetry's "...moral value resides in the emotional quality which, when integrated with the workings of intelligence is the index of spiritual vitality".[42] Eliot's mind was of rare distinction because he could analyse the need of the time and accordingly could bring about a revolutionary change in poetry. But his intelligence, as Leavis saw later, is not complete as his works lacked affirmation of life and therefore did not result in a fullness of life. His intelligence is not constructive. Poetry, divorced from life has no meaning for Leavis. Lawrence's emotions together with his intelligence resulted in works with a positive approach to life.[43]

Therefore, it may be said, that Lawrence's intelligence is constructive while that of Eliot is not. The difference lies only in their approach to life. This also shows that emotions, too, play a considerable part in making intelligence constructive. Here "emotions" means what Leavis earlier meant by "Interest". It is a profound concern having the urgency of personal problems—more than personal in significance. In *Woman in Love* Leavis appreciates Lawrence's use of intelligence to achieve spontaneous-creative fullness of being (206). "Supreme intelligence" of Lawrence is evident in the "self knowledge", which is brought out in *Woman in Love*, *Aaron's Rod*, and *Kangaroo*. The peculiar characteristic of his genius is revealed in the power of impersonalizing his "intelligence". The condition that makes this possible, says Leavis, is when "the artist, in an intensely personal exploratory way, is factually living the experience that goes into the art" (171). Thus Leavis believes that underlying creativity, awareness and impersonality is intelligence. In fact his meaning of intelligence is woven round awareness and creativity. Writing about Count Dionys, he says:

> Representing, in his dark unknowness, the profound energies and potentialities of life that the unconscious mind can only either serve or thwart, he represents, not the absence of 'consciousness', but rather the necessary vital intelligence that, serving the whole life, can detect and expose the usurpations of will and "idea". (17)

Count Dionys, Leavis says, represents the "necessary vital intelligence", and this intelligence can "detect" and "expose". This, if analysed keeping in view his earlier remark on the qualities of a poet, means that it is intelligence that brings about awareness and communication. Out of his experiences, an artist can "detect" and "expose" all that is relevant. "Detect" means to find out through investigation and "expose" means to bring to common knowledge. To "detect", an artist has to be sensitive. It is awareness of the relevant that leads to detection. The ability to communicate helps to "expose"—one who lacks the ability to communicate cannot bring things to common knowledge. Thus it is through intelligence that a person is aware and can communicate. Another thing that needs mention is that sensitivity and intelligence together work to form a piece of creative art. Sensitivity to experience, and intelligence to be aware and communicate is essential to bring most out of poetry: "Poetry matters because of the kind of poet who is more alive than other people, more alive in his own age" (*New Bearings*, 16). In other words the strength of poetry lies in the poet—his being sensitive and intelligent.

Thus intelligence, for Leavis, is not being opposed to life. It is experiencing life, being aware of the needs, communicating all that is relevant so as to affirm life. Leavis's definition of 'moralized fable' is very close to this view. Each character has to be assessed, judged, given value and evaluated. According to Leavis, in a moralised fable there is no figure or situation that is irrelevant or has little significance. Whatever the significance is, should be highlighted. There should be "a tact inclusive scheme". In Leavis's own words:

> I have called *The Europeans* a "moral fable" because a serious intention expresses itself in so firm and clear an economy of organisation and representative significance of every element in the book is so insistent.[44]

In *The Great Tradition*, Leavis says "...what again strikes us in the intellectual writer is an emotional quality...." What needs to be asked is where the emotional quality sets in the intellectual presentation of experience to give it "fullness of being" (Leavis appreciates in *Woman in Love* Lawrence's use of intelligence to achieve "spontaneous—creative fullness of being"). In Lawrence's novels, Leavis says, there is a serenely triumphant reign of intelligence—intelligence that moves beyond personal problems that give rise to it. It is then that intelligence is creative—so a creative artist's imaginative achievements are also achievements of intelligence (*DHL*, 175).

Thus it is through creative intelligence that a personal experience is impersonalized. Conrad achieves wholeness in art because his personal needs are not directly presented—it comes to us out of the "complex impersonalized whole" (*GT*, 43). Here his emotions are present but their presence is felt through the needs of the characters. George Eliot does have the genius of impersonality in her best works. In other works, we note it as an emotional quality, something that strikes as direct presence of the author's personal needs. Leavis does not underestimate the intellectual ability of George Eliot because she presents her emotions directly. He even praises George Eliot's intelligence. Therefore, to impersonalize a work of art—to bring wholeness—intelligence is essential. What Leavis saw and said in dozens of ways is that "values" in literature:

> ...without the bone structure of searching critical intelligence are outmoded and helpless denizens of some Cezonic era before mass-life, before the era of hugeness. Since this is so, ...Leavis has dared to instruct his generation in art of using intelligence.[45]

As Leavis grew, with him grew his meaning of the representation of life. It gained in depth and perspective. And as is clear from the above discussions, "life" became his key term and all the aspects that he viewed as great in the creative writers merged into his meaning of life. Rajnath, too, remarks that Leavis talks a great deal about ethical values, life and its possibilities in his studies of the novel, and it should be noted that the novelists in the great tradition are bound together by certain ethical values. The representative quality is a major aspect of his moral sense.[46] The poets and novelists—the creative artists who have gained prominence in the works of Leavis have all been praised for their representative quality. Some give a picture of the lifestyle, the others probe into the psyche of the character. They have a concern for life. Life and art cannot be dissociated. All great novelists show an intense interest in life. Their involvement with form is because of their concern for life. Writing about Jane Austen he makes this very clear. She presents life in such a way that her interest in composition completely fuses with her interest in life (*GT*, 17).

In a successful work of art the moral and the formal are one. Eliseo Vivas calls this fusion an "informed-substance",[47] and Leavis works to establish this. "But", Bilan says, "Leavis's formulation seems to bring the two apart by regarding the moral as prior to the formal, and certainly fits the more important".[48]

Despite this fact, Leavis does consider art incomplete without either form, or morality. In fact, he feels that only works of art can say with validity that "this is life".[49] Art presents moral values through its characters and situations. It need not state the moral values directly to make them known. Murry's views are quite similar.[50] Leavis praises Tolstoy, Jane Austen, George Eliot and Lawrence for presenting the relations between art and life in the way he appreciates most. Their concern for form is rooted in their concern for life. It is only then that art is creative. Art has to be representative to be creative.

The greatest creative writer for Leavis is undoubtedly Shakespeare. He has not attempted a detailed work on Shakespeare but he gives Shakespeare's example whenever he tries to establish the extent of greatness of an artist. This method hints at Arnold's touchstones. Murry too repeatedly cites Shakespeare's example in a similar way. According to Leavis Shakespeare is a measure,—the limit, the ideal in art:

> Shakespeare was a great living fact behind the English novelists of the nineteenth century; he can be felt, in different ways, as a vital informing power in their work and George Eliot was no exception.[51]

Establishing the greatness of Lawrence's style he compares him to Shakespeare "One wouldn't, it is true, call Lawrence, any more than one would call Shakespeare, a 'stylist'", and he calls him, "one of the greatest masters of what is certainly one of the greatest languages" (*DHL*, 26).

Leavis appreciates Shakespeare greatly for his poetic-creative use of language. The creative use of language is the Shakespearean use. In this Leavis concurs with Murry. It is close to the colloquial language. Its powers have been exploited by great artists like Shakespeare, Hopkins, Donne, Eliot and the later Yeats. The language of Milton, Spenser and Tennyson was divorced from spoken language and in this lay their weakness. A man's most vivid emotional and sensuous experience is inevitably tied up with the language he actually speaks (*New Bearings*, 71). This is what Leavis thinks creative language is. Experiences of a man are directly related to his language and if he does not use his spoken language, that is, if he uses idiomatic language he is insincere to his own experiences and thus is not able to represent his own time (*Revaluations*, 53). The language that Milton used does not come from within the writer, "Certain feelings are expressed, but there is no pressure behind the words". This accounts for the varying "deadness of speech" in Milton and shows how vital the role of language is for Leavis. The reason for giving such importance is that only spoken language is representative. Bilan in analysing Leavis's concept of language says:

> The notion of the poetic-creative or Shakespearean use of the English language is at the heart of Leavis's thinking about literature and involves three main points: first, a view of the proper relation between poetry and the spoken English language; secondly the claim that the quality of concrete realization characterizes the Shakespearean use, and finally, and most importantly, an insistence that poetic language is ultimately exploratory creative.[52]

This makes it clear that language has a vital role in creation. The richest poetic language is spoken language because it has its root in the emotions of a man and because it alone can present the experiences with sincerity. For Leavis "reality" and "sincerity" are synonymous terms. It is the weakness of both Milton and Shelley that they use language as a mere gesture. This is so because they err in using it impulsively. This can be referred to as "artistic insincerity" as it leads away from truth, from reality.[53] Thus an artist whose language is flawed and whose impulse is flawed cannot be great as he cannot be representative.

I shall analyse now Leavis' norms for representativeness. It shall be seen that he considers all great artists truly representative. Some poets are representative yet not genuinely so. Besides Shakespeare, the other artists that he considers great are Tolstoy, Jane Austen, George Eliot, Henry James,

Conrad and D.H. Lawrence in the great line of novelists. Amongst the poets he gives credence to Donne, Hopkins, Eliot. Other artists are also representative but they are not truly so because they are either flawed in language or impulse or they do not live up to the needs of their age. Tennyson, Arnold and Browning too are representative, but since they lack the ability to promote human awareness, their representative quality is ineffective (*New Bearings*, 71). They agree that the actual world is recalcitrant, and instead of attacking the situation they withdraw from it. Withdrawal was a Victorian characteristic but it failed to achieve the aim of poetry. Poetry that loses touch with the "finer consciousness" of the age as Victorian poetry does, has no meaning. For being representative it is essential to be one with the pulse of the time. Shirking away from it means being insincere to reality. This results in a picture of life that defies the genuine emotions and experiences, overlooks the possibilities of human behaviour and therefore the representativeness is not genuine.

Though Yeats exhibits the "inner struggle" of the nineteenth century mind, yet it serves more as a warning to poets of today. He has shown the general "state of civilization and culture", a state which he contends, makes waste inevitable for the sensitive. Though Yeats is gifted with rare qualities of intelligence and character, yet he is not as successful as he should have been because his approach to life in poetry is not constructive. The representative quality needs to have a positive approach to life. Similarly it is seen that Hardy has a philosophy but his approach towards the conditions of Victorian age is pessimistic. Leavis says his works are "particular evocations of either loss, the blindness of chance, the poignancy of love and its relation to helplessness, and the cruelty of time".[54] There he too fails to give a picture of life as Leavis desires.

T.S. Eliot, whom Leavis in his later works has criticised severely for his attitude towards life, had been a great influence on him in the early phase. Eliot's importance lay in the fact that he gave to English poetry a new direction. He understood the pulse of his age and both his form and content were representative of his time. Even when Leavis was highly critical towards Eliot he praised him for his representative quality:

> What I have been offering is both a recognition of Eliot's great importance and a severe adverse criticism. It is his using a major poet's command of the English language to bring home to us the spiritual philistinism of our civilization that makes him important to us.[55]

Eliot's originality and his intelligence together made him highly representative. This appeals greatly to Leavis as in his earlier criticism Leavis does not judge this aspect of a work. Therefore Eliot's lack of fullness of life does not trouble him. Eliot was sincere to his experiences and that was enough. In Leavis's later criticism Eliot's treatment is extremely severe. He is seen as a 'case', a symptom and (what Pound called Walt Whitman) "reflex" and seems almost to incur something of the strange "gratitude" Leavis accords J.B. Leishman in *Nor Shall My Sword*.[56] In Leavis' first chapter of *Thought Words Creativity* Eliot comes close to being a rather "distressing-model". According to Edward Neill, Eliots' own posture in *Four Quartets* as a creator who "unbelives in human creativity seems to make Leavis come close to calling him the "anti-poet's poet". Leavis admires his ability to be representative both in form and content. This is clear in his appreciation of Eliot's rhythm. Eliot's rhythm was influenced by the internal combustion engine. The combustion engine had undoubtedly a great effect on the civilization. Life had gained speed. His adoption of the rhythm of the internal combustion engine shows how fully alive he was in his own age (*New Bearings*, 71). Leavis appreciates Eliot for deriving his form from his age. That he expects this from all creative artists is clear when he says that the poet and the novelist both should be close to their contemporary world. That is, both should depict their time through the form and thought-content. The poet has an edge over the novelist as the "formal verse medium" can also help in representing the poet's own time. He appreciates Eliot's successful efforts to do so:

> We have here, in short, poetry that expresses freely a modern sensibility, the ways of feeling, the modes of

> experience, of one fully alive in his own age.... The poet is as close to the contemporary world as any novelist could be, and his formal verse medium makes possible a concentration and a directness, audacities of transition and psychological notation, such as are forbidden to the novelist. (65)

Eliot has been praised by Leavis for his "formal verse medium" for being highly representative of his age. The "seeming disjointedness" of *The Waste Land* is a feature of his own age. The "sense of absoluteness" that is necessary for a robust culture is absent (70). Therefore representation of age can be through the, verse form, the technique, the language, the allusions, the rhythm, since all work together to portray the spirit of the age.

Leavis feels that Ezra Pound is representative but not in the true sense. He presents various representative memories, and a representative experience of his life—tragedy, comedy, pathos, and irony, but he remained constant in one faith, the aesthetic. His main concern has been art. His real interest did not lie in life but in art. Even if he showed seriousness at times it was not enough to make his work truly representative.

A poet may be representative, yet not truly great in the Leavisian sense. This has been shown above. There are several reasons for this. As in the case of Pope and Dryden, Leavis finds that both are representative, but the distinction that Pope achieved is greater than that of Dryden.[57] Here the relationship between representative quality and the variety and range in a work of art is clear. Both belong completely to their time. Pope is a highly representative poet "...realizing in his poetry the strength of that actual concentrated civilization immediately around him" (37). Dryden's greater fineness and profundity of organization gave to his works greater intensity of art. This is the cause of Pope's greatness even today. "Dryden's was responsible, his effects are all for the public ear", says Leavis. His pamphleteering verse, though highly representative, cannot be called great poetry. Poetry demands more than mere representative quality to be great. This is where "form" plays its role. For poetry and novel, art and life cannot be dissociated. Weakness in any one aspect changes the entire nature of the work. Dryden's works are termed as "pamphleteering verse" by Leavis, whereas Pope's works are great because together with realizing the "strength" of the civilization, his versification too has its effect.

Wordsworth's ability to present the truth about life is commended by Leavis. His poetry is a picture of his essential "sanity and normality" for though he was a Romantic poet he was not an individualist.[58] Instead he dealt with essential human nature. Leavis is of the view that all major novelists, like major poets have to promote awareness of the peculiarities of life. Whatsoever may be the object of an artist's study—the nature of man, his psyche, the problems of his times, all create a picture of life. This is what Leavis is concerned with. The moral seriousness comes only when there is a "profoundly serious interest in life" (*GT*, 28). Therefore for moral seriousness an essential prerequisite is representativeness. But it alone cannot bring about "moral seriousness."[59] It is undoubtedly instrumental in making a novelist or a poet great. There is a difference between representativeness and "profound interest in life" as has been stated earlier. As this discussion proceeds, it will become clear that a work has profound interest in life only when seriousness accompanies the author's ability to represent life.

Tolstoy's works are a "piece of life". It is the range and variety of human experience together with depth and vividness in the rendering that makes his novels so great. For Leavis, a discussion of life means "...the thought about the nature, the meaning and essential problems about life" (*Anna Karenina*, 11). A work of art should be close to reality as this brings in moral interest. Tolstoy is the greatest kind of artist as his concern for art is the "...immense and focussed expression of the questing after significance that characterizes him in his daily living" (12). Discussing Tolstoy's art, Leavis says that Tolstoy's views on morality and art might have been the same as Lawrence's. He illustrates what Lawrence meant when he (Lawrence) said that a writer writes with his own "moral sense, for the race as it were" (12). In this attempt he states his own views on the relationship between art and morality:

> "Moral" of course, is an ambiguous word but Lawrence was thinking of that manifestation of his own vitality of genius, the distinctive preoccupation with ultimate questions—those which concern the nature of one's deepest inner allegiances and determinations, the fundamental significances to be read in one's experience of life, the nature and the conditions of "fulfillment". ...for the concern of significance that is the principle of life in *Anna Karenina* is a deep spontaneous lived question or quest. (*Anna Karenina*, 12)

Thus a question of life is an attempt to bring out a solution to the problems of life. Only the representation of life is not desirable in art, but there must be an effort to simplify things that are incomprehensible about life and give a positive view of life. Buckley states, "His concern for 'life' is a concern for the moral poetic vitality which can have varying manifestations".[60] It is due to this that Leavis considers Pope's use of language poetic-creative. This again is the reason why he considers Keats so great and Shelley whose grasp on the actual is vague, so insignificant. Shelley's philosophy of life should have been presented in a more concrete manner like Keats's was.

Leavis's views on Keats have been derived from Middleton Murry. Leavis believes that Keats' current evaluation, stemming from Matthew Arnold, seems right in essentials and that what is required is a sharper explanation, a more purely literary critical explanation which will find in the poetry rather than in the life or the letters the grounds for a higher estimation of Keats's potential.[61] Walsh rightly states:

> Leavis's analysis of Keats's Ode...enables Leavis to give a much tougher meaning to the connotation of the term Art as applied to Keats.[62]

Further Walsh remarks that Leavis considers the ode "To Autumn" Shakespearean and also believes that by this point Leavis had established his own strongly individual and positive sensibility. He even remarks that this "...is not to join in the extravagance of Middleton Murry". Walsh seems to have erred in his judgement here as it was Murry's views on Keats' "To Autumn" that Leavis appears to voice. R.P. Bilan, who has similar claims for Leavis, is rightly criticized by L.R. Sharma who says that there is an error in Bilan's claim. This is evident after going through the chapter on "Ode To Autumn". In *Keats and Shakespeare* (1925), written more than a decade earlier than Leavis's *Revaluation* Murry had already given the distinction of native Englishness to Keats.[63]

Representation on the philosophical plane only, is not acceptable, to Leavis. Philosophy alone cannot help the common man to simplify the problems of life. The answer to the question about life is to be represented through a poetic-creative use of language (*Revaluation*, 193). Bilan says that for Leavis the "body" and "substance" of the language is essential to make it useful.[64] What Leavis actually means by this will be made clear in this passage on "To Autumn":

> The "Moss'd cottage-trees" represents a strength—a native English strength lying beyond the scope of the poet who aimed to make English as like Italian as possible. So too with the unpoetical "plump", its sensuousness firmness—it introduces a tactual image—represents a general concrete vigour such as is alien to the Tennysonian habit, and such as a Tennysonian handling of the medium cannot breed. This English strength pervades the ode. (*Revaluation*, 193)

Tolstoy's presentation of the relationship between the individual and his social conditions appealed greatly to Leavis. To see how the moral judgement and perception was conditioned by the social norms is the main concern of Tolstoy. He believed that an individual's personality is influenced by a mixture of his own qualities and the qualities developed by the society. Leavis feels that "A study of human nature is a study of social human nature...."[65] and a novel must deal with it. Leavis's concept of representativeness includes the discussion of the relationship of man and society as this is where the seed of the culture of a nation lies.

Leavis sees in Jane Austen the portrayal of her own problems and characterises this as "her peculiar interest in life". Besides range, variety, depth, and vividness she created characters which were interesting, pleasant and delightful. Leavis feels that George Eliot, Conrad and Henry James were influenced by her works. It is true that they all deal with life, but with different aspects of human life. It should be noticed here that a novelist could be representative in many ways. But a novelist needs to remember, as has been said earlier, that there should be creativity in art and life should be assessed positively. In the pages that follow this will be made more clear.

George Eliot gives a picture of life of her times through reminiscences, but she deals more closely with the "inner life" of each character—the psychological and sociological aspects of her characters. Leavis says that the "inner life" should be presented impersonally. (This concept has been virtually lifted from Murry's critical system. This idea is to be found in *The Adelphi* essays which were written by Murry in opposition to T.S. Eliot.) This is possible if a mature intelligence than the character's, touches with subtlety the "intensities of inner life", or else there is an element of "self idealization" or "self pity" (*GT*, 55). Leavis finds such "self idealization" and "self pity" often in her works. Leavis says that through the character of Felix Holt, George Eliot's keen interest in political, social and economic history in the total complex movement of civilization is evident. George Eliot's greatness as an artist and novelist is attributed to her "psychological insight and fineness of human valuation" (*GT*, 65). This is a quality of mature art. *Middlemarch* is one such novel. It is a study of a society done with understanding:

> The sheer informedness about society, its mechanism, the sheer informedness about how different classes live and (if they have to) earn their livelihoods, impress us with its range and its real knowledge; that is it is knowledge alive with understanding. (*GT*, 76

Through this, he says, one can acquire true knowledge. The term "true knowledge" refers to the representative quality.

It is only through this quality of literature that man can get real picture of the life of that time. For this the artist should be "freely critical" like George Eliot and the attitude should be "complete and balanced". She achieved this as she understood the situation fully before presenting it. She knew "what she had to present comically and what not". Leavis finds this a rare distinction of a Victorian novelist. This also makes a work even more representative. She presented Klesmer with a comic element because she had depicted Klesmer as a philistine, showing her dislike for the "complacent unintelligent" (*GT*, 139) class. It is her greatness that she retained all provincial strength and virtue, and still escaped the limitations of provinciality. Meredith, who was profound about life, was an exhibitionist with little depth. Hardy's heavy fiction and provinciality, too, attributed to the same short coming. Thus a work of art must have a "criticism of life". It must depict the life of his time, but it should not suffer from the limitations of provinciality.

Henry James' ability to represent life distinctively, delineated essential characteristics of different civilizations—the national tones and qualities, the indices of radical differences of temper, tradition and moral outlook. His symbolism is a remarkable characteristic of his art and is derived from his "profound seriousness of his interest in life" (*GT*, 150). His representative quality is plain says Leavis, that is, there is no doubt about the qualities he stands for.[66] Madam Merle in *The Portrait of a Lady*, represents a social civilization. Felix in *The Europeans* implies a mature civilization and a sophisticated social culture, Leavis approves of James' positive valuation in art. He feels that the informing spirit of the drama is positive and constructive.[67] Leavis's admiration for bringing out positive values of a social order in a work of art shows his own respect for these values. Artists, in depicting life, must bring out these values to strengthen their art.

Conrad's genius was peculiarly alive in his time and he was very sensitive to the stresses of the changing environment. This is the main reason for Leavis's emphasis on sensitivity. An artist ought to be sensitive so that he may notice the slightest variation in the environment before the common men themselves are aware of it. Taking into account Leavis's views on the responsibility of the creative artists, it can be said that an artist not only has to record this change but also bring the virtues and the vices to limelight. He also must affirm life and present solutions to the impending problems. Thus sensitivity is a means to achieve greatness in depicting life.

Leavis regards the study of culture an almost religious act. *The Pilgrim's Progress* which belongs to popular culture has a religious quality which is the cause of its success according to Leavis. He says that *The Pilgrim's Progress* has a representative significance such as is found only in the works of a great creative writer. Leavis, therefore, believes that true representative quality can be regarded as an almost religious act. In *Nor Shall My Sword* Leavis once again makes this clear that morality in art that is achieved by representing "life", human nature, civilisation and culture, helps in achieving "religious depth of thought and feeling".[68] He believed that any culture worth having must foster the religious sense.

In his later criticism, Leavis regards Lawrence almost a symbol of greatness. His ability to present life by giving a picture of his time and going deep into the psyche appealed to Leavis. But more important is his affirmation of life. Leavis links Lawrence with the great tradition and refers to him as "a line running into the twentieth century".[69] Dickens and Blake link him to the twentieth century. This continuity seems odd as he regarded Dickens as the "great entertainer" and he disapproved of Blake's mysticism.[70] Dickens, like Blake, is a "vindicator of the spirit—that is life". Leavis regards Lawrence as a social critic. He says, "Lawrence belongs to the same ethical and religious tradition as George Eliot", the rural and nonconformist England (*DHL*, 303). *Sons and Lovers* being largely autobioghraphical, has dealt with personal relationships and we get the picture of the adverse effect of the age on the mind of man. His emphasis is more on the individual psyche and through it on society and civilization. Therefore, Leavis says, that he is recording in his presentation of provincial England what in reality was the actual civilization. As a recorder of essential English history he is a great successor to George Eliot.

Here it is to be seen that in many different ways Leavis feels an artist can be representative, nevertheless the question that strikes here is—why Leavis regards Lawrence a successor of George Eliot. Bilan puts forward a similar question, "It raises the question: is Lawrence as concerned to record English history as George Eliot? I think the answer must be no".[71] After discussing this, he says further that Lawrence deserves to be praised more for his exploration of the "new world" and his "exploration of the deeper life" of the psyche than, as Leavis would have it, for any recorder of a "living tradition" or of "essential English history".

Bilan's concept of history seems to be different from Leavis's. Bilan here finds the "individual" distinct from the "civilization", whereas, as it is stated earlier, for Leavis "a study of human nature is a study of social human nature".[72] Individual is a unit of civilization. To understand the individual or the human nature is to understand—of course only as deep as one should in literature—the unit of civilization. The problems of an individual that he focuses on are the problems evolving out of the society and are representative of society and civilization. It is true that he does not directly give the relationship of an individual to the history of the time but without a close analysis of the mind of the individual it is difficult to understand the depth, of the movement of that time. Lawrence's characters evolve from their time. In *The Rainbow* Tom, Anna, and Ursula give us a record of the contemporary mind. Leavis says that Lawrence knew very well that life is a matter of individual lives and that except in individual lives there is no life to be interested in.[73] Even in *The Common Pursuit* Leavis says that we should know that, "human life lives only in individuals" and it is only in individuals that society lives.[74]

Lawrence's insight into the problems and conditions of the age is admired by Leavis because he (Lawrence) was very sensitive to any change in the conditions of his age and also because his approach was positive. Lawrence considers the plight of an individual as the plight of the civilization. He calls Lawrence a social historian as he deals with the transition, with man's relation to the general development of civilization. Minor aspects of the culture like the importance of "English Sunday" cannot be illustrated in a better way in history. Thus the novel is an incomparable wealth as a social and cultural history. Analysis of the mind as done by Lawrence is related to the effect of the changing civilization on men. In Gerald, infact, he sees, "the malady of the individual psyche as the essential process of industrial civilization" (*DHL*, 164).

Leavis' main reason for deviating from Eliot was his negative approach to life. He believes that the greatest literature presents an affirmation of life. Leavis obviously believes that a creative artist is morally bound to create rather than present a repudiation of life. Lawrence's work, Leavis says, is different from Aldous Huxley's. "The disgust, the exposure, and the rejection" of Lawrence are utterly different from what one finds in Aldous Huxley. One can never be unaware of the affirmation, the positive attitude that gives them their "force". Bilan has discussed Leavis' views on affirmation of life. He finds a difference between the concept of life of Leavis and Lawrence and feels that Leavis has imposed his meaning of life while judging Lawrence's works.[75] Leavis' meaning of life is, as Buckley states:

> ...a kind of awareness of inner vitality, of capacity of growth, existing in a man who is not only unified in his being but has brought that unity to focus on "body". And that unity is not merely a unity within the individual but a means of uniting him, at some profound level of his person, with certain "supra-personal forces". Life as Leavis understands it, has a wide range of meaning.[76]

Rene Wellek has objected to the use of the term "life" by Leavis because it is first of all simply realistic art—not merely in a sense of copying or transcribing a social situation, a dramatic, objective rendering of life, of course, but as we find it in Shakespeare and the English novelists of the nineteenth century.[77]

Perhaps, if the views of Buckley and Rene Wellek, keeping in view what Leavis himself has said about life, are brought together it is possible to understand what Leavis means by it. Art has to present an "awareness of the possibilities of life" (*GT*, 10), and "Art is a manifestation of life or it is nothing".[78] Therefore only the art that is affirmative or as he calls it, normative, is great. Eliot is sincere in his art but his works are opposed to life. Edward Neill remarks rightly that though Eliot is closer to Leavis in time than to Arnold and though he is Leavis's "intellectual home" he started from, yet Eliot appeared to be alien to the later "Leavisean nub".[79] Eliot emerges, as Neill says further, in *Thought Words and Creativity* as a "pathogenic to count as cultural 'positive' Eliot 'unbelieves in human creativity' seems to make Leavis come close to calling him the antipoet's poet".[80] In his essay "T.S. Eliot As Critic" (1958) he argues for the first time that the negative approach towards life in Eliot's criticism involves him in a self-contradiction and "portends" a radical failure of wholeness and coherence in him, and consequently defeat of intelligence. His repudiation of Eliot's negative approach is in his assessment of "Four Quartets" in *The Living Principle*. He clearly mentions that it is due to Eliot's "fear of life and contempt for humanity."

Bilan questions Leavis's attitude towards the representative quality of a work of art.[81] He says that literature should be valued as a creation instead of a document and that the historical value of art is secondary. This brings to light the question of the relation between art and morality. For Leavis moral seriousness makes an artist great. "Interest in life" brings in morality. And therefore life has to be the main focus in a work of art. Leavis' main object is to enrich culture through art or at least to maintain a cultural continuity. This would make art a means of serving society. Keeping this in view, art has to give value to "life" to be of use to society. The works that do not affirm life might make men prejudiced to life; and they might lose faith in life. But to think that it is the social importance of a work that alone is valuable is not correct. Leavis, too, does not agree that this aspect of literature alone can make a work of art great. In art "aesthetic value is not separable from the moral one" (*GT*, 14).

As has been noted earlier every aspect of art that Leavis values is an outcome of the intelligence of the artist. But "talent" scores over every other aspect as without it there can be no creation. What Leavis implies by individual talent is left undefined. "Master pieces", he says, "arrive when gifted individuals occur, inspiration sets in, creation results" (*Common Pursuit*, 183). He does not say what exactly he means by "gifted individuals". It is definitely a quality that is of the poet and is not acquired. If this quotation is related to his discussion on the distinctive qualities of the poet (*New Bearings*, 16) it may be said that the poet's ability is to understand the potentialities of human behaviour, his being more alive in his time, his sensitivity, all are derived from the "individual talent". Leavis writes about this quality repeatedly, giving it various names—"gift", "genuine talent", "genius" (*Common Pursuit*, 184).

According to Leavis art has a function namely, "to communicate an attitude" (*New Bearings*, 16). If a work depicts life, affirms life yet cannot communicate, it cannot be referred to as art. It is the genius of the poet alone that can communicate to men the "attitudes". In fact talking about a poet, he says:

> He is a poet because the interest in his experience is not separable from the interest in his words, because, that is, of his habit of seeking by the evocative use of words to sharpen his awareness of his ways of feeling, to making these communicable. And poetry can communicate the actual quality of experience with subtlety and precision unapproachable by any other means. (*New Bearings*, 16)

He even remarks that the capacity for experiencing and the power of communication of a poet are indistinguishable from his awareness of what he feels. The sensitivity of a poet makes him aware of the needs of his time. Whatever he experiences he has the ability to put into words. The reason of Leavis's emphasis on form and technique may be to facilitate communication. Language itself is important to him because it is the most suitable medium of communication of attitudes in this age. William Walsh has elaborately sketched the relationship between language and society as Leavis understood it to be. He says that English literature can be read as:

> ...the self illumining chronicle of the state of the language. The life of language is recurrently refreshed by the people and by the poets who turn from its literary and mandarin forms to its use as a living tongue.[82]

The importance of language also derives from the fact that it can present feelings effectively. This is possible only when the words "seem to do what they say", as in Donne. Milton on the other hand has a language that is remote from speech, that is, his words "...are doing so much less while they seem, to be valuing themselves highly". According to Leavis, Milton's art is "incantatory", his use of language is remote from speech:

> Certain feelings are expressed, but there is no pressure behind the words; what predominates in the handling of them is not the tension of something precise to be defined and fixed, but a concern for mellifluousness—for liquid sequences and a pleasing opening and closing of the vowels. (60)

Shakespeare, Leavis says, has complete control over language. In *Macbeth* the theme is complex which is vividly and profoundly realized—not thought of, but possessed imaginatively in its concreteness, so that, as it grows in specificity, it in turn possesses the poet's mind and commands expression. Pope also exhibits a rare instance in which an exquisite symmetry of assumption, tone and manner exists between the artist and his time. Pope's vision of civilization has a just sufficient ground in the reality of the Augustan period to orchestrate its ideal aspiration with solid good sense.

Wordsworth's achievements owe much to his ability to communicate because he commands the kind of attention and permits no other (*Revaluations*, 146). This is because of the language and the exploratory tone and manner of this verse. Comparing George Eliot and Conrad, Leavis says that Conrad is a greater artist than George Eliot because of his communication ability. He transmutes fully into the created work the interests he brings in (*GT*, 44). Leavis further remarks that this ability was the gift of the environment of Conrad. He was a seaman and not a high level intellectual, as has been stated earlier. This has also brought wholeness in his work (*GT*, 44). The relationship between communication and wholeness can be understood. That the two are related is made clear by Leavis. Leavis has not stated clearly the meaning of "wholeness". The context in which he has written it shows that "wholeness" means a sort of completeness in art. There is some sort of balance between the philosophy and the communication of the attitude. This "wholeness" can be brought about when form and content are perfectly balanced so as to communicate the desired attitude completely. That is, form chosen is according to the content (*GT*, 17) This brings about a kind of "unity" in art. Bilan states, "For Leavis a novel can lack unity, form, wholeness and still be great".[83] This cannot be said with such conviction. Certainly unity, wholeness and form have not been given great importance, yet their impact has considerable effect on communication.

Form has been given the desired importance, though he found content more important. Without a good form a novel cannot be defined as a "moral fable". He also says that great novelists in the tradition are all very much concerned with form. They are original technically. He feels that style and form are indicative of the artist's view of life and says, "The chief preoccupation is with elaborating a beautiful style to apply to the chosen subject" (*GT*, 17). As Leavis proceeds he remarks that if a novel is great it cannot be said to be great because of its form but because of the moral preoccupation, that is, interest in life. According to Leavis a great novelist is always an innovator in form and method and is a servant of a profoundly serious interest in life. But the fact that all writers of tradition are concerned with form implies that form does help in making a work of art great and without a good form a work cannot achieve greatness.

Every work of art should in some way be original. Every age has some subjects that interest men of that age. The "original genius" is essential for a work of art to be great as it helps to present the "subject" of the age in a new way, thus making it interesting, and helping in communication.

Originality was lacking in the genius of the Victorian age. This stunted the development of poetry in that age (*New Bearings*, 62). From Tennyson to Hardy no poet had the originality which could give poetry a new direction. Leavis believes that if a poet has to be successful his poetry should keep in touch with the finer consciousness of its age. For poetry must change with the changing time and cater to the needs of the age (*GT*, 19). Explaining the concept of originality of Leavis, William Walsh says that new moments in literature are new uses of language. Chaucer, Shakespeare, Donne and Eliot all are examples of this (*GT*, 19).[84] The "new" mind requires a new voice, a new medium and it is the poet's genius that alone can provide it. But a writer's greatness is established when he represents a whole movement of civilization just as the prose of his period is the product of a whole new world. Originality will automatically evolve if a writer truly represents his age. For presenting values that have earlier been stated, originality of technique and thought-content is essential to communicate an attitude successfully. It should be noted here that Leavis is not disturbed by the changing times, but instead his vote is for adapting to the times. This is what he means when he says that poetry should continuously develop. Leavis asserts that an artist should accept from his predecessors all that he needs and at the same time be close to his age. A poet has an edge over the novelist as he can adopt his verse form to his age. Perhaps he wants the artists to follow the tradition and yet be original. Around this revolves his concept of the "great tradition".

Eliot's originality and intelligence together made his poetry so effective. Leavis realizes that to be as original as Eliot is a difficult task. Eliot was original both in style and content. His works were influenced by the scientific inventions of the age. As has been stated, the rhythm of his poems is derived from the internal combustion engine which had at that time influenced every sphere of life. He expressed without hesitation the "modern sensibility".

Originality also helps in communication as it does in Hopkins. The ability to "invent" is remarkable in him. Hopkins's language is simple yet not immediately comprehensible because the form of his poetry is unusual. In fact, according to Leavis, the form was deliberately so because he presumed to expect from the reader prolonged and repeated intellectual effort. Hopkins is really difficult, and the difficulty is essential. If we could deceive ourselves into believing that we were reading easily his purpose would be defeated (*Revaluation*, 122).

The originality of Donne is what draws Leavis towards Donne. Leavis praises both Eliot and Donne for their originality especially because they both had great influence on their successors. He feels that it is due to their originality that they have influenced the poetry of their age:

> The extraordinary force of originality that made Donne so potent an influence in the seventeenth century and a living poet in the most important sense. (*Revaluation*, 122)

The originality of Donne and Eliot was rare. Leavis does not expect each poet to be as original as them. An artist should understand and learn from a good artist. Originality should accompany this ability to learn from an artist. A good artist should imbibe from other great artists what he needs, but this must not be imitation. This helps in building a tradition, like James who brought a great deal from outside. He drew from English literature what he needed, and learnt in that peculiar way of genius which is so different from imitation. And he, in the real sense according to Leavis belongs to the tradition (*GT*, 122).

Leavis' concept of "tradition" developed quite early in his critical career. From the very beginning he thought in terms of "influence" of one artist on others of his own age or successors. Those artists who had great influence on others were according to him successful. There are, as we shall see, some artists who are considered to be so in the "great tradition". Amongst the novelists Jane Austen, George Eliot, James, Conrad and Lawrence are the main pillars of the English tradition. Much has been written and discussed on the "great tradition" by Leavis and his critics. My attempt will be to synthesize these views and bring out its meaning.

According to Leavis 'tradition' is a term which implies many things and often very little. To distinguish the major novelists in the spirit proposed is to form a more useful idea of tradition. Later he says that Jane Austen is the inaugrator of the "great tradition". Specifying what he means by it he says that tradition is something to which what is great in English fiction belongs. This shows that a writer who is historically significant is not necessarily in the great traditon. Feilding is historically important but is not in the traditon. He had influenced Jane Austen, hence Leavis considers him historically important. Tradition it seems, stands for a set of values that are picked up by an artist from his predecessors. These values may be those that have been already discussed above like originality, affirmation of life, communicative ability, as these are the lines on which he discusses the greatness of the artists in the tradition. But influence alone cannot establish a creative writer in the traditon. The above mentioned values have to be present to a considerable extent. Bilan says that for Leavis it means the continuation of literature and the formation of a tradition.[85]

Leavis repeatedly tries to establish resemblance between great artists or their influence on minor artists. Reviewing Adam Bede he says that an illuminating case of one of the major original artists learning from predecessors is George Eliot. She is deeply rooted in literature of the past and has also decisively influenced novelists coming after her, e.g. James, Hardy and Lawrence. She is at the centre of the creative achievements of the English language in the phase of its history to this day and incites pregnant reflections on vital continuity in art.[86] It is clear from the examples given above that Leavis appreciates the ability to learn from predecessors. Further he says that *The Europeans* emerges out of *Emma* and *Persuasion*. James has been influenced by Jane Austen. But it is primarily because of his affinity with George Eliot that he is in the "great tradition". There is no sense of reproof when Leavis says this. It also shows his admiration for the quality of being able to understand and absorb from a predecessor. In fact he looks forward for such extracts that can prove an artist's resemblance to another. Bilan disapproves of Leavis's opinion. He thinks that it is reopen to the question whether the kind of tradition Leavis wants to establish can be claimed simply on the basis of the relation between these two novels. James, in his essay on George Eliot, is revealingly critical of her, and the influence she has. He was aware that certain of his aims were different—he was more concerned with form and less with history. John Gross, too, shows dissatisfaction over the concept of tradition. According to Gross, the literary tradition could mean roughly one of the two things. It could be the loose broad historical continuity provided by the common culture shared by the writers of the same language or it could be region or social class. Leavis's "great tradition" is obviously not this. Alternatively, there are specific relationships between a group of writers in terms of influence, direct borrowing, strongly marked affinities, the use of similar forms and themes, and so on. Gross has some doubts. He insists that only five authors qualify for an assured place in the Leavis tradition, therefore the "comparative tenuousness" of such relationships between them is rather striking. He further says:

> ...if tradition is not a matter of historical continuity, nor of indebtedness then what exactly is it? ...he thinks they are immeasurably better than other novelists, and he is fully entitled to say so at the top of his voice. But to dress up a list of one's preferences as a tradition is another matter altogether.[87]

Bilan, too, finds Leavis's conception of tradition "unsatisfactory" and perplexing in many ways. Leavis's "great tradition" is his means of achieving a greater aim—a cultural continuity. Gross's view is flawed as he fails to realize that Leavis's idea of tradition is subservient to his idea of cultural continuity. It is the transference of the "values" from one generation of writers to the other that is of importance for him.

Tradition, as he says, is not a question of borrowing and resemblance, but if the salient features of the work are affirmation of life, representativeness, originality, the ability to communicate, and a poetic-creative use of language there is bound to be some resemblance. But since all the works are original they are not limitations. The influence is for the better and must not in any way be decried. The historical continuity inevitably emerges. To maintain a continuity of values Leavis never looks down upon the artist if he is influenced by his predecessors.[88] But he asserts throughout that originality is the key to greatness. They together form a tradition because they successfully communicate the culture and establish a bond between the people and culture. He says about literature that like the culture it represents it must have its life in the present—and that life is growth. Therefore "tradition", too, aims at growth in literature since it aims at affirmation of life and representativeness. This is probably the reason why he looks forward to English literature as a means of cultural continuity and believes that the focus of cultural continuity can only be in English. English literature is magnificent and matchless in diversity and range, and so is able to portray the changing life profoundly giving a continuity that is still alive.[89] There can be no substitute to literature.

As it has been discussed, F.R. Leavis insists on the use of literature as a means of cultural continuity. The purpose of literature goes unrealized if it is not understood or understood wrongly. Once Ibsen asserted, "A poet is precisely one who sees", Leavis implicitly added, "Yes, and we must teach seeing".[90] With this in mind all his works have been written. He has had a considerable influence on the criticism of today.

F.R. Leavis starts with the premise that true criticism of close scrutiny can never do injustice to a good work and that intelligence is essential for a useful, morally constructive evaluation.[91] Shaping the mind of the educated public, to tune the mind of the readers and to bring them to the level of artist is the aim of his criticism:

> Criticism, when it performs its function, not merely expresses and performs its function, not merely expresses

> and defines the "contemporary sensibility", it helps to form it to persuade an effective "contemporary sensibility" into being.[92]

This "contemporary sensibility" refers to the development of "literary mind", that is, an intelligence with the sensitiveness, the flexibility and the disciplined and mature preoccupation with value that should be the product of a literary training.[93]

Since he considers the place of criticism at the centre of the intellectual life of the civilization, he feels that critic cannot restrict himself to literature alone. It is difficult to dissociate from society. The critics must show how society is affected by literature. They also show the right path to creative artists. Hence a critic inevitably slips into discussing the conditions of society and civilization that underlie literature.

F.R. Leavis firmly believes that since literature is rooted in society, criticism, too, cannot be dissociated from it. His discussion with F.W. Bateson makes clear the extent to which social criticism can form a part of literary criticism. Criticism of literature, he feels, is not primarily criticism of society. Bateson says that a literary critic has a special insight into the society, and the function of a literary critic is to bring out a social diagnosis.[94] F.R. Leavis regards Bateson's views a betrayal to criticism and literature. It shows a disbelief in criticism and literature. The responsibility of criticism is in the field of literature. Social criticism forms a part of the body of literature. Leavis does not deny that the literary critic is concerned with the society but his foremost concern is with literature not society. The utility of criticism stands out when the created work is received by the men precisely in the spirit in which it was written—its reason of creation comes to light. Criticism is written so that a work of art is read understood and duly valued and has the influence it should have on the contemporary sensibility. Leavis is of the view that criticism must relate a work of any age to contemporary time—*Scrutiny* successfully did this.

Leavis gave the example of *Scrutiny* to relate how the involvement of the critics of the contemporary age gave real meaning to criticism. *Scrutiny*, through its volumes, presents the history of English literature. The systematic presentation of the critical achievement resulted in the revaluation of the past of English literature. This is so because it involved deep insight into the important events in the contemporary age and analysis of it and judgement too was given. The judgements of *Scrutiny* have proved to be quite correct. Therefore, Leavis desired that even the critic, like the poets and novelists should keep in mind the age while critisizing.

Leavis in his discussion with F.W. Bateson insists that literary history evolves from literary criticism. In his review of Bateson's *English Poetry and the English Language* he writes:

> ...critic, one gathers, is a description that he (Bateson) would repudiate. The nature of the distinction that, in his opening pages, he tries to elaborate between the critic and the literary historian is not clear, but he certainly intends a separation, and he calls his book *An Essay in Literary History*. Yet the kind of essay he undertakes could be successfully attempted only by a critic and would then be essentially literary criticism.[95]

Thus, he says that only a literary critic can write about literary history as he is the best person to judge the place of an artist, his development and his influence.

Criticism being a creative assessment of a work should keep in view the contemporary needs, a knowledge of the time and the values of the age. This is the work of serious criticism and the responsibility of a critic. The function of criticism is therefore neither analysis of society nor the formulation of norms or theory of literature. It implies the revaluation of art which reveals the contemporary sensibility in concrete form.

Leavis does not give much importance to psychological critics. He says that they have a very limited achievement. Psychoanalysis has been, for those interested in literary criticism, merely a

> ...nuisance, fostering in the guise of criticism all kinds of pretentious, impertinences and irrelevances—"explanations" of art, artists and the works of art.[96]

Very rarely, he says, there are critics who excel in this. The incompetent critics who have a vague purpose find it helpful as they get a vocabulary. Nevertheless I.A. Richards's use of psychology is appreciated by Leavis because he does not make use of technical psychology, but applies it. The psychologists do not find the use of pure psychological formulations in his works, yet his works could not have been written without a training in psychology. Leavis himself analyses the characters and also analyses the psychology of some. But his analysis never seems to go on an irrelevant track. The character is not analysed for its own sake, but there is some importance of that analysis. Importance is given to some characters for certain reasons, as in discussing Mrs. Transome's character, and also when Leavis explains the abnormality of Gerald (*GT*, 7).

Leavis probably tries to establish that psychological criticism should serve literary criticism in the sense that it must strengthen or add to literature rather than being for the sake of psychology.

Leavis also desires that literature should not be judged by the life of the author or the historical conditions of his age. He asserts that a critic fails to give adequate attention to what is before him if he observes or judges a work with the life of the author or the history of the age in view.[97]

Here it may be noted that to give largeness and depth to criticism Leavis used vocabulary from different social sciences. Kaufmann states that this is a reflection of his intense moral approach. Since he has not believed that the modern world's change can be prevented, his objective has been to confront it; one of preservation and practical continuity.[98] As a result, his work had to be sociological as well as conventionally literary. In fact his works are an illustration of his belief that the ground held by literature had to be enlarged if it was to survive. This explains the reason of his giving importance to social sciences in place of a purely literary judgement.

Leavis is of the view that a critic should be as close to the text as possible and be faithful to what is presented or realized in words on the page. According to Leavis:

> It should be enforced that literature is made of words, and that everything worth saying in criticism of verse and prose can be related to judgements concerning particular on the page.[99]

By this he means that a critic should be close to the text such that a critic does not, at any stage, be irrelevant. It does not mean that a critic must be involved with the artistic value of the words as he very clearly states:

> I don't believe in any "literary values", and you won't find me talking about them, the judgements the literary critic is concerned with are judgements about life.[100]

Ronald Hayman has elaborated his phrase "words on the page" with clarity.[101] He says that Leavis read, analysed, isolated images from their context, and pondered over the prose sense of the poem. The facts of the poet's life were irrelevant to the decision a critic or a reader has to take about the effectiveness of a poem. Leavis was "liberating", he says because he made us feel that nothing mattered except the arrangement of the words on the page, but that mattered enormously because the partnership between writer and reader could be creative.

To Leavis, as Steiner says, a critic is a "complete reader" and the ideal critic is the ideal reader. Steiner further says that Leavis himself realizes to the full the experience given in the words of the poet or the novelist. He aims at complete responsiveness, at a kind of poised vulnerability and consciousness in the encounter with the text. He proceeds with an attention which is close and stringent, yet also provisional, and at all times susceptible to revaluation. Judgement arises from response, he does not imitate it. Leavis here feels that:

> The critic's aim is first, to realize as sensitively and completely as possible this or that which claim his attention; and a certain valuing is implicit in the realizing.[102]

According to S.K. Aithal, Leavis's personal, creative response to works of art must not be confused with affective or impressionistic criticism. Leavis does, of course, think that the personal, appreciative approach is a basic factor in criticism. Leavis says:

> An approach is personal or it is nothing: you cannot take over the appreciation of a poem, and unappreciated, the poem isn't "there".[103]

But he does not make the poem an excuse for simply releasing his own personal thoughts and emotions. Rather, he always discusses the concrete details of the poem. He does not give us some vague general impressions about it. And he seeks to verify the truth of his reactions by collaboration. He claims that "aesthetic" is a term that literary critic should keep away from and:

> I don't think for, any critic who understands his job there are any "unique literary values" or any "realm of the exclusively aesthetic". (*The Common Pursuit,* 89)

This is what differentiated him from the American New Critics who were his contemporaries, as they tended to confine their attention to the play of words on the page, and neglected what deeply mattered to Leavis, the socio-historical contexts with which the words were written and their implication. The "unique literary values" that Leavis talks about are those values which he feels are against life. Literature cannot be a "unique" experience dissociated from life. Literature is footed in life, literature and life are interrelated. He believes in the moral concern of literature. But the New Critics believe in the "unique literary values". They feel that any moral concern of literature makes the approach fallacious. Thus calling him one of the New Critics cannot be justified. There is a tendency to refer to him as an English offshoot of the New Critics, but though he properly emphasized "the words on the page" he never did so to the exclusion of social and cultural considerations.

This means, as Thomas L. Jeffers says, that he was not a philosophic critic. His concern was not method but practice.[104] Rene Wellek's discussion with Leavis establishes Leavis's dislike for philosophy for he feels that it is abstract and poetry is concrete. Words in poetry invite us, not to "think about" and judge but to "feel into" or "become"—to realize a complex experience that is given in the words. This is the reason for his not being a philosophic critic. He gives more importance to the meaning of the words and, their implication and this is what he means when he says that "the words on the page" have importance. This is not the sense in which the New Critics used the phrase "words of the page".

Dr Raj Nath in his essay "F.R. Leavis: A Revaluation" also tries to establish Leavis's dissociation from the New Critics. He says:

> One sees very clearly the difference between Leavis and the New Critics: Leavis does not attempt, in the first place, that close verbal analysis that we find in the New Critics and secondly he includes in his critical fold many such elements (for example, the idea of morality and culture) as are alien to the New Critical system.... It has also been pointed out that unlike the New Critics, Leavis recognized the value of literature for life.[105]

Leavis, therefore, is not one of the "New Critics" as he is so often branded.

Leavis believes that a critic should be close to the text. His main dispute with the "theorists" and the philosophic approaches to literature is that they do not give "a fullness of response". He says that a critic of poetry should be a complete reader: the ideal critic is the ideal reader. The reading demanded by poetry is of a different kind from that demanded by philosophy. The critic-reader of poetry is indeed concerned with evaluation. The business of the literary critic for Leavis is to attain a "peculiar completeness" of response and to observe a "peculiarly strict relevance" in developing his response into commentary. The critic must be on his guard against "...abstracting improperly from what is in front of him and against any premature or irrelevant generalizing of it or from it". His primary concern should be to enter into possession of the given poem in its concrete fullness, and his constant concern is never to lose his completeness of possession, but rather to increase it. (*The Common Pursuit*, 213)

A response to the work must be presented but this is not enough. For the great cause that criticism has to work for, a single person's response to a work cannot serve the purpose. Criticism, he says, needs to be collaborative. Since it is a creative ability it must be a collaboration between public and private views. The critics form a part of the educated public. The views of a single critic on a work in isolation cannot fulfil the function of critics. A number of critics must evaluate with genuine interest, "...the functioning of criticism demands a fully overt kind of collaboration".[106] Through collaboration the views and perceptions of many minds meet. There may be agreement or even disagreement. No judgement may be absolutely correct, but it is through this that there can be a discussion on "values" in a work.[107] This helps to make criticism corrective besides being creative. The shortcomings of a critic's work may be noticed and corrected by another. The discussion of a work establishes a "value". This discussion is creative as different aspects of a work are assessed. In so doing a work is evaluated. Its significance is brought out. The "value" is discussed thoroughly by many educated and aware minds. Thus the process of collaborative criticism results in the establishment of a work of art and the "values of life". Buckley rightly says that Leavis has his eye on the audience.[108] I.D. Mac Killop also thinks that the classic Leavisian conception of criticism is of free communion with the artist's text, awaiting correction from other free readers.[109] This is precisely the way collaborative criticism works. Mulhern calls this concept of criticism "humanist" because it presents "immediated communication between critic and interlocutory reader, (a conception) logically dependent on the idea of human essence".[110] In such a critical communion minds meet, liberated from ideas which could be held by anyone else—ideas which belong in the background of artist and critic. Thus evolves "humanist" criticism.

I.D. Mac Killop insists that in humanist criticism the critic is expected, to identify with the artist and Leavis' criticism ought to be widely known as the criticism of artist identification. Mac Killop says that at first, artist-identification generates a particular type of writing in Leavis, second, the recognition of artist-identification might allow some of the distinctly romantic features of Leavis's work to stand out. This may perhaps be inferred from the statements where the critic's soul is referred to.

A striking quality of Leavis's criticism is his level headedness. His search for balance and reasoned response has been noticed by several scholars. Martin Jarrett-Kerr says, "He keeps his head" and states, the significance of the work. And Buckley says, "Relevance is a key word through out Leavis's criticism".[111] Since Leavis tries to establish the relevance of a work of art, he is always to the point, he keeps on searching for the relevance of work and therefore fails from straying away to discussions that have little concern. This, once again, emerges out of his moralistic approach to literature. Explanation alone is not sufficient. "See", he says, "what this poetry is doing; see what that prose is really upto".[112] In his own criticism this approach can be noticed. While comparing the images of Keats and Tennyson he tries to show the relevance of their images and the effect that it has on the reader.[113] Discussion of such images can easily take a critic away from his point, but Leavis "never lets it get out of hand". This is so because of his adhering so firmly to the "relevance" of the images.

It may be noticed that Leavis, while analysing a work, overlooks the irrelevant aspects, that is, those aspects that do not lead to his predestined conclusion. After attempting a close scrutiny of a work with generalizations he deduces a conclusion firmly linking it with what he had stated. The work on Conrad for example begins with "He has, of course, long been generally held to be among the English masters" (*GT*, 200). Leavis through each discussion in the chapter brings out the reasons for which he considers Conrad great. Through this his idea of greatness is also understood. He, in the end, concludes:

> ...if the criterion is the achievement in work addressed to the adult mind, and capable as such of engaging again and again its full critical attention, then Conrad is certainly a greater novelist than the four enumerated. (*GT*, 200)

Thus besides keeping firm grasp of the "words on the page", this too is a means to attain relevance. He even says that any and every thing that strikes a critic should not be stated, but there should always be the responsibility that a critic has to fulfil before him (*NSMS*, 19).

While writing about Samuel Johnson, Leavis states:

> But there is, for a critic, a problem of relevance: it is, infact his ability to be relevant in his judgements and commentries that makes him a critic, if he deserves the name. And the ability to be relevant, is not a mere matter of good sense; it implies an understanding of the resources of language, the nature of conventions, and the possibilities of organization such as can come only from much intensive literary experience accompanied by the habit of analysis. In this sense it certainly implies a specially developed sensibility. (*The Common Pursuit*, 114)

Leavis gives importance to relevance so that criticism achieves its objective. In the definition of a "moral fable" which is already mentioned Leavis makes it clear that no figure or situation should be irrelevant and no figure or situation should have little significance. Another reason might have been to successfully communicate to the readers without straying from the point. Anything that is irrelevant is liable to be rejected by the readers. Relevance too, is audience oriented and shows a humanist approach to criticism.

Leavis asserts that the "total value judgement" of a work should be brought out. Through an analysis of a work its relevance is brought to light. But even while judging the parts of the work the whole should be kept in mind. Through the analysis of part the whole has to be realized. All parts have to work to strengthen one particular value of life. Leavis, thus stresses that through the analysis of parts the core of the work can be reached, or that the whole is present in the part.[114] Allun Jones says that the determination of Leavis to never slide away into the abstract enables him to "imply" value-judgements without "dogmatically asserting them" [115] This, he says, has now hardened into a technique. This is definitely in keeping with the relevance of a work. As Jones says, it brings out two features of his criticism. First that even the analysis of parts is directed towards one conclusion and second that from the very beginning he has in mind the conclusion. Allun Jones also remarks that this technique often, "...afflicts the critic with a kind of literary myopia. A critic will always find in a text what he is looking for and often overlook what is there".[116] But this in Leavis cannot be considered to be a weakness. If a critic tries to establish a particular "value" through analysis of a work he cannot afford to move away from his line of thought and discuss other aspects of the work.

In his last phase Leavis merged literary criticism with general criticism of life and humanity so indistinguishably that he rejects the literary values completely. He believes that most literary critics are unsatisfactory practitioners because, not being like Birkin, "open to the deep source, to the unknown they are closed up in moral pride".[117] In this he is a follower of Wittgenstein's advice to give up literary criticism. "Technological Benthamite" is the coinage with which Leavis characterizes the way in which our civilization proposes to itself both problems and solutions which are themselves a sign and a complication of what afflicts it. Edward Neill says that the word has "enornous concomitants" in relation to the whole development of post-industrial civilization, and goes back to his early castigation of what could be called conventional radicalism and his belief that "Capitalism" and "Marxism" were united in the strife that divided them in an unseemly way. The social critic, Leavis believes, knows the reality of the world. Besides, this,

> ...he has no use of a distinct area where "literary values" can flourish. He is, infact, between two worlds one much like the other.[118]

A discussion of Leavis with F.W. Bateson that was published in *Scrutiny* may be recalled here.[119] "For Leavis", Bateson wrote later, "literary criticism was more important than literary history". Leavis himself said, "...we must look for our main insights into those characteristics of the 'social context' that matters most to the critic—to the reader of poetry".[120] This Leavis practiced in his own works too.

F.R. Leavis's efforts were not in vain. Though Leavis was to a considerable extent concerned with the society, he did not show notable concern with politics. Francis Mulhern's *The Moment of "Scrutiny"* (1974) which according to Edward Neill is the "most useful work on Leavis in recent years",[121] examines Leavis and his group from the political point of view. In the early years, he does find to some extent, a Marxist commitment in the editor of *The New Left Review*. The subjects that most concerned *Scrutiny* were left wing causes, antiwar, anti-fascist and anti-capitalist.[122] Leavis is quoted saying in 1932 that "...some form of economic communism was inevitable and desirable".[123] But as early as 1937, notes Mulhern, "...the Marxistant fringe had disappeared from *Scrutiny*".[124] *Scrutiny* was remarkable in its keeping a distance from politics as it never endorsed any existing political organization. It was a literary journal and it did not change its identity. Mulhern, nevertheless, finds it a weakness of Leavis and complains that *Scrutiny* "...failed to make the practical connection between 'culture' and organized politics".[125] The cultural function that *Scrutiny* served in the words of Mulhern was: "...to mediate the establishment of a new, professionally chartered discourse on literature in the new social layer into the national intelligentsia".[126]

Graham Hough also accepts the influence of Leavis and *Scrutiny* on educational practice.[127] *Scrutiny*, he says, was very effective because of its closeness to the class conflict. Lionel Trilling expresses surprise that so small a conflict could have generated so much emotion in Leavis's mind.[128] But in England class-issue was a very sensitive issue. Graham Hough assessing the achievements of the *Scrutiny* writes:

> *Scrutiny* was always inverterately hostile to elegant "belles" — "letters" and aristocratic literary establishment. An important part of the programme was to claim for the lower bourgeois the whole heritage of cultrue that had formerly been thought of as an upper-bourgeois preserve.... To break an obsolete

> barrier and to throw literary discourse open to wider social forces was one of *Scrutiny's* most genuine achievement.[129]

According to F.W. Bateson the *Scrutiny* revolution was primarily social.[130]

Leavis was, to a large extent, a critic who aimed at improvement of society by inculcation of a positive approach to life by helping man to move with the tide of time. He wanted to wipe out the disparaging effects of war—the fear of death looming low over the heart and mind of man, the growth of a negative approach to life and the development of class distinction in society. His tireless strife to achieve his objective was such that his criticism became almost indistinguishable from criticism of civilization yet maintaining its status of literary criticism.

NOTES

1. F.R. Leavis and Denys Thompson, *Culture and Environment* (1933; rpt. London: Chatto and Windus, 1964), pp. 1-2.
2. R.J. Kaufmann, "F.R. Leavis: The Morality of Mind", *The Critical Quaterly*, Vol. I (1959), p. 249.
3. Edward Neill, "'Give up Literary Criticism': The Last-Phase", *English* (Spring, 1984), p. 24.
4. F.R. Leavis, "'Literarism' vs 'Scientism'", *Nor Shall My Sword* (London: Chatto and Windus, 1972), p. 160.
5. *Ibid.*, "Mass Civilization and Minority Culture", *For Continuity*, p. 13.
6. R.P. Bilan, "Language, Literature and Continuity", *The Literary Criticism of F.R. Leavis*, p. 27.
7. Rene Wellek, "F.R. Leavis and the Scrutiny Group", *A History of Modern Criticism*, Vol. V, p. 251.
8. F.R. Leavis, "Summing up: 'Monstrous Unrealism'", *English Literature in our time and the University* (London: Chatto and Windus, 1969), p. 180.
9. *Ibid.*
10. *Ibid.*, "Mass Civilization and Minority Culture", *For Continuity*, p. 15.

11. R.P. Bilan "Language, Literature and Continuity", *The Literary Criticism of F.R. Leavis*, p. 28.
12. F.R. Leavis, "Pound in His Letters", *Anna Karenina and Other Essays*, p. 163.
13. *Ibid.*, "Mass Civilization and Minority Culture", *For Continuity*, p. 13.
14. Raymond Williams, "Two Literary Critics", *Culture and Society: 1780-1950*, p. 247.
15. *Ibid.*, p. 249.
16. F.R. Leavis and Denys Thompson, *Culture and Environment*, pp. 1-2.
17. F.R. Leavis, "Poetry and the Modern World", *New Bearings in English Poetry* (1932; rpt. New York: Penguine Books, 1979), p. 17.
18. Leavis, "Literature and the University: The Wrong Question", *English Literature in Our Time and the University* (London: Ghatto and Windus, 1969), p. 60.
19. W.J. Keith, "The Leavises", *University of Toronto Quarterly* (November 1985), p. 124.
20. Robert Boyers, *F.R. Leavis: Judgement and the Discipline of Thought* (Columbia: University of Missouri Press, 1978), p. 26.
21. R.J. Kaufmann, "The Morality of the Mind", *The Critical Quarterly* (Vol. I, 1959), p. 253.
22. F.R. Leavis, "Introduction", *Nor Shall My Sword* (London: Chatto and Windus, 1972), p. 18.
23. Leavis, "Introduction", *Education and the University* (1943; rpt. London: Chatto and Windus, 1965), p. 18.
24. Rajnath, "The Critical Achievement of F.R. Leavis", *English Studies* (October 1982), p. 420.
25. *Ibid.*, p. 21.
26. Lionel Trilling, "Dr Leavis and the Moral Tradition", *A Gathering of Fugitives*, p. 110.
27. Rene Wellek, "Leavis and the Scrutiny Group", *A History of Modern Criticism: 1750-1950* (London: Jonathan Cape, 1986), p. 252.
28. Eliseo Vivas, "Mr. Leavis on D.H. Lawrence" *Sewanee Review*, 65 (1957), p. 130.

29. Thomas L. Jeffers, "Review of the Leavises: Recollection and Impressions", *Western Humanities Review* (Spring, 1986), p. 86.
30. William Walsh, "The Arnoldian Middle", *F.R. Leavis* (London: Chatto and Windus, 1980), p. 143.
31. F.R. Leavis, "Johnson as Critic", *Anna Karenina and Other Essays* (London: Chatto and Windus, 1967), p. 223.
32. *Ibid., Dickens: The Novelist* (1970; rpt. Harmonds-worth: Penguine Books, 1972).
33. George Steiner, "F.R. Leavis", *Twentieth Century Literary Criticism,* ed. David Lodge (1972; rpt. London: Longman, 1975).
34. William Walsh, "The Arnoldian Middle", *F.R. Leavis*, p. 145.
35. J. Middleton Murry, "Flaubert vs Flaubart", *Discoveries,* p. 297.
36. R.J. Kaufmann, "F.R. Leavis: The Morality of the Mind", *The Critical Quaterly*, Vol. I (1959), p. 252.
37. "Two Kinds of Critics (a) F.R. Leavis", *Times Literary Supplement* (1967), p. 89.
38. Leavis, "Lawrence and Class", *D.H. Lawrence: Novelist,* p. 86.
39. *Ibid.*, "Poetry and the Modern World", *New Bearings in English Literature*, p. 17.
40. Rajnath, "The Critical Achievement of F.R. Leavis", *English Studies* (October 1982), p. 420.
41. R.P. Bilan, "Leavis's Revaluation of T.S. Eliot", *The Literary Criticism of F.R. Leavis*, p. 277.
42. Vincent Buckley, "F.R. Leavis: Reality and Sincerity", *Poetry and Morality*, p. 176.
43. Leavis, "Lawrence and Art", *D.H. Lawrence: Novelist* (1955; rpt. Harmondsworth: Pelican, 1973), p. 20.
44. *Ibid.*, "The Europeans", *Anna Karenina and Other Essays,* p. 59.
45. Kaufmann, "F.R. Leavis: The Morality of the Mind", *The Critical Quarterly*, I (1959).
46. Rajnath, "The Critical Achievement of F.R. Leavis", *English Studies* (October 1982), p. 423.

47. R.P. Bilan, "Basic Concepts of Novel Criticism", *The Literary Criticism of F.R. Leavis*, p. 117.
48. *Ibid.*
49. Leavis, "Anna Karenina", *Anna Karenina and Other Essays*, p. 13.
50. L.R. Sharma, "Murry's Theory of Literature", *In Defence of J. Middleton Murry*, pp. 112-22.
51. Leavis, "Anna Karenina", *Anna Karenina and Other Essays*, p. 15.
52. R.P. Bilan, "From Poetry Criticism to Novel", *The Literary Criticism of F.R. Leavis*, p. 94.
53. Vincent Buckley, "F.R. Leavis: Reality and Sincerity", *Poetry and Morality*, p. 169.
54. Leavis, "The Situation at the End of the First World War", *New Bearings in English Poetry*, p. 41.
55. F.R. Leavis, *The Living Principle* (London: Chatto and Windus, 1975), p. 205.
56. Edward Neill, "Give up Literary Criticism: F.R. Leavis—The Last Phase", *English* (Spring, 1984), p. 27.
57. Leavis, "The Line of Wit", *Revaluation*, p. 36.
58. *Ibid.*, "Wordsworth", *Revaluation*, p. 163.
59. *Ibid.*, "Anna Karenina", *Anna Karenina and Other Essays*, p. 11.
60. Vincent Buckley, "F.R. Leavis: Reality and Sincerity", *Poetry and Morality*, p. 160.
61. Leavis, "Keats", *Revaluation*, pp. 225-28.
62. William Walsh, "Critical Directions", *F.R. Leavis*, p. 64.
63. L.R. Sharma, "Murry's Influence on Leavis", *In Defence of J. Middleton Murry*, pp. 144-45.
64. R.P. Bilan, "From Poetry Criticism to Novel", *The Literary Criticism of F.R. Leavis*, p. 95.
65. Leavis, "Anna Karenina", *Anna Karenina and Other Essays*, p. 24.
66. *Ibid.*, "The Europeans", *Anna Karenina and Other Essays*, p. 62.
67. *Ibid.*, p. 63.
68. *Ibid.*, *Nor Shall My Sword*, p. 56.

69. *Ibid.*, *Dickens*, p. 275.
70. Rene Wellek, "F.R. Leavis and the Scrutiny Group", *A History of Modern Criticism*, Vol. V, p. 261.
71. R.P. Bilan, "D.H. Lawrence: The Grounds of Praise I", *The Literary Criticism of F.R. Leavis*, p. 222.
72. Leavis, "Anna Karenina", *Anna Karenina and Other Essays*, p. 24.
73. *Ibid.*, "Lawrence and Tradition", *D.H. Lawrence: Novelist*, p. 121.
74. *Ibid.*, "Literature and Society", *The Common Pursuit*, p. 185.
75. R.P. Bilan, "D.H. Lawrence: The Grounds of Praise II", *The Literary Criticism of F.R. Leavis*, p. 238.
76. Vincent Buckley, *Poetry and Morality: Studies on the Works of Matthew Arnold, T.S. Eliot, F.R. Leavis*, p. 209.
77. Rene Wellek, *A History of Modern Criticism: 1750-1950*, p. 252.
78. Leavis, "James as Critic", Introduction to Henry James's, *Selected Literary Criticism*, ed. Morris Shapira (London: Heinemann, 1963), p. xviii.
79. Edward Neill, "'Give up Literary Criticism': F.R. Leavis—The Last Phase", *English* (Spring, 1984), p. 27.
80. *Ibid.*, pp. 27-28.
81. R.P. Bilan, "Basic Concepts of Leavis's Novel Criticism", *The Literary Criticism of F.R. Leavis*, p. 133.
82. William Walsh, "Critical Directions", *F.R. Leavis*, p. 60.
83. R.P. Bilan, "Judgements and Criteria", *The Literary Criticism of F.R. Leavis*, p. 151.
84. William Walsh, "Critical Directions", *F.R. Leavis*, p. 59.
85. R.P. Bilan, "Basic Concepts of Leavis's Novel Criticism", *The Criticism of F.R. Leavis*, p. 140.
86. Leavis, "Adam Bede", *Anna Karenina and Other Essays*, p. 49.
87. John Gross, *The Rise and Fall of the Man of Letters* (London: Weidenfeld and Nicolson, 1969), p. 278.
88. F.R. Leavis, "'Scrutiny': A Retrospect", *Scrutiny*, 20 (1963), p. 5.
89. Leavis, "Literature and the University: The Wrong Question", *Literature in Our Time and The University*, p. 60.

90. Raymond Williams, "Our Debt to Dr Leavis", *The Critical Quarterly*, I (1959), p. 250.
91. R.J. Kaufmann, "F.R. Leavis: The Morality of Mind", *The Critical Quarterly*, I (1959), pp. 2-48.
92. Leavis, "This Age in Literary Criticism", *The Bookman* (October 1932), p. 9.
93. *Ibid., Education and the University* (1943; rpt. London: Chatto and Windus, 1965), p. 55.
94. F.R. Leavis, "A Selection From Scrutiny", Vol. II (Cambridge: Cambridge University Press, 1968), pp. 280-307.
95. Leavis, "Criticism and Literary History", *Scrutiny*, 4 (1935-36), p. 96.
96. *Ibid.*, "This Age in Literary Criticism", *The Bookman* (October 1932), p. 9.
97. S. Krishnamoorthy Aithal, "How Leavis Views a Literary Work and its Interpretation", *Critical Essays: A Presentation Volume for Prof. V.S. Seturaman* (Madras: Macmillan, 1987), p. 71.
98. R.J. Kaufmann, "F.R. Leavis: The Morality of Mind", *The Critical Quarterly*, I (1959), p. 249.
99. F.R. Leavis, *Education and the University*, p. 120.
100. Frank Whitehead, *The Leavises: Recollections and Impressions*, ed. Denys Thompson (Cambridge: Cambridge University Press, 1984), p. 151.
101. Ronald Hayman, "Introduction", *Leavis* (London: Heinemann, 1976), pp. x-xi.
102. George Steiner, "F.R. Leavis", *Twentieth Century Literary Criticism,* ed. David Lodge (London: Longman, 1972), p. 622.
103. S. Krishnamoorthy Aithal, "How Leavis Veiws a Literary Work and its Interpretation", *Critical Essays: A Presentation Volume for Prof. V.S. Seturaman,* ed. *S. Vishwanathan*, C.T. Indra and T. Sriraman (Madras: Macmillan, 1987), p. 73.
104. Thomas L. Jeffers, "Review of the Leavises: Recollections and Impressions", *Western Humanities Review* (Spring, 1986), p. 85.
105. Rajnath, "F.R. Leavis: A Revaluation", *Essays in Criticism*, pp. 161-62.
106. Leavis, *Nor Shall My Sword*, p. 112.

107. Vincent Buckley, "F.R. Leavis: Reality and Sincerity", *Poetry and Morality*, p. 158.
108. I.D. MacKillop, "F.R. Leavis: A Peculiar Relationship", *Essays in Criticism* (July 1984), p. 186.
109. Francis Mulnern, *The Moment of 'Scrutiny'* (London: NLB, 1979), p. 169.
110. I.D. MacKillop, "F.R. Leavis: A Peculiar Relationship", *Essays in Criticism* (July 1984), p. 187.
111. Vincent Buckley, "F.R. Leavis: Reality and Sincerity", *Poetry and Morality*, p. 158.
112. Martin Jarrett-Kerr, "The Literary Criticism of F.R. Leavis", *Essays in Criticism* (October 1952), p. 354.
113. "Mr. Eliot and Milton", *The Common Pursuit*, p. 16.
114. Leavis, *Education and the University*, p. 71.
115. Allun Jones, "F.R. Leavis and After", *The Critical Quarterly*, Vol. I (1959), p. 254.
116. *Ibid.*, p. 255.
117. Edward Neill, "'Give Up Literary Criticism': F.R. Leavis—The Last Phase", *English* (Spring, 1984), p. 30.
118. *Ibid.*, pp. 24-25.
119. F.W. Bateson, "The 'Scrutiny' Phenomenon", *Sewanee Review*, LXXXV (1977), p. 148.
120. Leavis, "The Responsible Critic", *A Selection from Scrutiny*, Vol. II, p. 293.
121. Edward Neill, "'Give Up Literary Criticism': F.R. Leavis—The Last Phase", *English* (Spring, 1984), p. 24.
122. Francis Mulhern, *The Moment of 'Scrutiny'*, pp. 70-74.
123. *Ibid.*, p. 89.
124. *Ibid.*, p. 71.
125. *Ibid.*, p. 318.
126. *Ibid.*
127. Graham Hough, "Criticism as a Humanist Discipline". *Contemporary Criticism*, eds. Malcolm Bradbury and David Palmer (1970; rpt. London: Edward Arnold, 1979), p. 47.
128. Lionel Trilling, "Dr. Leavis and the Moral Tradition", *A Gathering of Fugitives*, p. 109.

129. Graham Hough, "Criticism as a Humanist Discipline", *Contemporary Criticism*, p. 47.

130. F.W. Bateson, "The 'Scrutiny' Phenomenon", *Sewanee Review*, LXXXV (1977), p. 145.

5

The Critic as Moralist: Matthew Arnold, J. Middleton Murry and F.R. Leavis

Literature, if it is to have a positive value for the future, must have a definite function. This function must be distinct from the functions of all other disciplines. One of the chief functions is to reveal the relation between the individual and his surroundings. The relation between man and men, between him and the animals and flowers; between him and the dough he kneads and the soil he tills, between him and the stars, the forest the rivers; and between him and his machines and buildings; is for that moment the truth in the human consciousness. This truth is to be conveyed by the man of letters. The truth is to be garbed in the beauty of the work of literature—its form. Literature ought not to become propoganda but it should be what Arnold describes as the "criticism of life", it should indicate the truth of the moment. In this we see that the great value of literature is different from religion, philosophy and science. All of them endeavour to nail things down. Religion attempts to nail down its theistic dogma; philosophy to nail down fixed ideas and science to nail down its laws.[1] Literature if it nails down anything it is the ephemeral and everchanging moment. The less experimental forms of literature focus on large chunks of time and life. But in the moment or in "the slice of life" there are some universal features which have stuck inspite of life's changing nature. Literature captures this permanence in change.

This study makes an attempt to bring together the ideas and principles of some of the significant literary critics who have valued this distinctive role of literature. Moralistic criticism has always drawn the best minds, but in the latter half of the twentieth century it acquired a very positive role. Arnold, Murry and Leavis have been responsible for giving a new life to this approach of criticism. They have, as it were, made new openings which future critics could use or benefit from.

Till recently critics were of the opinion that Arnold, Eliot and Leavis formed a tradition in moralistic criticism. Michael Thorpe's presumption represents the widely approved view:

> Arnold's criticism is not systematic..."criticism of life", "highseriousness", "seriousness", "philistine", "provincial"... Arnold left it there: it has been the work of twentieth century critics to attempt a detailed demonstration of this.... Arnold's most influential successors here being, in their various ways T.S. Eliot, I.A. Richards, F.R. Leavis, Yvor Winters and Cleanth Brooks.[2]

Vincent Buckley's book *Poetry and Morality: Studies on the Criticism of Matthew Arnold, T.S. Eliot and F.R. Leavis* searches into their works but fails to give a sufficient explanation of the link between Arnold, Eliot, and Leavis. A close study reveals more disparities than similarities between the views of Eliot on the one hand and Arnold and Leavis on the other. I do not entirely negate Eliot's influence on Leavis, but to accept it as absolute would do injustice to Middleton Murry who I believe promoted the moralistic trend in criticism in the spirit of Matthew Arnold and left an indelible and vital impression on Leavis's approach to literature. When Buckley wrote his book it was too early to give a verdict on the ideology of Leavis as a large portion of his works had still to reach the stands. Buckley does not explain the shift in Leavis's later writings from Eliot to Lawrence. He simply avoids probing in those lines and writes:

> *D.H. Lawrence: Novelist* was published recently enough to put any account of it in danger of becoming a belated book-review. The danger is all the greater since it is so packed with matter relevant to my present interest, it so obviously endorses the chief values which Leavis detects in Lawrence, and it accordingly offers much invitation to debate.[3]

Instead of accepting Leavis's views on Eliot and Lawrence, he says that such statements should be deplored. Bilan believes rightly that whatever influence Eliot had on Leavis lies on his criticism of poetry, whereas importance of Leavis lies in his criticism of novel.[4] Sharron Greer Cassavant, who has studied Murry extensively writes aptly that Murry forms a link between Matthew Arnold and F.R. Leavis. The reasons behind this statement are not far to seek. But the fact remains that Leavis was influenced both by Eliot and Murry. As Steiner says, "Leavis' reorientation of critical focus...is rooted in the change of sensibility occurring in the 1920s and the early '30s" (*Encounter,* 18, 40). Both Eliot and Murry were critics who became eminent after the First World War, around 1920. Both were influenced by their predecessor Arnold; as a result they did have some similarities. They considered the twentieth century machine civilization to be a decayed culture threatening all human values. Both believed that the organic, integrated society was grounded in the peasant culture of medieval Christianity, where life was naturally tied to the soil and where class hierarchies protected man's spiritual relation to nature.

Between 1920 and 1930—the years which witnessed his rising popularity—Murry rose to the position of an established critic. But while in the years to come Eliot achieved universal acclaim, it was as if Murry's genius was nipped in the bud. It was largely due to his adverse relationship with the major critics of his time[5]—his misfortune that his works were first criticized by his adversaries—that he was reduced to a voice in the wilderness and he soon became the best hated man in the country. This was the chief reason that led to Murry's distorted image, which he certainly did not deserve. It took decades to wipe out the dust over his name and now critics have started changing their opinion about Murry.

Leavis, in the early years, appraised Eliot but as his criticism matured and as his ideology unfolded, his deep-rooted aversion came to light. In *New Bearings in English Poetry* Leavis placed Eliot at the apex of poetic tradition and praised him for his, intelligence, originality and his ability to represent his age in his poetry. The change in his attitude is apparent in *D.H. Lawrence: Novelist*. For the next twenty years Leavis' original acclaim for Eliot was replaced by a dissenting appraisal. This change in his attitude is one of the major developments of his later works. Leavis could never reconcile with Eliot's negative approach to life, his rejection of emotion and his dissociation of life and art. Rene Wellek remarks rightly that Leavis "...repudiated the so-called 'classicism' of his Eliotic youth and shifted to a new Romanticism".[6] Leavis, thus, voiced Murry's opinion in the decade long debate that went on between Murry land Eliot in which Murry spoke for Romanticism and Eliot for Classicism.

In the pages that follow I shall delineate the reasons of placing Arnold, Murry, and Leavis in the same tradition. The chapters on these critics have made clear that their meaning of morality is similar and that it can be attained in literature when art and life are inseparable. The function of criticism, according to them, too is humanistic.

Arnold, Murry, and Leavis have been involved with the cultural question. They aimed at establishing a "human culture". According to Raymond Williams, "The process which Arnold began, when he virtually equated 'culture' with 'criticism', is completed by Leavis."[7] Both firmly believed that culture was the end which criticism had to serve. Murry, too, was so deeply involved in the cultural question that he wrote:

> I have a feeling that I have been completely outside the mainstream of literature.[8]

Murry's literary criticism was devoted to humanity to such an extent that it looked close to social criticism. His desire to understand the artist's soul, his concern with political situation and with poets and prose writers whose effort was to make man more aware; and his writing works for the layman, all show his inexhaustible urge to work for "a human culture". It has been rightly said about his works that they,

> ...helped to articulate the consciousness of the age and to suggest paths for future literary and cultural development.[9]

F.A. Lea, too, considers *Heaven—and Earth* as a work which gives a general sense of cultural tradition of England.

R.P. Bilan considers Leavis to be the heir of Arnold precisely because both believed that there was a human culture to be aimed at.[10] In his last phase Leavis's criticism merged indistinguishably with social criticism, but it maintained its identity as literary criticism. If this is the criteria then Murry, too, is in the same line with Arnold and Leavis.

Murry has been accused for his "narrow nationalism", while Leavis is blamed for his "provinciality".[11] Both gave similar explanation—they believed that one's own cultural tradition should be first fully explored, only then is it possible to understand other cultures. But both, like Arnold, had regard for Greek, Latin, Russian and French literature.

Certain words like, "minority" and "tradition" in Leavis' works create a misapprehension that he is quite different, from Murry as we do not find these mentioned in Murry's works. It gives an impression of a direct lineage to Arnold and Eliot. Leavis' concept of minority differs from that of Arnold. For Arnold, minority is that part of every social class which escapes the limitations of habitual class feeling. Whereas for Leavis, minority is a "literary minority" which helps in cultural continuity. "Tradition" which has been picked up from the vocabulary of Eliot, has a different meaning for Leavis. For Eliot, tradition is a way of feeling or acting which characterizes a group throughout generations and it must largely be unconscious. Thus for him orthodoxy is a way of preserving tradition. Unlike Leavis, Eliot is a traditionalist. Leavis does not have this conservative dedication to permanence. Change is acceptable to him.

He insists on the need of understanding the idea of a living and changing tradition.[12] Probably because he understood the existing inappropriateness of the term, he later replaced it with "cultural continuity".

Arnold, Murry and Leavis's views on the process of growth of culture show a movement in the same direction. Arnold believed that culture could be strengthened by a reconstruction of society, and therefore he insisted on the transformation of philistinians for they could not be reformed.[13] Murry began with this in mind. To bring about reformation of society through literature and criticism was his aim.[14] His works are for the common men and aim at bringing about a definite change. Leavis, as has been mentioned above, believes that there should be a corresponding change in society with the time. For this he realized that a cultural continuity was needed.

Arnold, Murry and Leavis have been involved with the question of morality and their meaning of morality revolves around "life". For Arnold the very question "how to live" is a moral question. There should be a profound application of ideas to life if morality is to be achieved in literature.[15] Murry believes that a desire to "discern and to communicate" the truth about life is a moral intention. Morality in literature demands a faithful contemplation of human life. Avoidance of morality only makes a work uninteresting. Leavis desires a work of literature not only to represent life but to affirm it. Without affirmation of life a work of art does not have the desired effect on men and thus fails to serve the moral end. Literature is "...a servant of a profoundly serious interest in life—a moral tradition" (*GT*, 32). Great novels, he says, express an intense devotion to the pursuit of Truth. Eliot's "standing off from life", is what made Leavis move away from him. In Eliot's own words, "...an abstraction of life is a necessary condition to the creation of a work of art."[16] Therefore, life which makes a work of art moral has, unlike Arnold, Murry and Leavis, little meaning for Eliot.

Arnold, Murry and Leavis believe in the conscious involvement of creative works for the restoration of culture. Eliot, on the other hand disapproves of conscious involvement.

According to Arnold, poetry is a criticism of life and it has to make inert calm and tranquil (*CPW* III, 24). Besides, he has prescribed measures to the creative writers, like having poetic models, seriousness, criticism of life, so that their worlds can serve higher destinies. For Murry, it is the responsibility of the creative writer to communicate the truth about life to men, make them understand the facts of life like, "Beauty is truth, truth beauty."[17] Leavis has entrusted to the creative writer the entire work of establishing the cultural continuity. He believes that literature alone can do it. It is, therefore, essential for the creative writer to affirm life. As opposed to this, Eliot believes:

> I do not deny that art may be affirmed to serve ends beyond itself; but art is not required to be aware of these ends, and indeed performs to function whatever may be, according to various theories of value, much better by indifference to them.[18]

Arnold suggests that there should be poetic models before the modern writers so that their works are integrated. Shakespeare, according to him, is the right model as in him there is a "wholeness", hardly perceptible in modern age (*CPW* I, 9). Arnold has included him in his touchstone method. Murry and Leavis accept him as their ideal. Murry finds in his works a complete fusion of thought and emotion, art and life, such that communication is easily possible.[19] Leavis clearly states that in Jane Austen, Dickens, Hawthorne, Melville, George Eliot, Henry James, Conrad and D.H. Lawrence we have successors of Shakespeare. Comparison to Shakespeare was almost the highest praise that he could bestow on a writer. Murry and Leavis have presented the literary world with models other than Shakespeare. The very concept of great tradition is proof enough that he believed in setting models for the creative writers.

Arnold, Murry and Leavis firmly believe that form and content together make a creative work great. For Arnold:

> Truth and seriousness of subject and matter, falicity and perfection of diction and manner, as these are exhibited in the best poets.... (*Essays in Criticism* II, 110)

Murry, shares his views in this with Arnold for he says that content can be communicated with the help of form. Style is perfect when it is in accordance with the thought-content. It helps them to communicate precisely the emotion or thought. Leavis agrees with Arnold and Murry. The formal cannot be separated from moral, nor can art be dissociated from life. He finds Tolstoy to be a master of this. In the writers of the great tradition, too, this aspect is applauded. Eliot, as has been stated earlier, disapproved of this. He, as Leavis says, stands away from life:

> One may not have thought of comparing Eliot's creative work to Flaubert's, but Eliot's attitude to life is, not less than Flaubert's one of distaste and disgust.[20]

According to Arnold, Murry and Leavis, seriousness is essential for any work of art to be great. Seriousness of content must couple with seriousness of form to make a work of art effective. For Arnold, a work is capable of "higher uses" only if it is serious as it can only then interpret life. Murry, writing about seriousness says:

> Matthew Arnold set the fashion originally, and he picked it up from Aristotle.[21]

Seriousness in a work of art shows that it is moral, and that the writer is seriously communicating the "profoundest truth" that he feels about human life. For Leavis, interest in humanity implies seriousness. He, like Murry, criticizes Flaubert for his excessive concern with form and a resultant lack in seriousness. Arnold, Murry and Leavis regard comedy as serious as tragedy. Arnold does not demand humourless seriousness. Writing about Sophocles he says that Sophocles achieved "serious cheerfulness". When tragedy or comedy draws its strength from life, it is serious. Murry says that since both tragedy and comedy have the potential to illuminate, both can have high seriousness. Leavis affords seriousness to all the writers of the great tradition. He does not differentiate between tragedy and comedy. T.S. Eliot does not accept this for he regards George Eliot a more serious writer than Dickens because she wrote about tragic situation and Dickens' works were comical. That they differ from Eliot's view of seriousness is obvious here.

Communication of emotion, thought or values of life is one of the chief functions of literature. Arnold, Murry and Leavis accept this. The grand interpretative power that Arnold associates with poetry is the, ability of poetry to communicate effectively to men such values that can sustain and delight man (*CPW* IIII, 22). Murry in all his works gives immense importance to communication. The more complete the communication the greater is the artist. Leavis says that art to enact its moral significance has to communicate an attitude (*GT*, 48). Communication from the poet to the reader matters to them because they consider creative writers more aware and noble than the ordinary men. Arnold believes that poets have moral qualities which can be communicated through the style. Murry finds poets distinguished men as they are conscious of the all pervading beauty, he has full control over his emotions, and presents them in such a way that his own sorrows and joys remain aloof. He can truly perceive beauty in truth. Leavis finds poets more conscious of the changing times, they can understand human behaviour and can communicate an attitute for "...his capacity for experiencing and his power of communicating, are indistinguishable."[22] For Eliot on the other hand, literature is a communion rather than a communication. But just in case it is, it is the poem that is to be communicated and only incidently the experience and the thought that has gone into it.[23] Thus he is nowhere near Arnold, Murry and Leavis even in this aspect.

Since poetry is an ideal means of communication, according, to Arnold, Murry and Leavis, it can take the place of religion. Poetry can convey noble ideas more completely than religious works. Arnold first presented the idea of poetry replacing religion.[24] It has been adopted by Murry. The introductory chapter of *Keats and Shakespeare* reveals that poetry for him was religion that had taken the place of religion "petrified by its own formalisms"[25] Leavis regards literature religious because it conveys positive values to men. It is, therefore essential that it should affirm life.[26] Eliot is of the view that poetry "...is not the inculcation of morals,... and no more is it religious, except by some monstrous abuse of words."[27] The question of need for poetry does not bother Eliot. So he is not close to Arnold, Murry and Leavis. Buckley pointing out this difference, states:

> Whatever moral quality poetry possesses then, is intimately connected in Eliot's approach with the question of order. His investigation into this question is conducted sometimes by deducing knowledge of a process from the criticism of a wide range of poems. His approach in this is very different from Arnold, who tends to trace a relatively clear line from the quality of a poem, as utterance to the state of soul of its author, and back again.[28]

A reading of *Keats and Shakespeare*, or *Blake*, or *Aspects of Literature* shows Murry's endeavour to get to the very soul of his authors.

Leavis's view of art differs from Murry's. This is evident in the Lawrence issue which invited much interest from Murry Leavis and Eliot. Murry and Leavis both find Eliot and Lawreance antithetical to each other. Rejecting Eliot for his approach to life they chose Lawrence for his positive approach to life while Murry considered him a "prophet".[29] Leavis, too, regarded him as the greatest writer of all times. Eliot on the other hand, regards him as "a false prophet".[30] There did exist some misunderstanding in Leavis' mind regarding Murry's views on Lawrence. Murry did not regard Lawrence as an artist while, Leavis did. Art is not a positive quality for Murry for he considers it opposed to life. Art, undoubtedly, is closely related to morality, to life. A work is great only when both are inseparable. But by artists he means those writers who are not concerned with life. For him Flaubert and Milton are great artists. Leavis's stand is that a great artist is one who can create a work in which art and life are inseparable.[31] Leavis, too, disapproves of Milton and Flaubert for their lack of interest in life. They are not great artists in his sense of the term. Both appreciate Lawrence for the, same qualities but unknowingly.

Arnold, Murry and Leavis lay emphasis on emotion in poetry. For Arnold, poetry is moral ideas touched with beauty heightened by emotion (*CPW* XI, 48). As has already been mentioned, Murry believes that poetry is rooted in emotion, and it grows by mastery of emotion. Leavis, too, is concerned intensely with emotions, and believes that the artist's emotional life should be impersonalized. Buckley, explaining this, says that Leavis has dual meaning of the word impersonality. One that it is universalized and the other,

> ...we may call a general line of living, a servant of the poets' "essential interests", which are basically moral.[32]

Impersonality is supported by each of the three critics in question. Arnold's concept of disinterestedness, Murry's ardent praise of Keats's negative capability and Leavis' acceptance of Eliot's term "The Common Pursuit" are all evidence of the fact that the three did not favour a merely personal response. For Arnold emotions are not employed to serve the writer in any way but are a means to serve humanity. So they ought to be presented in a disinterested way. As has been earlier discussed, the term disinterestedness means that the writer's personal anxieties—joys, problems, unhappiness—should not interfere with the communication process. This term has been used by Arnold while defining criticism, nevertheless, its meaning is close to the concept of negative capability. At times Arnold also uses another term to express impersonality—self-control. About Keats he states:

> Character and self-control, the "virtus versque labor" so necessary for every kind of greatness, and for the great artist, too, indispensable....[33]

Arnold gives examples of those works like the letters of Keats to Fanny Browne that are wanting in self-control. They have the personal element to a great extent. But the best works of Keats, he says, have self-control. Arnold desires that the emotions should be universalized (*CPW* I, 2). The human actions chosen to be represented in poetry must appeal to the primary human affections; those elementary feelings which subsist permanently in the race and which are independent of time. Murry who is often mistakenly considered to be just a romantic, impressionistic critic, made it amply clear in his *The Problem of Style*, that the best writer was one who could blend the personal with the impersonal (*PS*, 32). In *Aspects of Literature*, he says in praise of Hardy, that Hardy's reaction to an episode had within and behind it his reaction to the universe.[34] These three critics did not support the rather impractical method suggested by Eliot in his "Tradition and the Individual Talent", where Eliot says that the poet ought to escape from his personality. Arnold, Murry and Leavis stood for a blending of the personal and the impersonal. Leavis's view is clearly stated in his discussion of Keats' impersonality.

> The immediately personal urgency of the preoccupation with suffering and death comes out plainly in the passage describing his nightmare race against the burning of "gummed leaves" but this personal urgency is completely impersonalized; it has become the life, the informing spirit of the profoundest kind of impersonality. There is no element of self-pity.[35]

Leavis's views on impersonality seem to be derived from Murry. Leavis believes that the artist cannot write in vacuum. There exists a relationship between the artist and his work. They both believe that the greater the artist the greater is his power of experiencing and of observing. Murry clearly says the greater the man is, the more completely is an event merged in his inward reaction to the event (*PS*, 32). Leavis, too, repeatedly expresses a similar belief. Writing about the distinctive qualities of poet, he remarks:

> He is a poet because his interest in his experience is not separable from his interest in words. (*New Bearings*, 17)

Comparing George Eliot and Conrad, Leavis says that George Eliot presented her own problems while Conrad presented his problems "out of impersonalized whole" (*GT*, 25). Therefore, at times he is greater. There is an emotional quality associated with George Eliot's works, he says. Her best works are impersonalized. Leavis insists that there is an emotional quality in an intellectual writer. Eliot, as opposed to this, shunned emotions at all levels. Leavis's objection to Eliot's view is given in his essay "T.S. Eliot as Critic", Eliot's view, he says, is a "wholly arbitrary dictum". He does not agree with Eliot that the more perfect the artist, the more separate in him will be the man who suffers and the mind that creates.[36] He says that a poem derives its "creative impulsion" from life and without full recognition of life there can be no intellectual appreciation of the artistic process or of art. Even while criticising a work, the life of the artist should not be dissociated from the work because in it lies the root of his art. Leavis believes that it is impossible to separate the artist and the man:

> ..."separate", for such a use is not a possible word, whether one thinks of Tolstoy or Lawrence...or Shakespeare—or George Eliot or Mark Twain. But when we recognize that the artist we implicitly propose is Flaubert then the proposition becomes intelligible, if not acceptible.[37]

The role of criticism in the creation of works of art, according to Arnold, Murry and Leavis is similar. They regard it as vital for the right understanding of literature for the recognition of truly great writers and for inculcation of fresh ideas. They believe that a critic should judge the works with some prescribed values in mind. Arnold's three estimates, and his touchstone method indicate this (*EC* II, 10). Murry's view is that the system of value judgement is essential to give direction to criticism and art.[38] Leavis practices this in his criticism and as a result he traces the great tradition. The writers that he incorporates in it have the prescribed values like seriousness, representative quality, unity of art and life, and affirmation of life. It is due to value judgement that work of these moralists has resulted in a reassessment and revaluation of literature. An example of Arnold's efforts has been the rising reputation of Wordsworth and Keats and the relative worth of Jane Austen, George Eliot, Henry James, Joseph Conrad and D.H. Lawrence. The reputations of Charles Dickens[39] and Thomas Hardy have suffered due to him. Today we are conscious of certain shortcomings in the works of these novelists.

According to Arnold, criticism is:

> ...a disinterested endeavour to learn and propagate the best that is known and thought in the world, and thus to establish a current of fresh and true ideas.[40]

In line with Arnold, Murry says that criticism should promote certain values of life[41] and that a critic should avoid, "momentary enthusiasm and passing disgusts".[42] Leavis proceeding in the same direction agrees with the establishment of values and even suggests collaborative criticism as a means to establish it.[43] He says that a critic's judgement may not be absolutely correct. Collaborative criticism is corrective besides being creative. This conception of criticism is truly humanistic.

By now it should be amply clear that Arnold, Murry and Leavis belong to a tradition of modern English criticism. It should seem fairly reasonable to conclude that Vincent Buckley's theory that the moralistic tradition includes Arnold, Eliot and Leavis is mistaken. It would not be an exaggeration to suggest that the three critics of this thesis comprise a group that is distinct from other groups or schools of literary criticism. They stand by certain values which will remain till man finds literature valuable and literary criticism remains a meaningful activity.

NOTES

1. D.H. Lawrence, "Morality and the Novel", *Selected Literary Criticism,* ed. Anthony Beal (London: William Hienemann, 1955), pp. 108-13.
2. Michael Thorpe, "Arnold's Critical Influence", *Matthew Arnold* (London: Evans, 1969), pp. 118-19.
3. V. Buckley, "F.R. Leavis: Impersonality and Values", *Poetry and Morality*, p. 205.
4. Cassavant, "Katherine Mansfield and the Antipodes", *John Middleton Murry*, p. 101.
5. L.R. Sharma, "Everything and Nothing", *In Defence of J. Middleton Murry*, p. 11.
6. Rene Wellek, "Review of William Walsh's book F.R. Leavis", *Modern Language Review*, 77 (1932), p. 712.

7. Raymond Williams, "Two Literary Critics", *Culture and Society: 1780-1950*, p. 248.
8. R.J. Kaufmann, "On Using an Obsessed Critic: John Middleton Murry", *Graduate Student of English*, 3 (Winter, 1960), p. 6.
9. E.G. Griffin, "Murry, Eliot and Style", *John Middleton Murry*, p. 42.
10. R.P. Bilan, "Language Literature and Continuity", *The Literary Criticism of F.R. Leavis*, p. 26.
11. E.G. Griffin, "The Englishness of Murry", *John Middleton Murry*, p. 99.
12. Leavis, "Towards Standards of Criticism", *Anna Karenina and Other Essays*, p. 223.
13. Arnold, "Letter dated November 14, 1863", *Letters to Clough* ed. Lowry, p. 240, *Culture and Anarchy*.
14. Kaufmann, "On Using an Obssessed Critic", *The Graduate Student of English*, 3 (Winter, 1960), p. 6.
15. Arnold, "Wordsworth", *Essays in Criticism,* II, ed. S.R. Littlewood, pp. 84-85.
16. Eliot, *Selected Essays*, p. 111.
17. Matthew Arnold, "Maurice de Guerin", *The Complete Prose Works of Matthew Arnold*, Vol. III, ed. R.H. Super, p. 24.
18. T.S. Eliot, "The Function of Criticism", *Selected Essays*, p. 24.
19. Murry, "The Nature of Poetry", *Discoveries*, p. 22.
20. Leavis, *D.H. Lawrence: Novelist*, p. 25.
21. Richard Rees, ed., "Seriousness", *John Middleton Murry: Selected Criticism 1916-1957*, p. 59.
22. Leavis, "Poetry and the Modern World", *New Bearings in English Poetry*, p. 16.
23. T.S. Eliot, *The Sacred Wood*, p. 30.
24. Matthew Arnold, "The Study of Poetry", *Essays in Criticism,* II, p. 1.
25. Murry, "Introduction", *Keats and Shakespeare,* pp. 1, 3.
26. Leavis, *Nor Shall My Sword*, pp. 56, 81 and "The Pilgrim's Progress", *Anna Karenina and Other Essays*, pp. 44-48.
27. T.S. Eliot, "Introduction", *The Sacred Wood*, p. IX.
28. Buckley, *Poetry and Morality*, p. 101.

29. Murry, *Reminiscences of D.H. Lawrence*, pp. 266-67.
30. Eliot, *Criterion*, 10 (1930-31), p. 769.
31. Murry, "Flaubert and Flaubart", *Discoveries*, p. 297, and Murry, "Dickens", *Pencillings*, p. 41.
32. Vincent Buckley, "T.S. Eliot: The Question of Orthodoxy", *Poetry and Morality*, p. 147.
33. Arnold, "Keats", *Essays in Criticism*, II, ed. S.R. Littlewood, p. 60.
34. Murry, "The Poetry of Mr. Hardy", *Aspects of Literature*, p. 144.
35. Leavis, "Keats", *Revaluation*, p. 144.
36. *Ibid.*, *Anna Karenina and Other Essays*, p. 180.
37. *Ibid.*, pp. 180-81.
38. Murry, "The Function of Criticism", *Selected Criticism: 1916-1957*, ed. Richard Rees, p. 4.
39. Though Leavis wrote an entire work on Dickens in 1971 but till then his statements about him in *The Great Tradition* (1948) had been widely read and accepted. Bilan says that he could never give sufficient explanation of Dicken's inaccuracies (R.P. Bilan, "Judgement and Criteria", *The Literary Criticism of F.R. Leavis*, pp. 161-62).
40. Arnold, "Function of Criticism in the Present Times", *The Complete Prose Works of Matthew Arnold*, Vol. III, p. 283.
41. Murry, "A Critical Credo", *Countries of the Mind*, First Series, pp. 183-84.
42. *Ibid.*, p. 183.
43. Vincent Buckley, "F.R. Leavis: Reality and Sincerity", *Poetry and Morality*, p. 158.

Bibliography

MATTHEW ARNOLD

Primary Sources

The Complete Prose Works of Matthew Arnold. Vols. Ed. R.H. Super. Ann Arbor: University of Michigan Press, 1962-1977.

The Note-Books of Matthew Arnold. Ed. H.F. Lowry, Karl Young and W.H. Dunn. London: Oxford University Press, 1952.

Letters of Matthew Arnold: 1848-1888. 2 Vols. Ed. G.W. Russell. London: Macmillan, 1895.

Unpublished Letters. Ed. Arnold Whitridge. New Haven: Yale University Press, 1923.

Letters of Matthew Arnold to Arthur Hugh Clough. Ed. H.F. Lowry. London: Oxford University Press, 1932.

The Poems of Matthew Arnold. Kenneth Allott. New York: Oxford University Press, 1965.

Poetical Works of Matthew Arnold. Ed. C.B. Tinker and H.F. Lowry. New York: Oxford University Press, 1950.

JOHN MIDDLETON MURRY

Primary Sources

Fyodor Dostoevsky: A Critical Study. London: Seeker, 1916.

Still Life. London: Constable, 1916.

Poems: 1917-1918. Hampstead, England: Heron Press, 1918.

The Critic in Judgment. Richmond: Hogarth, 1919.

The Evolution of an Intellectual. London: Cobden-Sanderson; New York: Knopf, 1920. 2nd ed. London: Jonathan Cape, 1927.

Aspects of Literature. London: Collins; New York: Knopf, 1920. 2nd ed. London: Jonathan Cape, 1934.

Cinnamon and Angelica. London: Cobden-Sanderson, 1920. 2nd ed. London: Dakers, 1941.

Poems: 1916-1920. London: Cobden-Sanderson, 1921.

The Problem of Style. London: Oxford University Press, 1922. Oxford Paperbacks ed., 1960.

Countries of the Mind. London: Collins; New York: Dutton, 1922. New ed. rev. and enlarged, London: Oxford University Press, 1931.

The Things We Are. London: Constable, 1922. New York: Dutton, 1930.

Pencillings. London: Collins, 1923. New York: Seltzer, 1925.

The Voyage. London: Constable, 1924.

To the Unknown God. London: Jonathan Cape, 1924.

Discoveries. London: Collins, 1924. 2nd ed. London: Jonathan Cape, 1930.

Keats and Shakespeare. London: Oxford University Press, 1925.

The Life of Jesus. London: Jonathan Cape, 1926. American title: *Jesus, Man of Genius*. New York: Harper, 1926.

Things to Come. London: Jonathan Cape, 1928. New York: Macmillan, 1928.

God: An Introduction to the Science of Metabiology. London: Cape; New York: Harper, 1929.

Studies in Keats. London: Oxford University Press, 1930.

D.H. Lawrence: Two Essays. Cambridge: Minority Press, 1930.

Countries of the Mind: Second Series. London: Oxford University Press, 1931.

Son of Woman: The Story of D.H. Lawrence. London: Jonathan Cape, 1931. New York: Cape and Smith, 1931. *D.H. Lawrence: Son of Woman*, issued with a new intr. London: Jonathan Cape, 1954.

The Fallacy of Economics. London: Faber and Faber, 1932.

The Necessity of Communism. London: Jonathan Cape, 1932. New York: Seltzer, 1933.

The Wanderer. Larling: J.M. Murry, 12 Issues, Dec. 1933-Nov. 1934.

The Life of Katherine Mansfield (with R.E. Mantz). London: Constable, 1933.

Reminiscences of D.H. Lawrence. London: Jonathan Cape. 1933. New York: Holt, 1933.

William Blake. London: Jonathan Cape, 1933. New York: McGraw-Hill, 1964.

Between Two Worlds. London: Jonathan Cape, 1935.

The Autobiography of John Middleton Murry: Between Two Worlds, New York: Messner, 1936.

Shakespeare. London: Jonathan Cape, 1936. New York: Harcourt, Brace, 1936.

The Necessity of Pacifism. London: Jonathan Cape, 1937.

The Pledge of Peace. London: H. Joseph, 1938.

Heaven—and Earth. London: Jonathan Cape, 1938. American title: Heroes of Thought. New York: Messner, 1938.

Studies in Keats: New and Old. London: Oxford University Press, 1939.

The Defence of Leadership. London: S.C.M. Press, 1939. New York: Harper, 1939.

The Betrayal of Christ by the Churches. London: Dakers, 1940.

Europe in Travail. New York: Macmillan, 1940.

Christocracy. London: Dakers, 1942.

Adam and Eve. London: Dakers, 1944.

The Free Society. London: Dakers, 1948.

Looking Before and After. London: Sheppard Press, 1948.

The Challenge of Schweitzer. London: Jason Press, 1948.

Kaltherine Mansfield and Other Literary Portraits. London: Nevill, 1949.

The Mystery of Keats. London: Nevill, 1949.

John Clare and Other Studies. London: Nevill, 1950.

The Conquest of Death. London: Nevill, 1951.

Community Farm. London: Nevill, 1952.

Jonathan Swift. London: Jonathan Cape, 1954. New York: Noonday Press, 1955.

Swift. (Pamphlet published for the British Council and the National Book League). London: Longmans, Green, 1955.

Keats. 4th ed. rev. and enlarged. London: Jonathan Cape, 1955. New York: Noonday Press, 1955.

Unprofessional Essays. London: Jonathan Cape, 1956. Fair Lawn, N.J. Essential Books, 1956.

Love, Freedom and Society. London: Jonathan Cape, 1957.

Katherine Mansfield and Other Literary Studies. Foreword by T.S. Eliot. London: Constable, 1959. Chester Springs, Pa.: Dufour Editions, 1960.

Not as the Scribes. Ed. with intr. by Alec R. Vidlen. London: S.C.M. Press, 1959. New York: Horizon Press, 1959.

Selected Criticism. Chosen and intr. by Richard Rees. London: Oxford University Press, 1960.

Poets, Critics, Mystics: A Selection of Criticism, Written between 1919 and 1955 by John Middleton Murry, Sel. and intro. by Richard Rees. Carbondale: Southern Illinois University Press, 1970.

Uncollected Works

Several essays and reviews by Murry appear in various numbers of *The Aryan Path*, *The London Magazine*, *The Adelphi*, *The Criterion*, *The Athenaeum*, *Rhythm*, *Nation and Athenaeum*, *Literary Review*, *Essays in Criticism*, *Blue Review*, etc.

For a full listing of Murry's uncollected essays see George P. Lilley, *A Bibliography of John Middleton Murry*. Toronto: University of Toronto Press, 1975.

F.R. LEAVIS

Primary Sources

New Bearings in English Poetry. 1932; rpt. Harmondsworth: Penguine Books, 1979.

For Continuity. Cambridge: The Minority Press, 1933.

Leavis, F.R. and Thompson, Denys. *Culture and Environment*. 1933; rpt. London: Chatto and Windus, 1964.

Revaluation. 1936; rpt. Harmondsworth: Penguine Books, 1972.

Education And The University. 1943; rpt. London: Chatto and Windus, 1965.

The Great Tradition. 1948; rpt. Harmondsworth: Penguine Books, 1966.

The Common Pursuit. 1952; rpt. Harmondsworth: Penguine Books, 1966.

D.H. Lawrence: Novelist. 1955; rpt. Harmondsworth: Penguine Books, 1972.

Anna Karenina and other Essays. London: Chatto and Windus, 1967.

English Literature in Our Times and the University. London: Chatto and Windus, 1969.

Leavis, F.R. and Leavis, Q.D. *Lectures in America*. London: Chatto and Windus, 1969.

Dickens The Novelist. 1970; rpt. Harmondsworth: Penguine, 1972.

The Living Principle. London: Chatto and Windus, 1975.

Thought, Words and Creativity. London: Chatto and Windus, 1976.

A Selection from Scrutiny, 2 Vols. Cambridge: Cambridge University Press, 1968.

Valuation in Criticism and Other Essays. Ed. G. Singh. Cambridge: Cambridge University Press, 1986.

Uncollected Essays

"The Influence of Donne in Modern Poetry." *The Bookman*, LXXIX (March 1931) pp. 346-47.

"This Age in Literary Criticism." *The Bookman*, LXXXIII (Oct., 1932), pp. 8-9.

"Revaluations (XI): Arnold as Critic." *Scrutiny*, VII (December, 1938), pp. 319-32.

"Revaluations XIII: Coleridge in Criticism." *Scrutiny*, IX (June 19-40), pp. 57-69.

"Hardy the Poet." *Southern Review*, VI (1940-41), pp. 87-98.

"Reflections on the Above (Criticism of Little Gidding)." *Scrutiny*, XI (Summer, 1943), pp. 261-67.

"The Teaching of Literature: III, The Literary Discipline and Liberal Education." *Sewanee Review*, LV (1947), pp. 587-609.

"Comment: D.H. Lawrence Placed", *Scrutiny*, XVI (March 1949), p. 44.

"Lawrence and Eliot." *Scrutiny*, XVIII (Autumn, 1951), pp. 139-43.

"The State of Criticism: Representations to Fr. Martin Jarrett-Kerr." *Essays in Criticism*, III (1953), pp. 215-33.

"Valedictory." *Scrutiny*, XIX (October 1953), pp. 254-57.

"The Responsible Critic: Note in reply to Mr F.W. Bateson." *Scrutiny*, XIX (Oct. 1953), pp. 321-28.

"A Note on the Critical Function." *The Literary Criterion*, V (Winter, 1961), pp. 1-9.

"James as Critic." Introduction to *Henry James: Selected Literary Criticism*. Ed. by Morris Shapira, London: Heinemann, 1963.

"Valuation in Criticism." Introduction to *The Image of Childhood* by Peter, Coveney, Rev. ed., Harmondsworth, Penguine Books, 1967.

"Wordsworth: The Creative Conditions." *Twentieth-Century Literature in Retrospect*, ed. Reuken A. Brower, Cambridge: Harvard University Press, 1971, pp. 323-41.

"Lawrence After Thirty Years." *D.H. Lawrence: A Critical Anthology*, ed. H. Coornbes. Harmondsworth: Penguine Education, 1973, pp. 398-407.

"Justifying ones valuation of Blake." *William Blake: Essays in honour of Sir Geoffrey Keynes*. ed. Morton. D. Paley and Michael Phillips, Oxford: The Clarendon Press, 1973, pp. 65-85.

"Memories of Wittgenstein." *The Human World* (1974), pp. 15-16.

SECONDARY SOURCES

Books

Abrams, M.H. *Literary Criticism: Idea and the Act*. California: University of California Press, 1974.

—— *The Mirror and the Lamp: Romantic Theory and the Critical Tradition*, 1953; rpt. Oxford: OUP, 1974.

Aithal, S. Krishnamoorthy. *Critical Essays: A Presentation Volume for Prof. V.S. Seturaman*. Ed. W. Vishwanathan and C.T. Indra. Madras: Macmillan, 1987.

Alexander, Edward. *Matthew Arnold and John Stuart Mill*. London: Routledge and Kegan Paul, 1965.

Allen, G.W. and Clark, H.H. Ed. *Literary Criticism*. New York: American Book Company, 1941.

Allot, Kenneth A. "A Background for Empedocles on Etna." *Matthew Arnold: A Collection of Critical Essays*. Ed. David J. DeLaura. N.J.: Prentice-Hall, 1973.

Alpers, Anthony. *Katherine Mansfield: A Biography*. New York: Knoff, 1954.

Anderson, Warren D. *Matthew Arnold and the Classical Tradition*, 1965; rpt. Ann Arbor: University of Michigan Press, 1971.

Armstrong, Edward A. *Shakespeare's Imagination*. Omaha: University of Nebraska Press, 1963.

Baldick, Chris. *The Social Mission of English Criticism*, 1848-1932. New York: Oxford University Press, 1983.

Baun, Paull Franklin. *Ten Studies in the Poetry of Matthew Arnold*. North Carolina: Duke University Press, 1958.

Beach, Joseph Werren. *The Concept of Nature in Nineteenth Century English Poetry*. New York: Macmillan, 1936.

Bentley, Eric. *The Importance of Scrutiny*, 1948; rpt. New York: New York University Press, 1964.

Bilan, R.P. *The Literary Criticism of F.R. Leavis*. Cambridge: Cambridge University Press, 1979.

Bowra, CM. *The Romantic Imagination*. New York: OUP, 1961.

Boyer, Robert. *F.R. Leavis: Judgement and the Discipline of Thought*. Columbia: University of Missouri Press, 1978.

Bradbury, M. and Palmer D. eds. *Contemporary Criticism*. London: Edward Arnold, 1970.

Browell, W.C. *Victorian Prose Master*. New York: C. Scribner's Sons, 1901.

Brown, E.K. *Matthew Arnold: A Study in Conflict*. Chicago: University of Chicago Press, 1944.

Buckler, William E. *Matthew Arnold's Prose: Three Essays in Literary Enlargements*. New York: AMS Press, 1983.

Buckley, Vincent. *Poetry and Morality: Studies on the Criticism of Matthew Arnold, T.S. Eliot and F.R., Leavis*. London: Chatto and Windus, 1959.

Bush, Douglas. *Matthew Arnold: A Study of his Poetry and Prose*. New York: Macmillan, 1971.

—— *Mythology and Romantic Tradition in English Poetry*, 1937; reprint New York: Pageant, 1957.

Butcher, S.H. *Aristotle's Theory of Poetry and Fine Art*, 1984; rpt. New Delhi: Allied Publishers, 1963.

Carroll, Joseph. *The Cultural Theory of Matthew Arnold*. Los Angeles: University of California Press, 1982.

Carswell, Catherine. *The Savage Pilgrimage*. London: Seeker, 1932.

Carswell, John. *Lives and Letters*. London: Faber and Faber, 1978.

Casey, John. *The Language of Criticism*. London: Methuen and Company, 1966.

Cassavant, S.G. *John Middleton Murry: The Critic as Moralist*. Alabama: Alabama University Press, 1982.

Chambers, E.K. *Matthew Arnold: A Study*. Oxford: Clarendon Press, 1947.

Couling, S.M.B. *Matthew Arnold and his Critics: A Study of his Controversies*. Ohio: Ohio University Press, 1974.

Culler, A. Dwight. *Imaginative Reason: The Poetry of Matthew Arnold*. New Haven Conn: Yale University Press, 1966.

Daiches, David. *Critical Approaches to Literature*. New Delhi: Orient Longman, 1956.

Dale, Peter Allan. *The Victorian Critic and the Idea of History: Carlyle, Arnold, Patel*. Cambridge: Harvard University Press, 1977.

Das, Manas Mukul. *Thomas Hardy: Poet of Tragic Vision*. New Delhi: Macmillan, 1983.

David, Arthur Kyle, Jr. *Arnold's Letters: A Descriptive Check-list*. Charlottesville: University of Virginia Press, 1977.

Dawson, Carl. Ed. *Matthew Arnold: The Poetry, The Critical Heritage*, London and Boston, 1973.

De Laura, David J. *Hebrew and Hellene in Victorian England: Newman, Arnold and Pater*. Austin: University of Texas Press, 1969.

—— Ed. *Matthew Arnold: A Collection of Critical Essays*. Englewood Cliffs: Prentice Hall, 1973.

Eagleton, Terry. *Literary Theory: An Introduction*. Minneapolis: University of Minnesota Press, 1983.

Eliot, T.S., *Selected Essays*, 1932; rpt. London: Faber and Faber, 1951.

—— *The Use of Poetry and the Use of Criticism*. Cambridge: Harvard University Press, 1933.

—— *The Sacred Wood: Essays on Poetry and Criticism.* London: Methuen, 1967.

Fairchild, Hoscie Moule. "Arnold". *Religious Trends in English Poetry.* Vol. IV: 1830-1880. Christianity and Romanticism in Victorian Era. New York: Columbia University, 1957.

Faverty, Frederic E. *Matthew Arnold the Ethnologist.* Evanston Ill: North-Western University Press, 1951.

Forbes Ducan. *The Liberal Anglican Idea of History.* Cambridge: Cambridge University Press, 1952.

French, Philip. *Three Honest Men: Edmund Wilson, F.R. Leavis, Lionel Trilling—A Critical Mosaic.* London: Carcanet Press, 1980.

Garrod, H.W. *Poetry and the Criticism of Life: The Charles Eliot Norton Lectures for 1920-1330.* New York: Russell and Russell, 1963.

Gates, Lewis E. *Three Studies in Literature.* New York: Macmillan, 1899.

Gomme, Andor. *Attitudes to Criticism.* Carbondale: Southern Illinois University Press, 1966.

Gottfried, Leon. *Matthew Arnold and the Romantics.* London: Routledge and Kegan Paul, 1963.

Green, Martin. *Science and the Shabby Curate of Poetry.* London: Longman, 1964.

Griffin, E.G. *John Middleton Murry.* New York: Twaynee Publishers, 1969.

Gross, John. *The Rise and Fall of Man of Letters.* New York: Macmillan, 1970.

Guerin, W.L., Labor, E.G., Morgan, L. and Willingharm, J.R. *A Handbook of Critical Approaches.* New York: Harper and Row, 1979.

Harding, F.W.J. *Matthew Arnold the Critic and France.* Geneva: Libralrie Droz, 1964.

Hayman, Ronald. *Leavis.* London: Heinemann, 1976.

Heppenstall, Rayner. *Four Absentees*. London: Barrier and Rockliff, 1960.

-—— *John Middleton Murry: A Study in Excellent Normality*. London: Jonathan Cape, 1934.

Holloway, John. *The Charted Mirror: Literary and Critical Essays*. London: Routledge and Kegan Paul, 1960.

—— *The Victorian Sage: Studies in Arguments,* 1953; rpt. London: Macmilan, 1952.

Hoopes, Robert. *Right Reason in the English Renaissance*. Cambridge: Harvard University Press, 1962.

Hough, Graham. *The Dark Sun: A Study of D.H. Lawrence*. Harmondsworth: Penguine, 1961.

—— *An Essay on Criticism*. London: Gerald Duckworth, 1966.

Houghton, Walter E. *The Victorian Frame of Mind, 1830-1870*. New Haven Connecticut: Yale University Press, 1957.

James, D.G. *Matthew Arnold and the Decline of English Romanticism*. Oxford: Clarendon Press, 1961.

Johnson, E.D.N. *The Allen Vision of Victorian Poetry: Sources of the Poetic Imagination in Tennyson, Browning and Arnold*, 1952; Reprint Hamden, Conn: Archon Books, 1963.

Johnson, Samuel. *The History of Rasselas, Prince of Abbissinia*. Eds. Geoffrey Tillotson and Brian Jenkins. London: Oxford University Press, 1971.

—— *Lives of the English Poets*. Edited by George Birkbeck Hill 3 Vols. New York: Octagon, 1967.

—— *The Yale Edition of the Works of Sammuel Johnson*. Edited by E.L. Mc Adam, Jr., Donal and Mary Hyde. New Haven, Conn: Yale University Press, 1961.

Jump, J.D. *Matthew Arnold*. London: Longman, 1955.

Kermode, Frank. *Romantic Image*. New York: Macmillan, 1957.

Knight, G. Wilson. *Wheel of Fire: Essays in Interpretation of Shakespeare's Somber Tragedies*. London: Methuen, 1930.

—— *Poets of Action*. London: Methuen, 1967.

—— *The Imperial Theme*. London: Methuen, 1931.

—— *Neglected Powers: Essays on Nineteenth and Twentieth Century Literature*. London: Routledge and Kegan Paul, 1971.

Krook, Dorothea. *Three Traditions of Moral Thought*. Cambridge: Cambridge University Press, 1939.

Lea, Prink A. *John Middleton Murry*. New York: Oxford University Press, 1960. Heritage Publishers, 1977.

Logoius, E. and Cazamian. *The History of English Literature*. Delhi: Macmillan, 1971.

Lemon, L.T. *The Partial Critics*. New York: Oxford University Press, 1968.

Lentrichia, Frank. *Criticism and Social Change* Chicago: University of Chicago Press, 1983.

Le Roy, Gaylord C. *Perplexed Prophets: Six Nineteenth Century British Authors*. Philadelphia: University of Pennsylvania Press, 1953.

Lilley, George P. *A Bibliography of John Middleton Murry*. Toronto: University Press, 1975.

Liptzin, Soloman. *The English Legend of Heinrich Heine*. New York: Block, 1954.

Livingston, James C. *Matthew Arnold and Christianity: His Religious Prose Writings*. Columbia: University of South Carolina Press, 1986.

Locke, John. *An Essay Concerning Human Understanding*. Edited by Alexander Campbell Fraser. 2 Vols. New York: Dover, 1959.

Lodge, David. *The Language of Fiction*. London: Routledge Kegan Paul, 1966.

—— Ed. *20th Century Literary Criticism*. London: Longman, 1972.

Lowry, Hward F. *Matthew Arnold and the Modern Spirit.* Princeton: Princeton University Press, 1941.

Lucas, F.L. "Matthew Arnold." In *Victorian Literature: Modern.* Essays in Criticism. Ed. Austin Wright. New York: Oxford University Press, 1961.

Madden, William. *Matthew Arnold: A Study of the Aesthetic Temperament in Victorian England.* Bloomington: Indiana University Press, 1967.

—— *Matthew Arnold: A Study of Poetic Temperament in Victorian England.* Bloomington: Indiana University Press, 1967.

Mairet, Philip. *John Middleton Murry.* London: Longman's Green, 1958.

Mansfield, Katherine. *Journal of Katherine Mansfield.* Ed. J.M. Murry. London: Constable, 1939.

—— *Katherine Mansfield's Letters to Middleton Murry 1913-1922.* Ed. Middleton Murry. London: Constable, 1951.

—— *The Scrap book of Katherine Mansfield,* Ed. J.M. Murry. London: Constable, 1939.

McCallum, Pamela. *Literature and Method: Towards a Critique of I.A. Richards, T.S Eliot and F.R. Leavis.* London: Macmillan, 1983.

McCarthy, Patrick J. *Matthew Arnold and the Three Classes.* New York: Columbia University Press, 1964.

Meckier, Jersme. *Aldous Huxley: Satire and Structure.* London: Chatto and Windus, 1969.

Miller, J. Hillis. *The Disappearance of God: Five Nineteenth-Century Writers.* Cambridge: Harvard University Press, 1963.

Mulhern, Francis. *The Moment of 'Scrutiny'.* London: NLB, 1979.

Murry, Mary Middleton. *To Keep Faith.* London: Constable, 1959.

Neiman, Frazer. *Matthew Arnold.* New York: Twayne Publishers, 1968.

Panichas, George A. *The Reverent Discipline*. Knoxville: University of Tennessee Press, 1974.

Pettet, E.C. *On the Poetry of Keats*. Cambridge: Cambridge University Press, 1957.

Plowman, Max. *Bridge into the Future: The Letters of Max Plowman*. Ed. D.L.P. London: Dakers, 1944.

Rahu, Phillip. *Literature and the Sixth Sense*. Boston: Houghton Mifflin Company, 1969.

Rajnath. *Essays in Criticism*. Delhi: Doaba House, 1971.

Rees, Richard. *A Theory of My Times: An Essay in Didactic Remembrance*. London: Seckert and Warburg, 1963.

Robbins, William. *The Ethical Idealism of Matthew Arnold*. London: William Heinemann, 1959.

Roberts, Ruth ap. *Arnold and God*. Berkeley: University of California Press, 1983.

Russell, G.W.E. *Matthew Arnold*. London: Hodder and Soughton, 1903.

Scott-James, R.A. *The Making of Literature*, 1928; rpt. Delhi: Allied Publishers, 1963.

Scott, Wilber. *Five Approaches to Literary Criticism*. New York: The Macmillan Company, 1962.

Sharma, L.R. *In Defence of J. Middleton Murry: The Critic as Moralist*. Allahabad: Dikshit Publishing House, 1986.

Stein, Walter. *Criticism as Dialogue*. Cambridge: Cambridge University Press, 1969.

Tate, Allen. *Reactionary Essays*. New York: Charles Scribner's Sons, 1936.

Thorpe, Michael. *Matthew Arnold*. London: Evans, 1969.

Tillyard, E.M.W. *Poetry Direct and Oblique*. London: Chatto and Windus, 1948.

—— *The Milton Setting*. London: Chatto and Windus, 1938.

Trilling, Lionel. *Beyond Culture*. New York: The Viking Press, 1965.

—— *Matthew Arnold*, 1939; rpt. New York: Meridian Books, 1955.

Tillotson, Geoffery. *Mid Victorian Studies*. London: Atholone Press, 1965.

Walsh, William. *The Use of Imagination*, 1959; rpt. Harmondsworth: Penguine Books, 1966.

—— *A Human Idiom*. London: Chatto and Windus, 1964.

—— *F.R. Leavis*. London: Chatto and Windus, 1980.

Warren, A.H. Jr. *English Poetic Theory, 1825-1865*. Princeton N.J.: Princeton University Press, 1950.

Weiman, Robert. *Structure and Society in Literary History: Studies in the History and Theory of Historical Criticism*. Virginia: The University Press of Virginia, 1976.

Wellek, Rene. *A History of Modern Criticism*. 6 Volumes. London: Jonathan Cape, 1986.

Wellek, Rene and Warren, Austin. *Theory of Literature*, 1949; rpt. London: Penguine Books, 1985.

Willey, Basil: *Nineteenth Century Studies: Coleridge to Matthew Arnold*. New York: Columbia University Press, 1949.

Wimsatt, W.K. *The Verbal Icon: Studies in the Meaning of Poetry*. London: Methuen, 1970.

Wimsatt, W.K. and Brooks, C. *Literary Criticism: A Short History*, 1957; rpt. New Delhi: I.B.H., 1974.

Wordsworth, William. *Wordsworth's Literary Criticism*. Ed. W.J.B. Owen. London: Routledge and Kegan, 1974.

Periodicals

Abrams, M.H. "The Deconstructive Angel." *Critical Inquiry*, III (1977), pp. 433-34.

Alaya, Flavia M. "Arnold and Renan on the Popular Use of History." *Journal of the History of Ideas*, XXVIII (1967).

Allot, Kenneth A. "Matthew Arnold's Reading List in Three Early Diaries." *Victorian Studies*, 2 (1959), pp. 254-66.

Babbit, Irving. "Impressions versus Judicial Criticism." *PMLA*, NSXIV, No. 3 (1906), pp. 687-705.

Bateson, F.W. "The 'Scrutiny' Phenomenon." *Sewanee Review*, LXXXV (1977), pp. 146-52.

Bantock, G.H. *Scrutiny*, Vol. XVII, No. 1, pp. 39-40.

Beer, J.B. "John, Middleton Murry." *Critical Quarterly*, 3 (Spring, 1961), pp. 59-66.

Bebnett, J.R. "The Problem of Style." *The D.H. Lawrence Review*, 2 (Spring, 1969), pp. 32-46.

Berryman, Charles. "Arnold's Empedocles on Etna." *VN*, No. 29 (1966).

Bount, Wilfred. "Blake and the Scholars." *New York Review of Books* (October 1965), p. 280.

Brick, Allan. "Equilibrium in Poetry of Matthew Arnold." *UTQ*, XXX (1961), p. 216.

Brisman, Leslie. "The Romantic Faith and the Primitive Logia." *The Arnoldian*, 5 : 2 (1978).

Brown, E.K. "Matthew Arnold and the Eighteenth Century." *University of Toronto Quarterly*, 9 (1940), pp. 202-13.

—— "The Critic as Xenophobe." *Sewanee Review*. XXXVIII, pp. 301-09.

Bruford, W.H. "Goethe and Some Victorian Humanists." *Publications of the English Goethe Studies*, 18 (1949).

Burgum, Edwin B. "The Humanism of Matthew Arnold." *Symposium*, II (January 1931), pp. 85-112.

Cadbury, William. "Coming to terms with Dover Beach." *Criticism*, VIII (1966).

Carnal, G. "Matthew Arnold's Critical Effort." *Essays in Criticism*. Vol. VIII (July 1958), pp. 256-68.

Casey, John. "Dickens and the Great Tradition." *Spectator* (24 October 1970), pp. 477-78.

Corke, Hillary. "John Middleton Murry." *Encounter*, 14 (January 1960), p. 75.

Couling, S.M.B. "The Background of 'The Function of Criticism at the Present Times," *PQ*, XLII (1963).

—— "The Evolution of Culture and Anarchy." *Studies in Philology*, LX (1963).

—— "Matthew Arnold's 1853 Preface: Its Origin and Aftermath." *Victorian Studies*, VIII (1964), pp. 233-63.

Davie, Donald, "F.R. Leavis', How to teach reading." *Essays in Criticism*, Vol. VII (July 1957), pp. 230-35.

De Laura, David J. "Arnold and Carlyle." *PMLA,* 79 (1964), pp. 104-29.

—— "Arnold Clough, Dr Arnold and Thyrisis." *Victorian Poetry,* VII (1969).

—— "What then does Matthew Arnold Mean." *Modern Philology,* LXVI, 1969.

—— "The Wordsworth of Pater and Arnold: The Supreme Artistic View of Life." *Studies in English Literature,* VI (1966).

Donovan, R.A. "The Methods of Arnold's Essays in Criticism." *PMLA,* LXXI (1956).

Dudby, Fred A. "Matthew Arnold and Science." *PMLA,* 57 (1942), pp. 275-94.

Ebel, Henry. "Matthew Arnold and Classical Culture." *Arion,* 4 (1965), pp. 188-220.

Eggensehweiler, David L. "Arnold's Passive Questions." *Victorian Poetry,* V (1967).

Eliot, T.S. "Poetry and Propaganda." *The Bookman*, LXX (Feb. 1930), pp. 595-602.

Farrell, John P. "Matthew Arnold's Tragic Vision." *PMLA,* 85 (1970), pp. 107-17.

—— "Matthew Arnold and the Middle Ages." *Victorian Studies,* XIII, 1970.

Fausset, Hugh. "Mr. Murry's Lawrence." *The Adelphi,* 2 (May 1951), p. 155.

Fogle, Richard Harter. "Beauty and Truth: John Middleton Murry on Keats." *The D.H. Lawrence Review*, 2 (Spring, 1969), pp. 68-75.

Ford, George. "Leavises, Leavis's and some Dickensian Priorities." review of *Dickens The Novelist*: *Nineteenth Century Fiction*, 26 (1971-72), p. 95-113.

Forster, E.M. "The Cult of D.H. Lawrence." *Spectator,* 147 (18 April, 1931), p. 627.

Forsyth, R.A. "'The Buried Life'—The Contrasting Views of Arnold and Clough in Context of Dr. Arnold's Historiography." *ELH,* 35 (1968), pp. 218-53.

Fraser, John. "A Tribute to Dr F.R. Leavis." *The Western Review*, 23 (1958-59), pp. 139-47.

—— "Leavis and Winters: Professional Manners." *Cambridge Quarterly*, 5 (1970-71), pp. 41-71.

—— "Leavis, Winters and 'Tradition'." *The Southern Review,* 7 (1971), pp. 963-85.

Gersh, Gabriel, "The Moral Imperatives of F.R. Leavis." *The Antioch Review*, 28 (1968), pp. 520-28.

Girard, Denis. "John Middleton Murry, D.H. Lawrence, et Albert Schweitzer." *Etudes amglaises,* 12 (July-Sept. 1959), pp. 212-21.

Greger, Ian. "The Criticism of F.R. Leavis." *The Dublin Review* (Third Quarter, 1952), pp. 55-63.

Gribble, James. "Logical and Psychological Considerations in the Criticism of F.R. Leavis." *The British Journal of Aesthetics*, 10 (1970), pp. 39-57.

Griffin, Ernest G. "The Circular and the Linear: The Middleton Murry—D.H. Lawrence Affair." *The D.H. Lawrence Review,* 2 (Spring, 1969), pp. 76-92.

Griffith, Philip Mahone. "Middleton Murry on Swift: The *Neo Plus Ultra* of Objectivity?" *The D.H. Lawrence Review,* 2 (Spring, 1969), pp. 60-67.

Harris, Terry G. "Matthew Arnold, Bishop Joseph Butler, and the Foundation of Religious Faith." *Victorian Studies* (Winter, 1988), pp. 184-208.

Heath, William R. "The Literary Criticism of John Middleton Murry." *PMLA,* 70 (March 1955), pp. 45-47.

Heyl, Bernard. "The Absolutism of F.R. Leavis." *The Journal of Aesthetics and Art Criticism*, 13 (1954-55), pp. 249-55.

Hirsch, David H. "Hard Times and F.R. Leavis." *Criticism*, 6 (1964), pp. 1-16.

Holbrook, David. "F.R. Leavis and 'Creativity'." *The New University Quarterly* (Winter, 1975), pp. 66-77.

Hough, Graham. "D.H. Lawrence and the Novel." *The Adelphi*, 30 (Third Quarter, 1956), pp. 365-82.

Houghton, Walter E. "Arnold's Empedocles on Etna." *Victorian Studies*, 1 (1959), pp. 311-36.

Howells, W.D. "Leo Tolstoy." *North American Review*, CIXXXVIII, p. 847.

Inglis, Fred. "Attention to Education: Leavis and the Leavisites." *The New Universities Quarterly* (Winter, 1975), pp. 94-106.

Jarret-Kerr, Martin. "The Literary Criticism of F.R. Leavis." *Essays in Criticism* (October 1952), pp. 350-67.

Jeffers, Thomas L. "The Leavises: Recollections and Impressions." *Western Humanities Review* (Spring, 1986), pp. 84-89.

Jones, Allun. "F.R. Leavis and After." *The Critical Quarterly* (Vol. I, 1959), p. 252-56.

Jones, John. "Murry Revaluated." *New Statesman*, 58 (12 Dec. 1959), p. 848.

Kaufmann, R.J. "F.R. Leavis: The Morality of Mind." *The Critical Quarterly*, Vol. I (1959), pp. 249-52.

——"On Using an Obssessed Critic: John Middleton Murry." *Graduate Student of English*, 3 (Winter, 1960), pp. 4-8.

Kent, John. "The Victorian Resistance: Comments on Religious Life and Culture 1940-80." *Victorian Studies*, 12:3 (1968), pp. 145-54.

Kermode, Frank. "On the Frontiers of Criticism." *Manchester Gaurdian* (10 June 1960), p. 8.

——"Some Reservations." *New Statesman*, 66 (1963), p. 568.

Kerrigan, John. "Arnold and Seriousness." *English* (Aut., 1981), pp. 263-83.

Killham, John. "The Use of 'Concreteness' as an Evaluative Term in F.R. Leavis's 'The Great Tradition'.' *The British Journal of Aesthetics*, 5 (1965), pp. 14-24.

Knight, G. Wilson. "Scrutiny and Criticism." *Essays in Criticism*, 14 (1964), pp. 32-36.

——"The New Interpretation." *Essays in Criticism*, 3 (1953), pp. 380-92.

Kushman, Keith. "Lawrence and Murry: A Twofold Vision." *The D.H. Lawrence Review* (Spring, 1987), p 45.

Lea, F.A. "Murry and Marriage." *D.H. Lawrence Review* 2 (Spring 1969), pp. 1-21.

Leavis, F.R. "Hardy The Poet." *Southern Review* 6 (Summer, 1940), pp. 87-98.

Leaner, Lawrence. "The Life and Death of Scrutiny." *London Magazine*, 2 (1955), pp. 68-77.

—— "Love Gossips or How Moral is Literature." *Essays in Criticism* (April 1964).

Lowe, R.L. "Two Arnold Letters." *Modern Philology*, 52 (1955), pp. 262-64.

MacKillop, I.D. "F.R. Leavis: A Peculiar Relationship." *Essays in Criticism* (July 1984), pp. 184-87.

Madden, William. "The Divided Tradition of English Criticism." *PMLA*, LXXIII, pp. 165-68.

Mc Luhan, Marshall. "Poetic vs. Rhetorical Exegesis: The Case for Leavis against Richards and Empson." *The Sewanee Review*, 5 (1944), pp. 226-76.

Meyers, Jeffrey, "Murry's Cult of Mansfield." *Journal of Modern Literature*, 7 (1979), pp. 15-38.

Milic, Louis. "A Quantitative Approach to the Style of Jonathan Swift." *The Hague* (1967), pp. 50-51.

Mill, J.S. "What is Poetry." *Monthly Repository*, 7 (1933), pp. 60-72.

Moore, T. Sturge. "Towards Simplicity." *Criterion*, 6 (November 1927), pp. 409-17.

Neill, Edward. "'Give up Literary Criticism': F.R. Leavis, The Last Phase." *English* (Spring, 1984), pp. 26-33.

Needham, John. "Leavis and the Poet-Saussureans." *English*, 24 (1964), pp. 235-50.

Nieman, Frazer. "The Zeitgeist of Matthew Arnold." *PMLA*, 72 (1957), pp. 977-78.

Paris, Rosemary. "Review of Katherine *Mansfield's Letters to John Middleton Murry*." *Furioso*, 1 (Winter, 1952), pp. 66-69.

Poole, Roger C. "Life versus Death in the Later Criticism of F.R. Leavis." *Renaissance and Modern Studies*, 16, pp. 112-41.

Pradhan, S.K. "Literary Criticism and Cultural Diagnosis: F.R. Leavis on W.H. Auden." *The British Journal of Aesthetics*, 12 (1972), pp. 384-94.

Peritchard, William H. "Discourses in America." *Essays in Criticism*, 19 (1969), pp. 336-47.

Rajnath. "The Critical Achievement of F.R. Leavis." *English Studies* (October 1982).

Rees, Richard. "The Politics of a Mystic." *The D.H. Lawrence Review*, 2 (Spring, 1969), pp. 24-31.

Robinson, Ian. "The Third Realm: Ten Years Work by F.R. Leavis." *The Human World*, 3 (1971), pp. 71-85.

Routh, H.V. "The Nineteenth Century and After." *The Years Work in English Studies, XIII* (1932), p. 303.

Schuchard, Ronald. "Elliot and Hulme in 1916." *PMLA*, 88, 1978.

Scott, Natan A. Jr. "Arnold's Version of Transcendence—the Via Poetica." *The Journal of Religion*, 59 (1979), pp. 261-84.

Singh, G.S. "Better History and Better Criticism: The Significance of F.R. Leavis." *English Miscellany*, 16 (1938), pp. 215-79.

Stanford, Derek. "Middleton Murry as Literary Critic." *Essays in Criticism*, 8 (Jan. 1958), pp. 30-67.

Tanner, Michael. "Literature and Philosophy." *The New Universities Quarterly* (Winter, 1975), pp. 54-64.

Thayer, C.G. "Murry's Shakespeare." *The D.H. Lawrence Review,* 2 (Spring, 1969), pp. 47-59.

Tims, Margaret. "A Biography of John Middleton Murry." *Aryan Path* 31 (Jan. 1960), pp. 34-35.

Todorov, Tzvetan. "Poetic-Truth: Three Interpretations." *Essays in Criticism*, Vol. XXXVIII, No. 2, April 1988.

Trethewew, Eric. "The 'Method of Jesus': Experience and Moral Life in Matthew Arnold's Poetic Theory of Interpretation." *The Arnoldian,* 9:2 (1982), pp. 6-22.

Trilling, Lionel. "Dr Leavis and the Moral Tradition." *New Yorker* (24 Sept. 1949), pp. 88-90.

Vivas, Eliseo. "Mr. Leavis on D.H. Lawrence." *The Sewanee Review*, 65 (1957), pp. 123-79.

Waldock, A.J.A. "The Status of Hard Times." *Southerly*, 3 (1948), pp. 33-39.

Watson, J.H. "A Good Workman and his Friends: Recollections of John Middleton Murry." *London Magazine,* 6 (May 1959), pp. 51-55.

Whitridge, Arnold. "Matthew Arnold and St. Bauve." *PMLA*, (1938), pp. 303-13.

William, Raymond. "Our debt to Dr Leavis." *Critical Quarterly,* I (1959), pp. 241-47.

Abbreviations of Periodicals Cited

PMLA	Publications of the Modern Language Association of America
PQ	Philogical Quarterly
RES	Review of English Studies
UTQ	University of Toronto Quarterly
VN	Victorian Newsletter
VS	Victorian Studies